CLASS OF HOPE AND CHANGE

A WALK WITH MILLENNIALS

Deji Komolafe

OverPond
CHICAGO

OverPond Media
P.O. Box 876
Chicago, IL 60680
info@overpondmedia.com

Book Cover Design by Mauricio Díaz
Book Layout ©2017 BookDesignTemplates.com
Copyediting and Proofreading by Seldon Writing Group, LLC
Ebook Layout by Nou Moua

Ordering Information:
Quantity sales. Special discounts are available on quantity purchases by corporations, associations, and others. For details, contact the "Special Sales Department" at the address above.

Class of Hope and Change: A Walk with Millennials/Deji Komolafe -- 1st Ed.
Paperback ISBN 978-0-692-97063-8
Ebook ISBN 978-0-692-05210-5

To my mother,
Whose body gave me life
Whose love gave me comfort
Whose determination gave me strength
Whose faith gave me peace

What was once impossible
Or at least unlikely
Now looks achievable
And will soon seem like destiny

Class of Hope and Change

Contents

Contents

Preface

What a time to be alive. This book could not have existed ten years ago. If you were a teacher, a coach, a counselor, or any adult engaged in the professional service of developing young people before 2007; once they grew up, you could only wonder what happened to them.

You may have gotten an occasional visit, call, or email from a few of them. You may have run into some of their parents or guardians and received an update on what they had been up to since they graduated/left. You may have seen something in the news about an accomplishment or an award they earned. You may have even reunited with them at a commemorative event 10 or 20 years later. In most cases, however, you would not have seen or heard from the young people you worked with ever again.

That was then. Over the past 10 years, advances in technology have reshaped nearly every aspect of life. The ability to stay connected and keep in touch with people from every season of your life is one of the defining aspects of this period in human history. For those of us engaged in the work of supporting, equipping, and empowering young people, this has been a paradigm-shifting moment. I am part of the first generation of people who have the opportunity and capability to not simply observe the maturation of individuals I knew as teenagers, but to routinely engage with them along their journey.

I have spent a significant portion of the first chapter of my adult life teaching, mentoring, and encouraging young people.

I have been around teenagers since I was a teenager. As a result, I have had the privilege of witnessing and, in my own small way, contributing to - the maturation of young people who span the entire age range of the Millennial generation. For the purposes of this book, the term *millennial* refers to people who turned 18 years old at some point during the first 18 years of the 21st century, between the years of 2000 and 2017.

For better or worse, this term does not apply to me. I fall into the "neither-land" between Generation X and the millennial generation. It turns out that this is an ideal vantage point for looking at this moment in history through conversations with young people who have come of age during the past ten years.

I have spent the last two years talking with millennials about their lives, their dreams, their struggles, and their ideas. This book includes excerpts from my conversations with 58 young adults I interviewed over the course of the past two years for the podcast documentary which accompanies this book. I have personally known nearly all of the individuals featured in this book since they were high school teenagers. A few of them have known me since I was a high school teenager. They range in age from people who were around 21 years old back in 2007, to people who are now around 21 years old in 2017.

This year marks the 10-year anniversary of several important events. The iPhone, produced by Apple Inc. and its iconic CEO, Steve Jobs, was announced to the public in January 2007. One month later, a junior U.S. senator from Illinois — Barack Obama — was announced to the public as a candidate in the upcoming U.S. presidential campaign. That April, close to 50 people were either killed or wounded on the campus of Virginia Tech University in what was, at the time, one of the deadliest mass shootings in U.S. history. A few months later in the fall, the reality show *Keeping Up With The Kardashians* appeared on television screens across the nation. As 2007 came to a close, economic reports revealed that there had been a historic rise in the number of home foreclosures that year, an ominous sign of the year to come.

Noting the 10-year mark since the occurrence of these historic events can elicit a wide array of passionate responses, depending on who you talk to. Statements like *"it has been 10 years already?!"* and *"it has only been 10 years?!"* can be delivered in whichever tone is necessary to communicate one's level of shock, awe, and/or horror. Nevertheless, each of those events from 2007 foreshadowed the ways in which technology, politics, violence, entertainment, and economic hardship would influence the daily lives of people, not only in the United States, but around the world.

These aspects of our national and global reality have intersected, in large and small ways, with the lives of the young adults you will meet in this book. This book was inspired by their lives, and by the lives of the young people who began to claim and create their space in our society during the past ten years. The title of the book is a nod to two of the foundational elements of youth: Hope and Change.

One of the primary ways young people nourish a society is by continually reflecting and rekindling hope. Parents and family members look into the eyes of their children, and are hopeful for their child's potential, their family's lineage, and the ongoing project of human life. We listen to young children speak with boundless aspiration about what and who they hope to be when they grow up. We watch as teenagers move with performed confidence through their adolescence, unsure yet hopeful about the future that awaits them. We react as young adults take their seats at the grown-ups table with a lot to say, hopeful that they represent a forward step in the evolution of human thought. Since hope is rooted in an opinion or belief about the future, young people are the protectors and defenders of hope. A society without young people will soon become extinct. A society without hope will soon implode. In order for any society to survive and thrive, it needs young people, it needs hope, and it needs young people who are full of hope.

One of the other primary ways young people sustain a society is by continually representing and requiring change. The words we speak, the clothes we wear, the food we eat, the places where we live, the places where we grow, the places where we heal; nearly every aspect of our daily existence is the result of humans who decided to do things differently from the people who came before them. No generation gets to press a reset button and return to the default settings of life on Earth. Each group of young people inherits the settings of those who came before them. Since every generation of young people begins at a new point in human history, they have a fresh set of information to work with while discovering and assessing the current reality created by the adults on the planet.

Young people are the agents of change: whether by force, by choice, or by default. A society unable—or unwilling—to change will survive only as long as everything in the world around it stays the same. We do not live in such a world. In order for a society to thrive and survive, it needs young people who are mentally prepared for a world that is constantly changing, it needs young people who are equipped to make change in the world, and it needs young people who are courageous enough to confront changes in the world which are detrimental to their existence.

The ideas of hope and change must be available and accessible to all. Individuals and groups of people are free to enjoy and explore the concepts of hope and change, but the ideas belong to everyone. More specifically, they belong to the young, to those who exist today, and to those who will exist tomorrow.

Back Then

At least we have great TV. In the past ten years, we have seen the fault lines in our society widen as advances in technology push us closer together, and social, cultural, and political differences pull us further apart. However, the one thing most people in the U.S. can agree on is that we are living through one of the golden eras of television entertainment. American viewers have a better chance of finding a TV show that they will connect with and relate to than at any earlier period in the medium's nearly 90-year history.

One side benefit of the explosion in serialized shows over the past 10 years, is that more of us now understand that before any conversation or debate about a show can begin, there are a few questions that must be answered: *What season are you on? What was the last episode you saw?* The answers to those questions determine the level of seriousness, passion, and attention we are willing to contribute to a discussion or debate about any given show.

Understanding the prior knowledge and experiences a person brings to a conversation *before* engaging their opinions is a useful skill, one that is helpful in areas of life far beyond the small screen. Context is everything. Whether we are talking about our individual life journeys, or our collective life journeys as members of a group of people defined by their region, culture, race, class, or religion; it is critical to understand ourselves in context. *Where I have been? What have I seen? Who have I known? When did I come to this perspective? How did I get here?*

We begin with a look back at the varied paths which have led us from the people we were to the people we have become.

FINDING MYSELF

Steven: *When I look back on the person I used to be...that person was hungry. He was even more ambitious than the person I am now. At that time in my life, all I knew was hunger. All I knew was my current situation. All I knew was being raised in the projects. All I knew was I had to get a scholarship to go to college or I wouldn't be able to go to college. All I knew was that I had to make it because I had no other choice.*

The dreams and the visions, the goals and the aspirations of that person in high school was something that...it was so big it scared me. I got into college and, as a lot of people do when they get to college, they want to get involved with the lifestyle of college. That person was still there, but I felt like I had to, you know, lower myself or dumb myself down to be able to blend in with the people around me.

It was slowly after I started to go through college, towards the end of college, that hunger started to slowly come back into my life...That person that I was in high school has always been there. [Now], I'm 24 years old. I'm a husband. I'm a father. I have a good career. I do want more for my family, and I do want to provide the lifestyle that I think my family deserves. And those dreams that I had when I was 17, when I was 18, now more than ever I know that it's actually possible and I'm in the best position to do it. So, I'm actually tapping into the person I used to be to go to that second gear in my life.

Salihah: *I think at the core I'm always going to be Salihah...But of course I've changed so much over the years. In high school, there was so much of me that was unsure about the future and what it is that I wanted to do. There's still some of that now. You never know what to* expect sometimes. You don't always know if things are going to go according to plan, but I definitely think I've embraced the unknown more, now that I've gotten a little older and a little more secure and confident within myself.

There are a lot of things that I've done that I don't think I would have done when I was younger in high school...Like when I was in college, embracing positions of leadership and trying out different things. In high school, I wasn't involved in any clubs or sports or activities. I kept to myself. I did my assignments, I read my books, and that was that. You get so used to doing certain things sometimes when you stop and reassess, you're like, "This is really boring. I feel really complacent. I feel too comfortable." And it's just like you know you're capable of more, you know there's more you want to do, so you decide to do it. When I was feeling that way in high school, I still didn't do anything about it. I was like, "I know there's more that I could be doing, but…" Too scared to make a change, you're worried about what people think about you, you know?

The older I get, I'm more worried about what I think about myself, and if I'm happy with the person I am and if I'm embracing my potential. When I was younger I was really stuck in a place where I cared a lot about what other people thought of me, and if I was fitting the image and the role that they had of me in their minds. But as you get older, you have to break outside of that and stop worrying so much about how people perceive you to be. So that's been helpful on this journey.

Erica: *The Erica of six or seven years ago was totally different from who I am now. I've had a wealth of life experiences that kind of curated who I am now.*

I would say six or seven years ago, I was completely lost. Very confused, very hurt, full of pain and anger. No one would have ever guessed that though, because to everyone else I was like the happiest

person alive, like nothing bothered me. But deep down I was like cry-
ing every day, and just hurt, and in lots of pain from home experienc-
es with parents, a lot of emotional abuse and all those kinds of things.
I would say that this path has been a very treacherous one.

I've had people along the way who have helped me to embrace who
I am and truly learn to love myself. I was very hard-headed and I nev-
er really liked to listen to other people. I was one of those people who
said I had to experience something on my own and then [decide]
whether or not to do something. After going through years of that
phase and realizing that everything that I was trying to do wasn't
really working for me, my turning point was two years ago… it's
been a journey to get to this point. There were certain things we had
to work on…sometimes it's so hard to let go of the things that we
know, and to walk into the unknown. So, I would just say this whole
process has been one of faith and learning to trust and believe that
God has my back.

Amadu: I would say that many of my friends - if they know me well
- would say that I'm introverted. Specifically, more of a thoughtful
introvert, so I'm often observing the scene, taking it in. Not necessari-
ly needing to judge per se, but just understanding what's going on
around me. That's always been a characteristic that I've had. But
even with that, when I began to show who I was, it wasn't necessarily
considerate of those who were around me. It was more of, 'well, I
know how you guys are, so I can play this way.' It was more of a
chess game. I can play this way and get what I want.

Whereas now, after going through college…I guess it was sopho-
more year where it hit me…I used to be very driven by success and
accomplishments. Thinking about, 'what am I going to do?' and 'who
am I going to be?' And not really about 'what am I going to do for
others?' But I changed my mindset from 'how much money [am I]
going to have and what aesthetic success will I achieve?' to 'who can I

actually help? What impact will I have on society?' For some reason, I'm not gonna lie, there was a point in time where I felt that my academics somehow suffered from that. Maybe because the new goal wasn't driving me enough. I'm not sure what it was, but I ended up still kicking it back into gear around my junior year...I was like, "Yo, I really, really want to do something for others." Whether that be just for my own personal community where I'm from, Bed-Stuy...or if it's for like all Black people...or for just everyone universally. There's something more to life than just getting money and having riches and fame, or whatever it may be.

Noor: *There wasn't one big change, or one big thing that happened. There were so many events that made me change and made me the person I am today. There are lots of things that were important to me ten years ago, like talking about brands and fashion. I used to be obsessed with makeup, with fashion. I would go and spend a lot of money on my makeup. Chanel is my favorite, Dior as well...those are the top two. I used to be obsessed about fashion and my looks.*

I'm not saying that it is no [longer] important to me. Of course, it is [still] important to me now, I am a woman and I love to dress up and look really nice. But the way I look at it now is different than the way I looked at it back then. When you're so obsessed about something like makeup or fashion, it also takes away energy from some important things in your life. I feel like back then I didn't focus much on other major aspects [of my life] like I am now.

Daphne: *Back in 2007, I was in high school. I would say a sophomore or a freshman, I believe. I was definitely another person. I was surrounded by a lot of young females, a lot of people. And at that point in my life, I wasn't where I needed to be. I knew where I wanted to be, but I wasn't there mentally. I always wanted to be doing what everybody else was doing, 'cuz I thought that was cool. I don't know. Hon-*

estly, looking back on it, I can say that I wasn't in love with myself. I was in love with what people wanted me to be, not who I wanted to be.

And then I realized, I'm destined to be Dafna; I'm destined to be me. And I'm not like every other girl. I'm not like every other young woman. I have to be me, and I have to go down my own path...follow my own rules and do what I have to do for myself. Because at the end of the day, when everybody leaves you, who do you have? Yourself. So, if you're not happy with yourself, nobody's going to be happy with you. You can't try to be Person A or Person B and not be who you need to be. So, I feel like I have to find that love in myself. When I look in the mirror, I have to be able to say, 'I love that girl. I really love her.'

Janelle: *Seven or eight years ago...so that's about middle school? Around that time, I had always been in predominantly Black schools, so I've always been a person who was aware of my Blackness, but I wasn't as aware of myself as a woman. Which is really weird to me, because you'd figure being a woman, I would notice certain things being said to me. But I realized a lot of things.*

Like I didn't realize how bad our society was with misogynistic views until it was time for me to get a job. I got to 18 years old, and I was looking for jobs before I got to college...I was just like, wow. I was never aware of the fact that - as a woman - people were going to talk to me a certain way, or treat me a certain way. And I realized it, but I didn't think of myself as a feminist or a womanist who would actually care about these ideals that I instill in myself now. Now I actually feel like I need to have these arguments with people about protecting my 'woman-ness'! I didn't think about it before.

There are a lot of issues with being a woman today. Being a Black woman, that situation in general is just like, 'wow, like you just made me really aware of the fact that I'm a Black woman.' I guess it wasn't at the forefront of my mind when I was younger.

Toshawna: *Well 2007 was my entrance into high school, and now I'm about to exit college. I wasn't as self-sufficient...and confident. I didn't have that in 2007. Maybe a little bit, but not [enough] to go out on my own. I think the first couple years of high school, it was just like people-pleasing to some extent while still being in my own space.*

It's been a journey in that sense, because I was trying to find myself throughout the first couple of years of high school. After high school, not even probably until the end of my sophomore year of college, did I start finding myself and being comfortable with who I was. That's another thing you have to get accustomed to in high school: being you and being comfortable with being you. I don't think I got to that [point] until actually coming to college where everything is just so free. Especially coming to a school as diverse as the one I go to, it's really liberating. You don't feel as bound by social norms and the need to fit in as much as in high school. So, I think that has changed me a lot.

James: *Back ten years ago, I always thought everything was done without much effort, so I wouldn't really put too much effort into [anything]. When I wasn't good at something, I'd be like, "man I'm not good at anything." But I didn't realize, I [hadn't] put enough effort into it. Whether it was exercising, playing video games, or just doing something in school...I didn't have the patience to understand [that if I] put some effort into it, I could do it.*

Now, it's like everything is starting to click. So, I push myself harder and harder because I want more. I want to be faster, stronger, smarter...I want everything now. I have the patience to wait on it, but

I'm driving myself to get to levels I didn't think I'd even be able to reach.

Camille: *Back then, I was very shy. I really secluded myself. I was real quiet. That was years ago. Growing up in a very strict Caribbean household, it was kind of hard to voice your opinion. I feel like now, I'm much more outgoing. I don't really hold my tongue for anyone...in a good way. I just tell it like it is. I voice my opinion more.*

FAMILY

Raven: *Seven years ago, my dad passed when I was in eighth grade. I think the biggest change in me has been that I went from being very privileged to being more understanding, I guess.*

My mom is a single mom, so that really changed my perspective on a lot. Especially because he was murdered. I was very green to how the world worked and how wrong the world worked. I didn't find it fair that my mom had to be a single mom. I didn't find it fair that she had to struggle. But I see that there are a lot of people out there who have to struggle, for different reasons.

I feel like there were a lot of barriers against me, just because I didn't have my dad. I had to basically grow up and understand a lot about this world. Like sometimes, a lot of people don't have dads for a lot of different [reasons]. I lost my dad to violence. This violence was probably caused by this man not having the means to do anything besides...I guess...go out and kill someone. And this [lack] was because of where he grew up. And where he grew up is due to, I guess, institutionalized racism. So, there are a lot of things that I see [how] the points connect. Before, I was really angry, I didn't understand why my dad wasn't there. But after looking deeper into it, I've learned a lot about acceptance in the past seven years. And forgiving, because I could have just lived my life hating this guy.

And because my mom had to basically raise me on her own, [I've gained an] understanding of how to struggle, respect for what my mom has done, and respect for a lot of people who do it - whether it's by choice or not by choice: single fathers and mothers. [I've learned] responsibility, because my mom had to work a lot more, I was responsible a lot more for my little brother. [I learned about] being a role model, because I had to be there for my little brother. I guess I was a lot more selfish [before], in that I didn't care about too much of anything [except] myself and getting what I wanted, making sure I was fly! And I realize now, that's not what's important in life.

A lot of the people who you hold dear to you and close to you are what's important. And I didn't really notice that until losing my dad, that no one is guaranteed in your life. One of the things I've gotten over the last seven years, is to forgive. One, because of the man who murdered my dad. But also, two, to forgive people who you love...and people who you don't love. Because no one is always going to be in your life, and ultimately, you've gotta live your life not having regrets, not having malice in your heart. Your days on this Earth are numbered, so just live your life happily and not angry at anyone, because at the end of the day, you only have one life to live.

Ebonee: *Seven years ago I think I was 15 or 16...it doesn't feel like it though. It feels like just yesterday I was 15. It feels like I'm a 30-year old woman. Being 15 and 16...man, listen...I didn't care about much. A lot of stuff that I should have cared about, I didn't care about. I was too focused on being 'grown', as my mother would call it.*

Everybody wants to be grown. You know, you hit teenage years, you start feeling yourself. You get you a little boyfriend...can't nobody tell you nothin'! I stress family more [now]. Before, when I was 15 and 16, I didn't want to sit around my house and bond with my mom and my sisters, and go here and go there. No, I wanted to be out with my friends, I wanted to go see my boyfriend.

That has definitely changed. I definitely enjoy spending time with my sisters. I enjoy having those talks. I enjoy chillin' with my family, that's what I like. Because family is all you have, you know? Losing my mom and losing my dad, it made me appreciate my family way more. There are a lot of things that I didn't get to do with my mother and my father that I should have. I was being stubborn, I was being a teenager, I was being me. I didn't care about getting manis and pedis with Mommy. No, I wanted to go with my friends...and we were going to get our nails done.

FRIENDS

Kiana: *Back then I was probably a little worse with my anxiety than I am now. Over the years through different life experiences, I've learned how to accept certain things and how to adjust to certain things. I realized what I deserve and what I don't deserve.*

I definitely am not the same as I would have been seven years ago, because I would have not really talked, and been a little more in my shell. It gradually became [a part of me], because I basically became fed up with a lot of things that I was dealing with. So, I was like, 'Uh-uh this cannot continue to happen.' So, I started speaking up and saying how I felt about anything...to anyone. Originally, when I first developed this new attitude, I was feeling good about it. I was like, "People are getting where I'm coming from. I don't want to say it again; I'm not dealing with this nonsense!" But I started to kind of abuse it a little bit. I started going off...and I realized that I can't be doing that.

So, I had to take a little bit of a back seat from myself and just reflect a little more, and think a little more. Before I started speaking up for myself, I was always thinking about everyone else and their feelings, and not mine. My feelings had always taken a back seat, so that's when I started. I got fed up, and started putting my feelings first. Now it's kind of on an equal balance, I'm thinking about myself and you at the same time. So, I'm not going to go off on you, but I'm still going to let you know how I feel.

Aquillia: *In 2007, I would have wondered why people weren't taking more pictures of me to put on Facebook! And then I would have wondered if I looked good in them, and please don't put them on Facebook if I don't! That's what I would have been doing.*

I did not think highly of myself at all. Most times I had a lot of acquaintances, and that wouldn't have bothered me then, because I would have looked like I had a lot of people [who] knew me or wanted to hang out with me, and that would have been cool with me. But the people [who] knew me in high school - like really knew me - the difference with them is that they [still] know me now. They have my number. They have my address. And those are the people [who] I want to connect with. And I think back then it was more about why more people didn't want to connect, you know?

I was younger [than my classmates]. I wasn't exactly the lame, but I wasn't the really cool person, so it's like I was in the middle. This was my life: "my parents won't let me go to the hotel after party when you turn 18. I gotta be at home. That's so lame."

And I really felt self-conscious about all of those things...My group of friends, we have been friends since we were little, and we were just not really outgoing. We stayed within ourselves. We're really different, my friends, we're a special bunch. And by that, I just mean that we have a lot of jokes people don't think are funny. Some of us are awkward. At some point in time I just thought, 'if I didn't have this group of friends, who would I be friends with?...If you don't like me, you're missing out!'

IN SCHOOL

Krystal: *In 2007, what was I?! A sophomore in high school? Nothing was important except for school and boys, and whatever I was wearing to school the next day. I feel like there was nothing that was of deep substance that was important.*

It was one of those things where I knew that I wanted to help people but I wasn't really doing anything about it. I wasn't acting on anything much. We'd do little stuff here and there but nothing like, profound. At least in my opinion, I don't think I was doing anything off the wall. I feel like I was a regular teenager, I was worried about boys, talking on the phone, running around, like nothing bookworthy.

Khalid: *Six to seven years ago, I was in junior high school on my way to high school. Back then I wasn't concerned about the issues that we're going through now. I was more concerned about passing my classes, going to school, girls and everything. But where I'm at now, I'm more politically aware, and I guess racially aware, of what is going on in the world. What we're still facing, and what we still have to do.*

Malika: *14 or 15...one of those ages...as a freshman in high school, I was still trying to figure out how to fit in and how to make friends. And I was awkward. I...Oh god, just thinking about it, I'm cringing...I lived mostly for others in the sense that I always tried to impress other people or receive their validation on everything that I did.*

I always had strong opinions. I was always known for that as a student, but it was always simple to just change so that I could be like everyone else. So that if someone brought up an opposing view, I was like, "you know what? That actually sounds better, so I'm gonna tag along."

It didn't really start developing into something that I caught and stopped doing until towards the end of high school. It was just a place where I...I don't want to be again. Yeah, I'm far from it. I don't even know how I got here.

Mikal: *Looking back at 2007/2008, I was living in New Jersey with my granddad. I was a very awkward young man back then. I'd just gone through puberty, I was getting used to the new shape of my body...I was like an inch taller.*

It was weird back then. I was only there for a year, and my grand-dad was the biggest prude. He didn't want us doing anything but reading books, and he really believed in getting an education and making a better life for yourself. But right outside the window, on that block, there were drug-dealers. Every single day you'd hear gun-shots, and it was just a weird thing to live in.

A year after that, we came out to Canarsie [in Brooklyn, NY]. While we were in Canarsie, that's when I started going to Bedford [Academy High School]. I think being at Bedford, there were a lot great role models there. Maybe I didn't appreciate that at the time. I was a little bit younger, I didn't know as much, and I didn't know how to appreciate that at the moment.

Brother [Learie] Corbin - he's since passed - he was a great influence on us. He used to come out to some of our shows, and he always showed us love. He would mentor us and give us great advice. I think that had a huge part in developing the man that I've grown into. Through college, and to the point where I am now, I've always kept his words with me and I always respected the man that he was. Having role models like that can definitely help build you...turning that awkward young man into the stud that I am now wasn't an easy task!

Chelsea: *Six or seven years ago...I was a freshman in high school. I was hanging out with the wrong crowd, the wrong people, seeking validation from everyone. You could see how that could be problematic, because you really can't please everyone, and in an attempt to do so you only end up hurting yourself. I never went to class. I was basically setting myself up for failure. If you were to ask me about yoga and meditation back then, I would really look at you like, "are you serious?! Are you really asking me this right now?!" I wasn't lucky, but I was fortunate to know the right people.*

There's this guy, Seneca the Younger. He was a Roman philosopher, and he said, "luck is what happens when preparation meets opportunity." So, I got to this point...part of it was knowing the right people. But the second part was being open and allowing them to guide me in the right direction. That's pretty much what made all the difference for me.

There were two people in particular - Marquita Speller and Craig Richardson. I have no idea what they saw in me as a freshman, but they helped me get out of that school. And that really made all the difference for me. Changing my environment, changing the people who I hung around with...I'll definitely always be grateful for that opportunity. I really don't know where I would have been had I stayed at [the other school].

I think part of me being open to guidance is showing vulnerability. Showing that, "okay I know that I really suck right now, but I'm okay with you helping me." You'll meet those people who know they're not on the right path, but they make it seem as if everything is okay, or as if they know everything. I think part of it for me was being okay with knowing that I was not content with where I was. I knew that some change needed to happen. And they kind of met me halfway.

Joshua: *In 2007, I was sophomore in high school. I transferred from a high school...it wasn't really a good school. The students weren't really motivated to perform well. And my grades...I was getting A's and the teachers would look at my grades and they'd be like, "whoa, this is* new." That was so foreign to them, because no students were as motivated to perform well.

So, I talked to one of the vice principals. I was like, "I don't think I'm doing really well in this school." So, she talked to some people and the next semester I was able to transfer. So, I feel like I've always wanted to be surrounded by students who are motivated, who thought about their futures, and didn't just go to school as a place to go to. That's how I felt back at my old school.

Faith: *In 2007, I was just entering high school. I was transitioning from junior high school where my grades and my performance in school weren't bad, but I could have done way better. My family knew it. I knew it. But I was focused on fitting in.*

I've always believed that we are created to be exactly who we are. And I was always trying to just fit in because I was always that young lady that stood out. Not necessarily in a bad way, I just stood out. I wasn't partying, I couldn't go to the parties. I wasn't doing the whole boyfriend thing because my grandmother knew everyone in my school, everyone knew me in my school, so there was nothing that I could do. Even up until I got into college, my first year in college my grandmother was like, "Oh, I'm going to come to the school and I'm going to talk to x, y, and z" and I'm like, "why are you coming up to the school?! It's college, and nobody really cares right now!"

But I always had that in my life, so it was very hard for me to try to be in with everybody. I knew that when I came home, that wasn't going to work. So, I was transitioning from that...and when I got to high school I made a vow in between that transition and said, "When I get to high school, it's a fresh start, and I'm going to do my thing." And from freshman year to senior year, I did my thing because I just made up my mind that I was going to be very successful, and [that] I was going to be exactly who I'm supposed to be.

Rima: *Well, I was actually home-schooled. When my mom brought me home from Senegal, she was like, "Oh, we'll do home school." She didn't want to put me in a school, she felt like it wasn't the right thing to do. But home school...um...I had no discipline, I guess?! Maybe. I don't know. Whatever it was, home school wasn't working out. And after much convincing and [talking] with the principal of a nearby high school - whose son and my little brother were classmates in a private home school - I ended up at my [high school].*

When I was home-schooled for the first half of 9th grade, it was terrible. Like I wasn't doing anything! To be quite frank, I was on lesson three when I should have been on lesson 13. But I was also home-schooled for 4th grade and 5th grade, and that was a little better. I had a teacher, so-to-speak. My mom was more heavily involved, and one of her friends - who was like a Ph.D. or something like that, or she was getting her Ph.D., I don't quite remember now - was teaching me as well. So, I had more of a schedule then. For 9th grade, I was expected to go out there and take it head on, as someone would if they were going to college. But home-schooling is not the worst...I was the random kid in the neighborhood who didn't go to school. My little brother, however, has been home-schooled his entire life and he has a group. They were kids in various grades, but they were a group nonetheless.

Alberto: *I was born in New York City. At the age of four, we moved to Providence, Rhode Island with my mom and my dad. That's where I was raised until the age of 14. At the age of 14, that's when my mom decided to take my sister and I to the Dominican Republic. One, it was better for my sister, who had a skin condition at the time. Two, I was really into playing baseball, and the Dominican Republic is like the motherland of baseball players...When I came back from the Dominican Republic to New York, [since] I didn't have the opportunity* to attend to attend high school in the Dominican Republic, the first thing I had to do was get my G.E.D.

I signed up for classes - a two-month crash course at [a local] community college - where we squeezed in four years of high school into two months. And I say two months, but it really wasn't two months because my classes were only two days a week, and they were only three hours each day. We covered four years of high school in 48 hours. My dad has a pet grooming business, so before I started school I would go to the pet shop with him all the time. I would wake up around 5:30 or six o'clock in the morning, and I would make sure to put in an hour and a half to two hours of studying with the G.E.D. prep book. Then I would go to work. I would come back, shower, and then continue to study for like another two to two and a half hours before I went to bed.

...To be honest, I received my G.E.D., and it was great and everything. It was a lot of hard work, but I knew there was still a lot that I had to do. So, in my mind at the time, I wasn't focused on celebrating that stuff. And thinking back, I think something we should all do is celebrate each step we take. Because whatever effort it took, it took effort to get to that step. And I think that everything should be celebrated.

Devin: *All the standard societal personality types, you will find in the tech world. It is literally no different...Society sees us as wizards, geniuses, magicians because we can fix their items and get their email working again. Or make an application. Or change the background on their monitor. But in reality, we just devote the time to study and work towards what we love messing with.*

And a lot of that is actually born - for the majority of people I've met in tech field and from my personal experience - [out of] being shunned from that typical societal hierarchy in school. 'Cuz I was bullied a lot in school. The love for tech was already there, but in ele-

mentary and middle school I was bullied a lot. So, I turned to technology and video games to pretty much ease that pain. And that is the case for a lot of people. They turn to all that to get away from society.

Growing up, it wasn't that tough to keep holding on to these interests, because I felt like I didn't really have a choice. It's what kept me sane during the middle school years...growing up, the school life was particularly kind of rough. Not only for holding on to my interests, but from being one of six Black kids enrolled at a school, because my mom decided to put me in Catholic school due to bullying in public school. Great school, but the fact that I could count on my hands the number of Black [students] and students of color enrolled at the school was kind of disheartening.

And it really didn't help with the whole "getting a group of friends together" in middle school. Because for most of it, I didn't fit in with the other kids of color in my class. I stayed on talking terms with them, but especially as we got older and hit puberty, the bullying got serious. I just retreated into tech and video games.

When I was super young, [I remember] taking trips to FuncoLand with my older brother, shopping for video games, playing Street Fighter against kids at the arcade machine in the Chinese restaurant on my block...as I started getting older and going to arcades on my own...from 2007 to 2009 is really when I got competitive into gaming and I was playing games like Street Fighter III and Street Fighter IV. And the community there was very supportive, but in a school of hard knocks sort of way.

FINDING MY PATH

Christina: Back in '07/'08, that's when I was really trying to figure out what I was going to do. I graduated [from college] in 2007 and was really in this limbo. I had this degree in psychology, and I can't do anything with it unless I go get my master's degree. I really have *this passion where I want to get into the medical field, but I can't do well on this [MCAT] test, what am I going to do?*

Me and my cousin moved into an apartment together. So, I was like, I need to work. I need to figure out what I'm going to do with my life now that I'm in this limbo area. I was excited to have just come out of this great experience at college, but at the same time I was discouraged because my plan didn't exactly go the way that I had envisioned when I applied to college. It was a little discouraging, because I was coming back home to live, and hopefully, to try to find a job.

I was not really sure where I was going at that point. It was kinda just sitting down and trying to make a plan. Like I said, there's more than one way to your goal, so things just kind of fell in place and I just kinda worked hard and tried to figure out where my passion lied, and how I could get there.

Leodus: *In 2007, I knew I wanted to be an entrepreneur, and I was hungry. I had all the energy in the world, but I was not necessarily as mature as I am now, and I was not streamlined [in my focus] like I am now. I didn't know what I wanted to do in '07.*

It just happened to be a situation where the real estate market crashed in '08. And so, buildings were going for nothing. It's just like the stock market, when stuff falls down and stuff is cheap, you can grab a piece of it. You grab as much as you can, and when values go back up, now all of a sudden, you've become rich. In a way, it was luck...I would have come up with something.

I had a vending company too. Even if I had a bunch of vending machines all around, eventually that would have made me enough money to [the point] where I didn't necessarily have to be anywhere. It actually might have been easier, now that I think about it...I think I had a lot of raw talent but I didn't know how to really utilize it. I didn't know anything. Looking back, I got out of college and I didn't know anything. I didn't know anything about life, business, nothing.

But I wanted to know, so I made it my business to find out everything I needed to find out.

Haniyyah: *I was 13 years old, I was in high school, and...I mean, I don't even think I know who I am right now exactly for me to say who I was in 2007. I don't think at that point anyone really knew who they were. At that point, we were all just listening to what people were telling us...and following instructions.*

And so, I think I was receiving information. I think I was doing whatever I wanted to do with that information at the time...I was a sophomore, and at that point I didn't even know what I wanted to do with my future, which I didn't figure out until I was a senior in college...But I definitely think there were a lot of mentors along the way that supported me to get to the point where I am today.

Kasim: *It's like as I grew up, [my goals] evolved each time. There was a time I wanted to be a doctor, I wanted to save people's lives. But as I got older I got turned off by that because you've got to go through eight years of medical school. That's when I was like, 'Okay, that's not a passion!' I was like, 'Hold up, hold up! Y'all didn't tell me that part! Obviously, that was [in] the fine print!' I was like, 'I guess I don't have a passion for this after all' because I got out of that plan real quick! I was about that life until I saw that!*

After that whole doctor stuff went through the roof, I was just like, 'man, I don't even know what I want to do.' But the one thing I know that I want to do is...be successful at something. Meaning I want to find something I'm good at, that pays a lot, to the point where I can provide for my family on a life-changing type of spectrum...like [where] we're living luxuriously.

Another thing that pushed me towards that [is being] a fan of hip-hop. And although if you look at these hip-hop videos, most of the time they have negative images associated with them, but I just see the amount of fun these rappers have in these music videos and I'm just like 'nah yo, look at them! They're just living beautifully right now!' I want to push [towards] something like that, or at least have the ability to do something like that whenever I want, you know? So, I use that as a drive.

Jonel: *I don't think you would have met the same person seven or eight years ago. Back then, I never really thought about the future that much. I definitely never imagined living here [in Japan]. I always thought it was a great idea, but not something I could actually make come true.*

I feel like seven or eight years ago, I was a very limited person. I only saw what other people did and was like, 'okay I can potentially do that.' But I never saw beyond that...Out of my friend group, I was the only one learning Japanese. My other friends were learning Chinese, so we had that kind of Asian influence in us. But we couldn't really communicate with each other, which is what I kinda wanted. I wanted someone to learn the language with me so we could be like, "hey!" and talk to each other throughout the day and stuff. But it wasn't until I got to college that I found people who were also interested in the same things I was interested in.

Ethan: *Seven years ago, I was 13. I've always been ambitious. I remember telling everyone in my house, "I'm gonna be rich one day! You'll work for me!" And they were always like, "oh? What's your plan?! What are you going to do?"*

And originally the plan was, go to the NBA, you know? I loved basketball. That's when I was 12. And then I turned 13 and all my friends hit their growth spurts, and I was still 5'2", and everyone was like 5'7" and up. This is when I was keeping up with everything. High school ball, college basketball, the NBA...I was into it like that was a destined thing. I did intense research on it. I saw that the aver-

age point guard was like 6'2". In 9th grade I was already taller than my dad, my grandpas, and my uncles. So, I was like, 'Uh, this might not be the thing for me.'

Since then, it's been a constant pursuit of trying to identify what it is I want to do. As the journey continues, I would say everything I've developed a strong interest in, or love for, I will be doing, or will incorporate into what I'm doing. Except for playing professional basketball. That was a crucial point in [my] life. I guess you could say that's when it all kinda started.

Jasmine: *How old was I?...How old am I now?!...Seven years ago I was 17 years old. I was a junior in high school. Junior year of high school was rough! I'll never forget the day [my friends and I] collectively went to the guidance counselor's office and just sat down like, "We want to drop out!" It was really dramatic because we were applying for the SATs or something like that.*

Back then, I had everything planned out and how it was going to happen. I was going to graduate. And then I was going to go to college. I was going to major in history, but do it on a pre-med track. Get into medical school. Be a doctor. And live happily ever after.

That didn't happen, and that's exactly how I got to this point right now, 'cuz I learned that life does not go as you planned. At all...I was 17, and planning my life 10 to 15 years [in advance]. That didn't go as planned...that's when I had my mini-crisis that I wasn't going to [medical] school, the year after I graduated.

I had to take a year off. [I was like], 'Oh my gosh! What am I going to do?! I'm a failure at life! Everything is not going as planned!' It was real dramatic at that time. Well, first I cried. I cried for like a day or two. And then I got it together, because I was like, 'I can't just sit here and do nothing. I have a college degree, I'm not about to sit at home and sulk. I have to do something and prepare myself to try again and get it together.' So, it was really an internal thing for me.

Silver: *Back in the beginning of high school, I was definitely lost. I didn't really feel like I had the principal direction that I wanted to go in. I was just following the path that the government set out for me. But I still think that there was a part of me that didn't grow up, and was the kid in me that wanted to have fun before anything else. That was pretty much it, that was my number one priority.*

It was a good thing and a bad thing. It came with some strengths and some weaknesses...but I do think that wanting to have fun is very important.

There's something about having that childlike innocence that can really help you communicate with the world. Especially if you're trying to get into television, because your audience is going to be children; and if you don't know how to talk to children, if you don't know what it means to be a child, then you're not going to succeed. That's when you enter that territory when you're like one of the suits, and you're trying to have those test audiences where you just bring kids in and show them shapes and colors to see how they react because you don't know what kids want. There's something about being able to go back into that inner child and being able to let them out...sparingly.

If you try to go about everything [by thinking about] the most responsible thing to do, or the most logical thing, then you'll probably miss out on the solutions to problems that may not seem clear to the traditional adult. I think any problem can benefit from some creative problem solving, and no one knows how to solve a problem like kids.

Quaneesha: *Seven years ago...I had just entered [high school]. I had no clue about what to do in life. I didn't have any goals [about] what I wanted to be. You know how people sometimes say, "I want to be a police officer." I didn't have any plans on what I wanted to do. I just came into [high school] with an open mind.*

Acting wasn't on my mind then. I used to watch it and say, "Oh okay, that's cool. I [might] want to get into it." But it wasn't some-

thing that I was like, 'You know what? I'm gonna go into high school and start something. I'm going to be a part of something.' No, seven years ago I was like a blank page. I was just trying to figure out what life would be like. It was scary, like 'oh my god, I'm entering high school! I don't want to be an adult. I don't want to grow up.'

It wasn't until I was in Ms. Johnson's history class. Ms. Johnson and I figured that I would be a lawyer. She did law and I looked up to her like, 'She's such a great woman! Oh my god, she's awesome! I would love to do law.' That's when I just felt like I wanted to be a lawyer and that's what I wanted to do. You couldn't tell me I wasn't going to be a lawyer. I was going to graduate college and I was going to go to law school. That's all I wanted to do.

Neiko: *Who was I in 2007? I was an 18-year old immature kid who had signed up for the United States Navy. Where was I? I was in Guantanamo Bay, Cuba, serving the country. [Being in the military] instilled in me a lot of discipline. Don't get me wrong, I had discipline, but the military instilled more discipline into me that I really never saw. It helped me to become a more positive and a patient person.*

You know, especially with having kids, being positive and having patience is the key. So, it's helped me with that. I tell people all the time when asked about the military: if it's for you and you want to try something different, then make it happen. But, if you know you don't want to do it, school is the best thing. That's how I feel.

THINGS CHANGE

Courtney: *[Back then], I was fearless. I was controversial. I was just...so young. I wanted to experience everything. I thought everything was within my reach. Not to say that it isn't now, but I just thought that it was so much more within my reach.*

I thought it was so close. I thought it [would take] just a couple phone calls, and a couple connections, and I would be in New York or in L.A. pioneering some new cultural channel. I was dating, and I thought love was something that you see in movies. I thought relationships were something that you see in music videos. It was just so different.

Marriage to me now, having kids, it's...hard work. It's hard work and responsibility, and that was lost on me seven years ago. I always said, "I want to have a family. I want to be like the Black '7th Heaven!'" That's what I always used to say. It was lost on me, the work that goes into it.

Patrick: [Back then] I dreamed that when I turned 21 I'd be in college, having a lot of fun, partying and having a good time. Now I'm working a full-time job, partnering with my wife to try and raise our son in this day and age. I'm a lot different from who I was. I think differently.

When you join the military, once you get in the door, your mentality changes. How you look at things changes. It's the smallest things sometimes, that we didn't think were dumb or immature back then, you look at it now and...it annoys you a little bit more. I wouldn't say [the military] forces you...it encourages you to be an adult at a very early age. It spurs your mind to develop a little bit faster.

I'm very different from how I was back then. I had to understand that eventually I was going to grow up, eventually I was going to have to make the sort of decisions that I'm making now. One of the biggest things I say when I get paid is "man, I wish I was a teenager back in high school with my parents, because I didn't have these types of responsibilities." Having a lot of responsibilities changes you a lot. It definitely does.

Shanai: *I may have had the same personality in some ways, but I've definitely grown. I would say that I was a child seven or eight years ago. Coming to a place of adulthood is something that changes a person anyway. Something I'm grateful for is the ability to continuously progress as a person.*

I wish I could take some days off [from adulting]! I don't enjoy the bills and the things that come with it! I've been saying I think we all, as a country, should have a week every so often, to restart. No adulting. I think we'll all benefit from it and enjoy it.

Ashley: *I was the planner. I had my life planned out up until retirement...this was in high school. I knew when I was going to get married, when I was going to have my 2.5 children. I had it down. And then that plan went out the door, and I had to cope with that. I had a moment of awakening where I was like, 'oh my gosh, my life is not at all where it should be.' And I freaked out...and then I was like, 'It's not where I thought it would be, but I am in such a good place. And I didn't plan this good place, but it's awesome. So, let's just keep rolling with it, because it's turning out pretty good.'*

Bernadette: *You wouldn't have met the same person last year, so definitely not six or seven years ago. You know, people can tell you certain things, but sometimes you really just have to live. My mom is extremely overprotective. My grandmother is extremely overprotective. I'm an only child. I was my grandmother's first granddaughter. My mom tried her best to prepare me for the world as much as she could, sheltering me from some things that she probably shouldn't have sheltered me from.*

College taught me some things...I left from college so empowered like, 'I'm about to take over the world! I'm going to be able to get whatever job I want to!' And then life hits. It takes about 10 weeks for your diploma to come in the mail. As soon as it came in the mail, I swear life took off. Losing a job (my first job right after college) and really liking that job and thinking that this was going to be my career, working in mental health. And then seeing, 'this is not what I thought it was going to be.' Like what I read in textbooks about what it was going to be, and when I actually experienced it, it [wasn't] the same thing. I had to regroup and take jobs in different areas to see what I wanted to do.

Some people are born knowing their passion. Some people learn their passion over their experiences. I feel like I've learned a lot of things through experiences. My perspective is completely different. I'm a big planner. I'm going to over-analyze everything. I like to plan out things...that's how my approach was to everything in life. I had a five-year plan. I had a two-year plan. I knew where I was going to be...It was very easy to be so confident, and pumped, and motivated when things are going your way.

But then, when things are not going your way, and you're getting a "no"...maybe not even a "no", but a "not now"...I feel like in the last two years, through the experiences that I've had, I've really had to think about it like, I really need to stop planning everything...Yes, some of those things are going to happen, especially when you have steps for how you're going to get there, but it's not always going to happen the way you think it's going to happen. Like if I say right now, "Oh when I'm 40, I'm going to be doing this." I can work towards doing that, but who knows what's going to happen at 37.

Jared: *[Back then], you would have met a confused people-pleaser. You would have met a chameleon. Who I was with, and what I was around, is what I would conform to in efforts to find myself.*

...Whether it was a group of people who dressed a certain way, or authority figures that said I had to get these certain types of grades [in school]. I was across the board. Like I could be affiliated in some street gang, but then I could be getting straight A's and B's as a re-

cruit in high school playing football. I never made sense. If you were on the outside looking in [you'd be like], "Why is he acting this way [when] he can do this?" I was just...it made no sense, looking back on it. And that's why I say I was people-pleasing. If you're getting A's and B's...why are you getting kicked out for a gang-related fight? Like, it just doesn't add up.

So, I was pleasing the streets; I was pleasing my parents, but at the end of the day, I wasn't pleasing anybody if you look deep...and it took me a long time to figure out that all that was overrated. You don't have to know where you come from to figure out who you are, and what you want to be...I was across the board confused, but I played the part I needed to play. And for the people who weren't smart enough to see it, I had them fooled. That's what landed me in the penitentiary. If you knew anything about me and my family, that's the last place I should have been.

Kevin: *Life has changed me over the last seven years. My dad always told me life is your best teacher. Some people make mistakes and don't learn. Some people make those mistakes over and over again; versus [other] people who made a mistake, maybe didn't understand it, maybe made it that second time, but they learned and they progressed, and got better [because of] it. That's kind of been what has changed me over the past seven years.*

Back in 2007, I was working at a very popular company at the time. It was just hitting the ground running, and I was thinking, 'Hey, this is pretty good. I started off as a regular representative. My work ethic ended up getting me to be on the management team, and here I am.' I was maybe 20 or 21 at the time, and I'm making $16.72 an hour. I had just come back from school in Mississippi - I had unfortunately dropped out - and I was thinking like, 'man, I dropped out of school, but I'm at $17 an hour at 20 years old. This is going to be pretty good! I know a couple of adults who don't make this amount.'

The reason why I bring that up is that I was kinda...shallow. Again, those life experiences. I had never experienced a layoff, which this company did.

This was a grand company, I'm thinking 'wow, this is going to be great!' And here I was...I worked there a total of two years and then they shut down the whole call center and outsourced it to Toronto. That was my welcome into corporate America. It really made me realize at that point, 'man, just working a job is not going to do it.' After the layoff, I decided to get back into school after dropping out in Mississippi. I will admit, they did take care of us. There was a situation where - I guess because the job was outsourced - there were a lot of different benefits. It's called the [Trade Adjustment Assistance program] under the Federal Trade Act. So, I was able to go back to a two-year school, and get it paid for...I actually finished up not too long ago, to get the associate's degree.

It was good...it takes a little prayer. I know it sounds cliché, but you can't lose your faith. I just asked God to help me through it. Sometimes I feel like I shouldn't think this way, but I always think how it could be worse. I lost a brother in 2006, my second brother. My first brother got killed in 2004. So, I mean, it could be worse. I was still living, I was only 21 at the time, I still had opportunities.

Tobi: *I do think, to some extent, you would have met this woman. I've always been an overachiever...In terms of my dreams, being passionate, and all that, I was kind of the same person. I would say [now] the passion is times ten, for sure.*

The past few years have been very monumental in terms of who I am today...being around people who challenge me. That has played a key part in the person that I've grown to be. I had my mom, who played a very important role in who I am today. I had her around me, constantly telling me all these things that I needed to hear to keep me

*going. As you grow up, that doesn't really happen anymore, so I had
to find that voice to keep me going.*

*When it comes to reading…[back] then, you would have had to pin
me down to get me to read. In the last week actually, I bought six
books. I'm kind of embarrassed and kind of happy to say that. That is
a massive, massive difference. Doing research at university helped me
a lot. The things I was able to find out, and the things I was able to
unravel, it just completely blew my mind. I'm different from the person I was. I ask a lot more questions. I used to ask questions then, but
[now] I ask a lot more questions with the aim to find, or create a solution to those questions.*

Family Life

It starts at home. We have all heard this statement before. It is nearly impossible to have any kind of extended conversation about children and/or teenagers without someone uttering those four words. We use it to talk about nearly everything kids do, from how they interact with peers and teachers in school, to how they behave in public, to how they interact with authority figures.

Ironically, this statement is rarely used to describe the ways in which we as adults - the designers and keepers of all the spaces where children find themselves - interact with the youngest members of our society. This is unfortunate, because not only do children and teenagers have to deal with the consequences of adults' decisions about what kind of society they will grow up in, but their lives are negatively impacted each time we fail to examine whether our collective behavior matches our proclaimed beliefs.

What we each bring from our homes into the broader society determines what kind of country we live in. It determines who we allow to represent and lead us. It guides the formal laws we create to govern how we will live peacefully in each other's presence. It undergirds the informal norms we create to govern how we will engage with each other. It determines how much civility will exist in our civilization.

It starts at home, but what is *it*? What are the experiences, values, beliefs, and ideas that are most heavily determined by the homes we come from? What are the life perspectives that we absorb from our home environments? Who are the people in our homes we look to for these things? Who are the people in our homes who brought these things to us?

It starts at home, but where is *home*? Is home the place where we sleep? Is home the place where we feel free to rest? Is home where we find the people who most closely share our DNA? Is home where we find the people who most closely share our values?

The spaces we call home, and the people we call family.

SETTING THE FOUNDATION

Ashley: *My family has always been really important to me. The more I talk to people outside of my family, the more I realize how rare my family dynamic is. Growing up, I didn't know the difference between my mom's side of the family and my dad's side of the family. They were all just family. And they would get together, and nobody argues, nobody fights...we just have a good time. And I have a big family and we're all really close, so they have been the constant in my life and have always been really important to me.*

I'm sure a lot of other people can relate, when everyone else turns their back on you, you gotta have somebody who's still down for you through whatever. No matter what you do, no matter what, they're still down for you. And that's my family. They definitely allowed me to get to this place, and just loved me and accepted me for who I am. And if these people can accept me for me, then gosh darn it, everybody should! And if you can't, that's okay, because I've got them. And so, however you define family, you need family. They don't have to be biological, but you gotta have your people.

Alberto: [My mindset] really has a lot to do with a combination of a couple of things. One is my family - my mom, my dad, my uncles - everybody who represents my family. The people around me, my community, my environment...I've always seen people work hard. I've never had the privilege to be around people who always had it their way, or always had it easy. I grew up seeing that everything takes hard work...It was always an uphill climb for me, and for the people around me.

...[When] I was 13 or 14 years old...I was with my mom and my stepdad...I call my stepdad my dad because he was the one that raised me. I get along with both of my dads. Both of my dads have been there. My mom has been there. That's always something that I tend to put out there, I'm very grateful for my stepdad and my dad. So, I was with my mom, my dad, and my three sisters. We weren't rich, we just led normal lives...I was always with my family. It didn't matter which side of my family I was with, I've always been pretty close to my family.

Who I am today, hasn't just been [because of] my experiences, it's also been the support that I've had. Something that I always like to mention is the support that I've had, [and] the family that I've gained through my life experiences. Whether it's my nuclear family, whether it's...just everybody. Sometimes I feel like anyone who has supported me through my process, I call them family, just because of how close I [hold] them. I tend to not forget the little things that people have done for me, you know?

Katie: [My family] just lets me be me. We're all so different, and it's helpful that I've never felt compared to anyone else. I grew up with three sisters and I think whenever you have siblings, there's always that danger of comparing yourself to your siblings. Sometimes I think that just happens a lot in families, and I don't know how my parents did it, but I've never felt like I had to live up to my older sisters, and I *hope my [youngest] sister doesn't feel like that either. We were all just kind of free to explore the paths that we wanted, and I think that I was on the usual path.*

Right after high school, I went to college...and kind of wandered off that path. And there were definitely questions and challenges like, "well are you going to finish? What are you going to do?" And there was definitely pressure - from myself mostly - because you don't want to let down the family or anything like that, but I think there was a lot of grace given for me to grow. I think they realized it sooner than me, that there is no set plan. Sometimes - or many times - life does not happen like you want it to. And I think the family realized that even before I [did]. Realizing that, letting me come to terms with it, and now I am where I am because I was allowed to make mistakes and re-cover. It's really nice to have that, because I know a lot of people don't.

I grew up in a unique situation, with all girl [siblings] and no brothers, and people always kind of bemoan that fact like, "Oh it must have been super hard, the bathroom must have been a disaster!" and it's like, "Well, no...everyone calm down. You think that was a big thing happening in the house? Like, not enough bathroom time for all the girls?! We all showered and got dressed and made it to church relatively on time every Sunday, okay?! So, we're good!" The whole idea of freedom, since I didn't have any brothers, I didn't know any other way to be. This is just kind of how it was...I feel like my parents were very good at making it known that we were loved and giving us a path to finding self-love as well. Loving who you are, and loving who you are becoming.

Kasim: *I gotta give it to my parents too. They tried their best and they really kept me away from [negative] stuff. They sat down with me and weren't afraid to talk to me about all the images that are por-trayed [in the media]. I could listen to rap music, but I don't neces-*

sarily have to take it to the head or think that it's like the only way out, you know?

There are way more options out there, it's just that they are not as highlighted as [becoming] an entertainer or an athlete. I feel like those are two lanes that - especially African-American men - choose to take. They feel like those are the only two lanes to get out of what you would [call] the 'hood. But there are many other ways. That's how I kept that balance, my parents and my family. They made it known, they proved to me that those are not the only ways to get out...I've got to give it to them.

Jasmine: *I think I've always been like that. I think it's the way I was raised. I'm going to do what makes me happy, and I know myself best. I know what I want. I know what's going to make me happy. I know what's best for me. When it comes to other people's approval, it never really mattered to me...except for my parents. So, I would tell my parents and get their advice like, "hey, do you think this is a good idea?" And they've always been so supportive.*

...You know, parents have hopes for their children, and they really wanted me to be a doctor. But they saw the struggle, and they saw what it did to me. They saw that I had another place which was just as good, so they were like, "We're going to roll with it." And that's all I needed. Once I had that stamp of approval from them, and they were behind me 100%, everybody else's opinion didn't matter.

Leodus: *I was going to college and everything, but I knew that college was just a backup for me. I had entrepreneurial parents. So, I never saw them have to get up and go to work. I never saw them get fired or laid off. I've always seen them getting up when they got ready, and coming home when they got ready.*

If they wanted to have lunch at home every day, and wear sweatpants to work...I've never seen them 'have' to do anything. So, when somebody is watching that their whole life, they don't really think it's impossible to have their own business. I saw them having their own real estate. I saw them having their own businesses.

Aquillia: *I haven't seen dad, mom, and grandma together, in this generation. I haven't seen divorced mom and dad together, and still having grandmas of the mom and dad be close. I've never seen that before. In spite of themselves, in spite of their own relationships, they all held it together. And even more than that, they all thrived and loved each other for real while they were raising us. Which didn't have to be the case.*

It was so important because all three had different strengths and weaknesses. My grandma, we knew we could go to her always for food, shelter, and prayer...regardless. My mom didn't cook when we were younger - not like she does now, it's great! My grandma would be the one that would [bring] food, even if we were three blocks away. [She would say], "It's too cold for you to walk," and she would come and drive us from her house and take us. She would cook dinner and all this stuff. We just knew that we had that comfort too; and then when my mom came home, mom could help with homework. Mom can stay up 'til 5am with you to do science projects. Mom would go to youth group with you, and be involved in youth group. And then dad would give you all the life advice. You didn't even need to ask for it, he'd give you all the advice! And he'd show up at report card pickup, because he wanted people to know that you had a dad. They were all very present.

We lived with my mom and she essentially made the final decisions on our lives, but we didn't get to her final decisions without all sitting down together and saying, "This is what's in front of us, what are we going to do now?" We'd all decide it, and then mom would say 'yay' or 'nay', but it didn't happen without each other. She would always counsel with them first before we decide on something.

Rima: *I don't think I'll ever see things completely through American eyes. My household is very multicultural, from language, from my brothers' wives...there's not just a single, 'Hey we're just Puerto Rican over here and we're African-American here.' My brother and my stepdad speak Arabic. The wife of one of my brothers speaks French and she's Nigerian, but she grew up in London. The wife of another one of my brothers is Senegalese, so I grew up with her and knew her before they even got married.*

Massamba: *I would say from 2007 until now, there hasn't been much change within myself. And that I would credit to my upbringing back in Africa. First of all, my parents are Senegalese, but migrated to the United States. I was born in the U.S. In my early childhood, [when I was] maybe around two or three years old, I was sent back to Senegal.*

And from there, my grandmother became my guardian. So, her mentality [regarding my upbringing] was, if I was outside playing with my friends and peers and people my age, she felt that they might be a bad influence. So, I mostly stayed at home studying. My grandmother was very strict about that. The only time I got to go out was when I went to the praying place, to the market, or to school. So, I got used to that. She instilled that habit in me... and it started when I was very young. That's why I say between 2007 and now, I really haven't changed, because that was my routine then, and it's still my routine now.

Camille: *From the time I graduated from high school, up until now, life has really hit me in ways that I wasn't expecting. I feel like, after all this stuff, I keep pushing. I keep putting my best foot forward. [The persistence] has always been there. I've always had a really great support system when it comes to family telling me to never give up and to keep the faith. Having a good support system is key...family and my really close friends.*

Before my godmother passed away, she always told me to keep focused, to never let small things get in the way, and to keep my head in the game...I feel like family has become more important to me. Kind of having somewhat of a...not a broken family, but [one where] everyone doesn't see eye-to-eye...I feel that unity and union is very important growing up in this day and age. 'Cuz a lot of people are really disoriented and they don't really have their family. They don't really have anyone to support them.

Christina: *My base has been my family and friends, who've always been supportive. My parents were really supportive. They talk about me like, "Oh, you're a career student," but in the end, they've always really supported me...and I had an aunt too, my Aunt Cindy. She was a really big supporter of me. If I told her, "Auntie I want to go to medical school in the Caribbean," she was like, "oh yeah, go! You should do it." Everything that I wanted to do she was my biggest fan like, "you can do it. Whatever you need to do, do it." And she gave me options when I got discouraged. Even now when I get discouraged, she always makes the glass half-full instead of half-empty. It's always good to have that base. I would just say my spiritual family, my daughter, all that just really motivated me. I have good people around me, and it's always good to have that extra support.*

Neiko: *A man's word...being able to go off of your word...the word to me is the biggest thing. Because nowadays, you got a lot of people who say, "I'm gonna go by my word" and it never comes through. To me that's what makes a man, is by [being able to] go off his word. That has to be taught. I had my uncle who would always tell me, "Your word is everything. Nothing else really matters in this world but your word. If you don't have that, you have nothing." And look-*

ing at him - he's now in his sixties - his word has been everything. He gets so much stuff off of his word and I love it. And as I just watch him steady grow and be that man that he is, I see what he was saying. As a kid, I really didn't listen to him - just like most kids who don't listen to their parents - but as I've grown and gotten older I actually see what he means by that.

James: *I'll say it like this...Every man looks to somebody else, an older man, somebody they respect, as what I call an alpha male. That's who they learn from. That's who they turn to. That's who they need. Men need their alpha male.*

...The person I follow is my uncle. He's my alpha male. He's the guy that believed in me ever since I was a child. He always believed in me, and knew I would be something. Even when I didn't see it in myself. He's my alpha male. And now that I've learned that, I think I'm ready to step up and become an alpha male myself. I look at it as you always had somebody to turn to. When you had a question, you could ask him anything. Whether it was personal, whether it was something general, you had someone to teach you [about] life. You had somebody to teach you before you could make the mistake yourself.

My uncle always told me, "When you learn from somebody else's mistake, you can learn a lesson without actually having to deal with the pain or the trouble behind it." Just having that extra drive from having somebody pushing you to be your best, somebody [who is] giving you that guidance. Because if you don't have anybody guiding you, you're probably just a loose cannon. You've got no direction.

...So, to have that person always there telling you what you need to know and just giving you that extra push...even if he has to drag you and take you across the finish line, he was going to do it. You were going to get where you had to go because this person was going to make sure [that] when you start slacking off, they were there to put their foot in your behind because that's what you needed. They were

there to talk to you. They were there to teach the meanings of every-thing. I'm forever grateful and till this day I still thank him for teaching me everything he did. He taught me the value of a dollar. He taught me the basis of being a man, which helped me to become who I am now.

Kevin: *Coming up, I was the one kid - out of my crew - who used to have to say "yes sir, no sir." I'm not saying other kids didn't say that, but out of my little crew in the little neighborhood that I grew up in, it sounded so abnormal [to them]. They were like, "man your dad is super-strict! You gotta say 'yes sir' and 'no sir'?!" My dad, let's say I [answered] "yeah", he would just automatically go deaf! He didn't hear it. It was like:*

    Me: "yeah"
    Dad: [silence]
    Me: "oh...yes"
    Dad: "What?!"
    Me: "Yes, sir."
    Dad: "Oh okay, alright."

That's something so small, but I look at it today like that helped me a lot. Just something so small.

I take pride in situations where people will come up - let's say we're out in public - and say, "oh, that's your son? He's very respectful. You don't see that type of stuff nowadays." That thing right there, the whole having respect for your elders...'cuz if you respect yourself, you're going to learn to respect others. You're going to respect your elders...most of the time you would do that. So, I would say that the best thing [my father] taught me, was to respect myself and respect others.

Felice: *My dad always told me that the one thing he taught me was how to be self-sufficient. I remember him showing me a home video* one time, where I was trying to get on a swing. And I was struggling. So, I asked him, "Daddy can you help me?" And he goes, "No, you figure it out." And there have been plenty of other types of videos, or instances, I can remember where something I'm sure I could have figured out myself, I kind of tried to reach out to them like, "Can you help me?" And their answer was, "No." And it seemed mean or harsh at the time, but it got me to the point that as a young girl with disabilities, I was able to go 1,000 miles away from both my parents, to go down south and go to school; because they taught me to learn how to do things my own way.

Devin: *I grew up in a fairly comfortable middle-class family, single-mom helping me out. She worked - and she still works to this day - in telecommunications. So that's I.T. technical support, except for phones. So, I was exposed to this computer technology lifestyle and environment before I could walk. She would always take me to work with her. I essentially grew up in a server room, because she would always take me when she had to do stuff with the servers. I grew very friendly with the I.T. guys. I would always sit in her lap while she was working on the computer, so that's how that love was engrained in me; 'cuz it was something I saw my mom doing and I was like, "hey, I want to do that one day."*

Joshua: *I look at my mom. She came here - this is when I was like two - and we were very poor. We were on welfare. She would have to clean the streets and stuff like that. This is while I was very young, so I don't remember it clearly, but she tells me about it all the time. She was focused. She went to nursing school. She got her degree, she went back to become an R.N.*

Now we're in an apartment building. She's not cleaning streets anymore. She works in a hospital. And to see her go through all of that, and I'm growing up in America...I have no excuse. I have no excuse to not succeed, because she literally came from nothing, and she worked here cleaning up streets, and now she's doing well for herself and she's supporting three sons. So, I have no excuse, you know? That's how I feel about it.

STRENGTHENING THE FOUNDATION

Quaneesha: *Growing up with my sister, we weren't as close as we should have been. My mom used to tell us all the time, "I can't believe you guys are not as close."*

What I tell people is, having a twin sister is having a sister who just happens to be your age. I don't really think that we look alike...people say, "oh, you guys look alike! You look just alike!" all the time. We weren't the twins who had to have matching everything. We had our own personalities. We had friends in common... I think I mainly just steal her friends, because she's more diverse with her friends...also, my sister is more of an emotional person. I'm not as emotional.

...We didn't do things together. We really didn't. Now that I think about it, we didn't spend that much time together. Like in high school, people would be like, "Where is your sister?" And I would go, "I don't know, she's probably out with her friends." It wasn't one of those, 'Wherever she's at, I'm at' type of things. It wasn't until college when I went away to school. I only went to Long Island, [New York], but I dormed on campus. That's what made us closer, being away from each other. Like really away, not with each other in the same household. It made us hang out more, and essentially, do what twins do. It made our bond stronger [even though] we have two different paths in life.

... I think that most twins - because they are twins - are forced into doing things together. They don't have a sense of their own identity, because [people around them] are like, "You're gonna look alike.

You're going to do things together. You're going to go everywhere. You're going to have the same life." So, most twins have the same friends…Some people [even] work in the same place because they don't know how to be separate. It's like, we know how to be separate, and we still speak to each other on a day-to-day basis. But we have our own lives and we're okay with having our own lives and that doesn't bother us.

Jonel: *I think my sister really helped me [expand my mind]. I was really interested in Japanese, and the culture, and the anime, and she was like, "Why don't you just learn the language?" At this time, I was watching anime for, I don't know, five hours a day…maybe even more. I was using subtitles to watch it, and [my sister] was like, "Why don't you just learn the language so you understand it without having to read the subtitles? That makes more sense to me." So, she's the one who really pushed me. She got me into language classes, which is something I never thought I could do. Learning Japanese [seemed] strange to me. She really pushed me into doing what I actually wanted to do, but was afraid to do.*

Shantel: *Another thing that has stayed really constant has been my relationship with my family. With my parents, with my sister. Some siblings are super-close, they do everything together all the time. Me and my sister may not [be together] all the time. There have been days during the week when either she'll come home late from doing things, or I'll come home late from doing things, and we won't see each other. We'll see each other for a few minutes in the morning, and then we'll go about our business. We'll kinda text, kinda talk that day…but definitely we'll stop and be like, "you and me need to go out and have dinner together." I still feel like I'm very close with my sister, I still feel like I have a lot of good conversations, a lot of thought-provoking conversations.*

And then with my parents, [they're my] biggest supporters. My parents did not go to college, but they are so encouraging with education and just to see what me and my sister have achieved education-wise and how that makes them so happy and proud, like that was enough for me. Not to say I wasn't doing school for me, but I was kind of doing it for them too. It's just that sense of support.

When life is coming at you, and people are coming at you with such negativity or discouragement...it's that idea that when I go home, I have three people guaranteed to have my back...Having that backbone of support that no matter what else the world thinks, I've got three people who've got my back regardless.

Atisha: *One thing that I have to stay [consistent] with in order to get inspiration is keeping contact with my family, and most of my family lives in Guyana. So, I'm always talking to them, I'm always asking them to send me pictures because I can't be there. It's really...I feel so detached from my country that I just need to feel like I'm still there with them, and that they still remember me. All of my little cousins, I want them to know me, and I want them to know who I am, not just that they have a cousin named Atisha who lives in America, but they don't really know me. So, I like to stay in constant contact with them.*

Patrick: *Being away from my actual family, coming to another state...you wanna have someone to lean on. And family is very important to me. I'm in the military, and a lot of other people do this in the military, but it's nice to have something to look forward to at the end of the day when I get off of work. Coming home to a wife and a kid is the best thing in the world. A lot of people don't want to do it, and there's a lot that comes with it... I would say don't get married too young, unless you're ready for that kind of responsibility, because it is hard.*

Marriage is a whole other job in itself. There are times when you are not going to get along. Times when you're just like, 'man, I wish I was out alone by myself.' But like I said, it's a joy to come home to a wife and son at the end of the day. When it's just been a long day, you just want to come home to hold someone. Or to a cooked meal. You're not coming home wondering, 'What am I going to cook today?' or 'What am I going to eat today?' It's a joy to come home to a home-cooked meal. When your wife has figured out the whole menu for the week, it's something special.

Phillip: *My wife is a powerful woman. We both did a 180. We were both so different and diverse in our pasts and what we've been through with our parents, what we've been through in our neighbor-hoods.*

What we thought about family, what we experienced and thought worked for our families, what we thought didn't work, disciplinary actions, how to talk to one another, communication, what not to say to one another...we were off. But through our trials and tribulations, we're hitting our strides of happiness and growing together. We feel like we've been together – honestly, we have - but we feel like we've been together for years. Just being married finally, and being a house-hold...having that American Dream of waking up on a beautiful summer morning, and opening the door to take the mail, and seeing kids on the block...That's [how] I grew up. And to give my kids that experience, that's the ultimate joy. To give them what you had.

Erica: *Well my current book is* <u>The Five Love Languages</u>. *It's pretty interesting. It's really helping me learn how to interact with people in general. [Learning how to] read people better and getting to know them on a different level. It's opening my eyes to a lot, just truly understanding why certain people are receptive or non-receptive to certain actions and behaviors.*

So far, I would say - and this has helped me tremendously as well because I am currently in a relationship - the book talks about two phases of love. There's that 'in love' phase in the beginning where you're head over heels with the person, and all you want to do is talk to them and you're just crazy about them. But the book explains that this isn't really love, and that you don't truly enter the whole 'love' phase of the relationship until you just want to make that other person happy. Where you're totally not involved with self, and it's all about what you can do for that other person. [The book] explains, that is truly when you love someone. And I thought that was pretty interesting, because sometimes we can get that mixed up.

Dante: *Most of what I'm doing now in my work, involves my friends and my family. Someone asked me recently about success, and I really feel like I'm successful now because I'm living the life I want to live. I don't think anything will change beyond that, that's really what matters to me. The life I want to live, specifically, is to affect my friends and family. And I know for a fact that no matter what happens, I'm definitely shaking up a storm among the people I can touch. That's all I can really ask for, so I don't really worry too much beyond that. I'm happy there.*

Erin: *I'll say this, the four friends that I have now, I don't even call them friends to be honest. I call them my cousins. That's my definition of a friend, a cousin. I don't know where I get that from, but every time somebody is like, "Is that your friend?" I'll be like, "No, that's my cousin." 'Cuz at the end of the day, they're like my backbone. When I'm going through something, whether it's like a little thing with a boy, or school, or situations with my mom...I know I can go to them. Alright, I've got it! The definition of a friend is a judge-free zone. They're my judge-free zone, regardless of the topic.*

College

I like graduations. I liked being among fellow graduates during my graduations. I liked sitting in the audience watching my family and friends' graduations. I liked sitting on stage among fellow educators, hugging and high-fiving my former students during their graduations. I even liked riding the subway in New York City on days when I spotted a stranger wearing their cap and/or gown on their way to their graduation.

High school graduations are my favorite. They are celebrations of a life chapter that has come to its end. They are beautifully democratic, like marathon finish lines, as the people with the highest scores get to celebrate just as much as those with the lowest scores. They are temporarily unburdened, like sports championship celebrations, by demands of future success. For at least that one day, it is enough to declare *"I did it!"* or *"We made it!"*

High school graduations are reflective. There is an acknowledgement that what has come to an end will not happen again, and in the midst of our fast-paced world, we pause to acknowledge this once-in-a-lifetime moment. There is also an awareness that many of the friendships and relationships, which were as essential to our teenage lives as the ones in our families, are also about to change dramatically. Until ten years ago, high school graduations were one of the rare moments in life where we lost so many people who were important to our life story all at the same time.

High school graduations reveal the stark contrasts between the singular, school-centered world that students graduate from and the wide range of worlds that students graduate into. In my work with high-school aged young people, I like to tell them that everyone goes to college. For a number of people, college means the realities and pressures of earning a living after high school. For others, college refers to the ups and downs of life as a struggling artist or aspiring entertainer. Some people find their college experience in the discipline and self-sacrifice of serving in the military. Others will find their college experience in the discipline and self-sacrifice of being a young parent.

For the rest of us, it's off to campus.

ON CAMPUS

Janelle: *I feel like in high school, there aren't a lot of like-minded people like there are in college. In college, I feel like you have more people who are goal-oriented, so you kind of know where they're going, even if they still are kinda lost. There are some lost people in college, I won't lie about that! People in college are little more like-minded than people in high school, so I feel like some friendships drift apart more in high school because we just see it as something...I don't know...I don't think it's on purpose, but we sort of the see the friendship or connection as temporary. Whereas in college it's like, 'okay, I'm getting my life started and I need to network and I need to be able to maintain connections.' And then you have the friends who sort of think like you, so now you're like, 'okay maybe these [might] be some long-term friendships.' I just think it's easier to maintain connections in college than it is in high school or any time before that.*

I don't know, I think it's just the way that we start to think after a while, and our maturity. In college, you're kind of not done growing, so you kind of grow together. Whereas in high school, some people can like slow down and some people can grow apart and be on different paths. But in college, I feel like you're all kind of on that one path where you're like, 'I know where I want to go in life. I know what I'm doing.'

Jason: *You have Black people [who] come from a variety of places. When they told me I was going to go an HBCU, [they said] it's not going to be diverse. Are you kidding me?! Do you know how diverse Black is? Just the color in itself is diverse! And when you put our people in a box like that, and you treat us like a monolith, like we're just one thing, it takes our humanity away.*

Christina: *I'm lucky to [be able to] say that I went to an HBCU, and I'm able to have connections with everybody all over the world. I feel like wherever I go, I know somebody there...and that's kind of motivating to me also. So, on social media, on Facebook, when I see people who I went to college with and they're achieving all this greatness, it really motivates me. We kind of motivate each other...I'm blessed to have a lot of people around me [who] are about doing stuff.*

Amadu: *Everyone since I was young said, "Oh my god, Amadu is so smart! Oh my god, Amadu is so gifted!" So, you get the idea that, 'I don't even have to try, I'm good!'...but I was still humble. I wasn't a child who necessarily gloated or ran around saying I was the best or anything. I was never like that. However, in my mind, I did have a little bit of a cocky, overconfident kind of attitude.*

That was immediately changed as soon as I got to college. A lot of kids had opportunities that you would dream of, you know? In fact, they had opportunities that you could not dream of, because you did not know that they were possibilities...It was interesting to see where people come from and how much more 'advanced' people were...in academics.

I say it that way because although there were people who I met or interacted with who had more knowledge than I did, it did not necessarily mean that they were smarter than me. I determine smart by the ability to learn. So, you [may] know more, that means that over our [life] time span, you have learned more and picked up more information than I did. However, I choose to be a little bit better at connecting new pieces of information. So, although you have this huge repertoire of information, you may find it very difficult to actually put pieces together. Whereas I was pretty good at that. I learned that I was decently capable of doing that, so that helped me out a lot. That helped me stay in the game even when some of my close friends actually had to drop out of college, I was able to stay in because I just had that grind.

I would always go hard. One thing that I do still find interesting is that when I went to college, just because I realized that people were 'better' than me didn't make me want to be less. I know people who were like, "Damn, these people are so much more advanced than I am, and maybe I'm just like an average student." I'm like, "average?! Oh, I'm not an average student!" I have no problem discussing how some people may have had opportunities that we didn't have, but don't get me wrong, that doesn't mean I'm just going to sit here and stay in third place! Nah, I'm still going to go hard either way, you know?

Tobi: *I moved to [England] about five years and two months ago, for my undergraduate. I moved here to study economics and finance...up north, that's where my university was. I was in England for two years, I went to Paris for a year to do a study abroad program, and then I returned to England for another year. I finished my under-*

graduate; I went on to do my master's in international development. So, education brought me to the U.K.

When I went in, it wasn't really a thing of 'oh my goodness, I'm going to LSE!' I found a [major] that I really wanted to do, and it was apparently one of the best schools to do it in. But then I got in there, and we were being told, "You are the best of the best in the field. This is what LSE means." And when you speak to people and you're like, "Oh, I go to LSE." And their reaction is like, "Oh my goodness! You must be super smart!" And I'm like, "Uhh...no."

Kiana: *When I first started attending college, it was definitely different for me. Throughout my whole [life] growing up in Brooklyn, I never really went to school with anyone other than Black people. So, when I went to college I was just like, 'okay, this is different.' I was loving it at first. I wanted the change, that's why I went away to school.*

But I soon saw the differences between...should I say...White culture and Black culture? The way...how do I say this correctly without sounding wrong? I don't know...just the way they go about certain things is different from how I would. So, I don't know...it was weird to me that they didn't either take me seriously or just treated me differently. So, I was just like, 'okay, this is different, and I have to adjust to this.' It was a little hard for me to try to connect with different groups because I felt like they weren't as accepting of me. Eventually, I just let that go. It depends on the person, not really whether you're White or Black or whatever, 'cuz people act how they want to act. When it came to the [campus] protests and things of that nature, there were a lot of people who participated. There were a lot of White students that were with us, there were a lot of Black and Latino [students]...everyone. We came together in times of need.

Toshawna: *I've always been open to new experiences and I've always been interested in learning new things. So being in a diverse community was exciting for me, because I'm not around people who are just like me all the time. There's something new to learn all the time. Today I could be speaking to someone from Marrakesh, and the next day I could be speaking to someone from Shanghai, or someone from a small village in a southern African country.*

Erica: *[Back then] I didn't really care much about other people, so to speak...when I say that, I mean that I never really cared much about that stuff because I wasn't really exposed to it or open to it before. I was just so used to being private and being confidential with everything that came to me...College was a huge eye opener for me.*

I grew up my whole life in predominantly Black neighborhoods, Black schools, like everything. I wasn't really exposed to much else. It wasn't until one particular experience in college. I did this program for a week after the school year finished, called LeaderShape. It was pretty much a program where about 50 to 100 students - I'm not quite sure of the number - we all just came together and it was to help build leadership skills. We did that through team-building exercises and really making ourselves vulnerable to one another. And on the second-to-last day, I can't remember the activity verbatim, but essentially, we sat in groups of two or three and we just spilled the beans about a personal issue. And it was so interesting that I sat there with the two other girls who had two completely different social class and cultural backgrounds [from me], and we could relate on so many different levels, where we had gone through some of the same things in our lives. To me that was mind-blowing, because I would have never guessed that before. That kinda just opened up my eyes that we're all just humans, no matter where you come from, or [your] background or anything. We all go through the same things essentially.

Stephanie: *When I went to college, and I got to experience people from different states and different countries...in my college experience, sometimes some of my friends didn't get a chance to come back. They decided to transfer to go someplace else...I miss [one friend in particular], because she taught me to be more thankful and more respectful, and to be more present. I'm so used to being here in America where water comes right out of the sink, whereas [in my friend's home country] Swaziland, they had to go get water. And I noticed that every single time I was around her, I learned to be more thankful. And in being more thankful, and having a spirit of thanksgiving, I learned to be more pleasant. In learning how to have a spirit of thanksgiving, and being more pleasant, I learned how to be a better person and a nicer person to others. It was contagious.*

And I had another friend who was from Texas and she was a wild girl, and I was like 'uh, she's always got boys in her room. I don't want to be in there today, because something may happen.' Or somebody came in there and they smelled like something they shouldn't smell like, like some type of smoke or what-have-you. And I don't want to get in trouble with that. I'm not judging her, I'm just saying, "You know what? Her surroundings right now are not what I need"...I wanted what was more contagious for me.

Alberto: *Once I started school at [my community college], it took even more hard work for me just to be at the college level. Remember, I wasn't able to finish high school, and then I took a crash course on high school to get my G.E.D. So, I didn't have those habits that I needed in order to succeed in college. I had to work even harder just to get through my first semester of college. I took six classes my first semester. They weren't the most difficult classes in the world, but at the same time for me they were the most difficult classes in the world, because of where I came from.*

It was a steep learning curve, but I was able to pass my classes, end up with a very nice G.P.A. and move on to the next semester. Then things got a little more complicated, because I was now fulfilling that standard that we all have for rigorous classes. I remember just studying for most of my days, and I wasn't used to just studying all the time. And I remember having to cut back hours at work and not being familiar with the whole, 'oh wow, I can't work because I have to study for this.' And I had to do it, and it definitely paid off...I've had to work hard throughout my life to get to where I am now. It wasn't, 'just go to class.' There was always something attached to going to that class or just dealing with everything else.

...When I started at [my community college], I was in a room full of people [with] one person who had four kids, but still had a 4.0 G.P.A., and had two jobs. I was in a room with somebody who had the same struggles as me. I was in a room with [people] who came from the same community that I came from. I was in a room with [people] who spoke my language. I was in a room of people who understood my struggle, and I understood theirs. I was in a room with people who, even though we had different goals, we had the same hustle. I feel like, in terms of [making] friends, that's what changed a lot. I was able to bond more with the people in my community college. Not just the students, but also the faculty.

One thing that I wish people would know is that community college is a very special place. It's an opportunity for all of us, and a second chance for most of us. The reason why is that community colleges are filled with faculty members, professors, and resources, and all these programs. And it's to build a foundation for you to move forward to your next step. Whether that next step is a job, or whether that next step is you moving forward to your four-year school, which is my case.

One thing that I can definitely say is that 99% of the people who walk onto community college campuses have a story. If not 99%,

99.9% of them. There's a reason why they're there. It's not because my dad and my mom have money and they're paying my tuition. It's not because of that. It's not because I have good SAT scores. It's not because I had the best grades in high school. It's because of something, whatever that is, it's something. There's a whole bunch of [people like] me - in different versions - on community college campuses. A lot of us fail to acknowledge our struggle and to acknowledge our path. I went through a lot of things in my life, and I'm sure that a lot of us have. But I wouldn't have it any other way. If I had to go through my same struggles all over again, I would.

FINDING MY WAY

Bernadette: *It's kind of a lot of sacrifice. It's really an issue of 'how bad do you want it?' I work with some campus students, but mostly with students who are taking classes online. I have students who are 18 and 19, fresh out of high school. But I also have people who have returned to school. Especially those students who have returned to school, I ask them, "How bad do you want this? It's going to take sacrifice. It's going to take long nights. You're going to be exhausted some days, but how bad do you want it?" And a lot of the responses are: "Oh, but I have work" and "I have my children" and "I have this."*

You had all those things when you signed up for school, so it's really about prioritizing and really managing your time. You can do whatever you want to do in your day, if you manage your time appropriately. A lot of us do not know how to manage our time. So, we get overwhelmed, because we don't have a good balance. You have to readjust your time management. Like the way that you manage your time before you have kids is not going to be the same way you'll manage your time when you have a child. The same way you manage your time [differently] when that child is a baby versus when they're three. It's not going to be the same.

So, I tell my students that you have multiple priorities in your life, but look at it as if you had triplets. Each one of those children needs attention. They each need a part of you. So how are you going to be able to dedicate a part of you to each one of those things? So, work and school, and your children, are your triplets, so what are you going to do to make sure that one of them is not feeling neglected?

Casey: *I guess now I'm more focused on the end game. Back in high school, I was definitely living more in the moment...When I was younger I played chess, and from playing chess I learned to look forward and look ahead in terms of planning things, and planning the next move in life. Now I'm a college student, I'm in my junior year, and I'm beginning to try and network with alumni from my school and apply for internships for job opportunities that can help me later on. Right now, they might not be available to me, but during my senior year they definitely will become available to me. I kinda just want to springboard past the slow part of coming out of college and looking for a job, and hopefully [I will] have everything set up by the time I do graduate.*

Krystal: *When I first went to college, I just got exposed to all these different things and I just wanted to dibble in everything. I was on like four executive boards at the same time. I was taking a full course load, and all this other stuff, and I'm like, "What am I doing?!" I can't give myself to 20 different causes. You have to pick one, you have to narrow down. It's the same thing career-wise and life-wise, you have to find something and commit to it. If you keep putting your hand in everything, you can't help anyone like that. You can't give someone a hand, if you're handing them out to everyone. You can't help yourself in that way either.*

...Time moves on. I'm a big person on that. It's easy to get stuck in high school, but it's way easier to get stuck in college. Like, move on! Life goes on. Trust me, it's going to be okay...you're not in the same mind frame. You have to move on. You just have to. There are other things that you can give besides what you gave before, but you're not opening yourself up to those opportunities because you're stuck in the past and being complacent in what you like.

Felice: *I was always that person, or that kid, who grew up [getting] everything I ever set my eyes on. It was like, "That's mine!" And then I got to Spelman, and it was like the biggest dream for me. I had wanted to go there since I was in fourth grade, and when I got in, I kind of had this setback at the end of my senior year when I found out I would have to come back for an extra semester.*

It hurt me, because I was like, "This is not a part of my plan!" That was a big, humbling moment for me because it was that moment when I had to realize that life doesn't always go according to your plan. Sometimes you gotta re-evaluate that plan and look at it differently, and realize that just because it didn't go the way you wanted it to go, doesn't mean everything else is going to be that way and that you can't achieve everything that you wanted.

What wound up happening was that I did that last semester, and it wound up being one of the best semesters I ever had at college. That extra semester that I wasn't even supposed to have. It was humbling for me because it made me realize, okay just because society feels like you're supposed to graduate in four years, and you're supposed to [do] this, that, and the third...doesn't mean that if you don't achieve [that], you're less than.

Atisha: *I'm already in college studying fine arts, and it's one of those careers where you have to be worried about if you're going to find a job or if you're going to succeed or what's going to happen. All of my friends who I talk to, sometimes they don't want to think about what's going to happen after they graduate. They don't want to think about making money, because it's very frightening. But I feel like I've chosen this for myself, and I have to do this. It's this or nothing, because I can't see myself being happy doing anything else.*

Haniyyah: *I think I said I wanted to do business when I was a sophomore [in high school]. And then I did an internship on Wall Street and I was like, "You know what? This is great for people who love it; but this is not for me." So, then I decided that I needed to pursue something else, 'my mom is in education. Maybe that's what I want to do.' So, I had this idea that maybe I wanted to teach in an elementary classroom.*

I really didn't narrow down what I wanted to do, so when I was looking at colleges, I looked at liberal arts colleges because it gave me that option to take different courses before I actually decided what my major was going to be...what my degree was going to be in. So instead of wasting the money and going to medical school, or just going full time for teaching and getting certified, I took the time to really get to know myself. Because nobody in high school - I mean, there might be some people who do - but my 2007 self did not know exactly what she wanted to do in life. I knew [about] college, that was the option. My mother was like, "You're going to college and there's not really [any] ifs, ands, or buts. You're going. For what? I don't know. But you're getting a degree. You're getting a degree in something." And that's what happened. I didn't know, and I was okay with not knowing. I was okay with that.

Jason: *I'm in my third year of college and I'm contemplating what I want to do after college. Like what are the next steps? It's interesting because I have to rely on the information I'm learning at Howard [University] to sustain me [after] graduation, and [for] the rest of my life, essentially. The education we receive...is like the foundation - supposedly - for my future success.*

...I would say there's definitely a little anxiety in terms of what I'm going to do after college. But I realize that people graduate from college regularly and they have to deal with the same anxiety. So, it's like, just make up plans, make up solidified plans for how you want to continue. Yes, anxiety is a natural part of life, but if you just stay stagnant you're not going to get anywhere. You have to plan. You have to execute. Pray, and just work towards it.

Steven: *In college, I got to meet a lot of people, I became friends with a lot of people. I slowly saw my dreams...I slowly felt my potential...I slowly saw that the person I could be was dying and it was only by seeing people doing the things I knew I could do, but not doing [those things] as great as I could have done them.*

And I remember having a conversation with two of my mentors who, to be honest, were some of the major reasons I got through college...I think the thing that saved me was that I developed a skill, and that was to find some amazing mentors in every aspect of my life. After my first semester of college, I did terrible. [These two mentors] kind of grabbed me by the throat, sat me down and said, "This is not you. Everybody else here may think that you're the guy, and you're popular, and you're having a good time. But I know that your family at home is not eating as well as they could be eating. I know that you're living a life that you've never experienced before, but don't forget." To me it was like, don't forget that my mom still lives check-to-check, that my dad still lives check-to-check, and that I could be doing better. And that took me back.

You see that comfort and that lifestyle was still there, and it was a fight and it was a battle. I do believe that once comfort sets in, it's one of the biggest enemies to defeat. It takes a strong purpose and a strong 'why?' to get out of that stuff. And it took me my entire college career.

Maya: *I was in my junior year of college. That was the first point where I had to deal with the changing of friendships. The friendships I had my first two years of college were changing a little bit and it was really hard. It was hard because I had gone from the point of being friends with these girls, and hanging out all the time, and I came back for my junior year and everything was set. It was really going to go down! I had my car at school, it was about to be super-epic. And then I just realized...I kind of had an out-of-body experience, and I just had to look back like, "What am I doing? Do I want to be drinking for no apparent reason other than the fact that we can (kind of) because it's a Monday?"*

And that kind of took me...I retreated and was spending some more quiet, reflective time alone. But it was also great because at the same time I was making a friend that would allow me to build other friendships, with people who are some of my closest friends. I lost some friends, our relationships changed, but I also gained these new friends in that time.

IS IT WORTH IT?

Joshua Jackson: *It's okay to go to college. There's nothing wrong with that. College actually disciplines you. But I think people need to go to college with an end goal in mind. Where you're not just spending money, and wasting money to get an education, but where you have clearly defined goals about where you need to go and where you want to go. That career adviser or career center that they have at schools, they will be able to point a person in the right direction as well. Once they get that degree, now it's crunch time. Get to where you need to go quickly, because there are people who are already doing it at 18. [A college graduate] is 21 or 22, and at that age it's like, "Okay, I got my degree, what's happening now? What's next?"*

Maryka: *I'ma be real, I feel like college is a scam. I feel like [with] our unemployment rate...so many people are getting laid off. Jobs aren't...you're not guaranteed a job as soon as you're done with college. So, an engineering major can go out in the world and get a job at Toys 'R Us, and he's thousands of dollars in debt. And it's like dang, he probably wishes that he would've [gone after] fast money, and that probably would've worked out better for him than this.*

Honestly, I'm at a point now where it's like, you can always have that thing that you love to do. Whether that's music, whether that's rapping, singing, dancing, all of that. You can always do that, but as far as college...it's so much money that you should be going into a field where you know that ultimately, I will have a good job in which I can pay off this debt, so that in the end it is worth it. But I feel like a lot of college students - more than 50% of college students - won't find a job.

[College administrators] should know that a lot of us come from real crazy foundations. A lot of us come from families where we're in the 'hood and we're just trying to eat for the night. We want to get sent to college. We wanna to go to college, because society said that's what we should do to make money and be a good citizen of this country. But it's just like, a lot of us are going into major debt while trying to achieve this goal, so it's just real bittersweet. You want us to look at the light, but we're struggling trying to take out loans and stuff like that.

So honestly, I wish I could tell them, "Can you give us more financial aid? Or can you make things less expensive for us?" My best friend isn't in school, and it's because she can't afford it. She comes from a single parent household, and they have mortgages, and the government says your mom is making enough money...but it's just like, "Yeah, but we have bills." And sometimes you get behind on bills just because you're living life and you have a family to feed. I just wish that those people who are running the colleges...like how we visit their schools, maybe they can visit our homes and see where we come from. Maybe that can give them a different perspective...I don't know. I don't know what the business aspect entails in colleges, and how it really works, but I just wish that like how we have school orientation...they come to our houses and they can see what we live in, and they can have a perspective on how they bill us...they can have that background of where we come from, you know?

Steven: *To me, the traditional sense of an education is only 5% of the education that we need. 'Cuz I realized a long time ago that my life will be based on the 95% of things that I do outside of the class. Even my grades were based on the 95% of things I did outside of the classes. If I studied outside of class, I'd have good grades. If I practiced the problems, I would do well on the problems. If I formed groups, then I would have a better social life in college outside of the classroom. If I was active, then I would be more informed.*

The classroom - to me - is just a small percentage of education. I don't know exactly when the traditional sense of education [came about], but when you think about human beings on this Earth, and how long we've been in existence, the traditional sense of the classroom is very short in comparison. So how did they teach each other? From the caveman to the modern-day man, how did they make that transition without the classroom? Is that traditional sense even really needed?

Joshua: *One thing I noticed [studying in France] is that they love their students. The student has power over there. They view their students as products to be invested in, products to be improved upon. Whereas in America, students are...I feel like students are - in a sense*

- indentured servants. We rack up this huge debt and we're expected to work for the rest of our lives to pay off that debt.

While I was in France, there was even this department where if you're studying at the college and you're staying in one of the dorms, they actually pay you based on a percentage, to help you cover the costs of the rent. So, my rent was a little under 300 Euros, but I was able to get 50 Euros. It didn't matter that I wasn't a French student, but they cared that I was studying at a French school. So, they were able to help support me and that was so that I could save money for any other thing. I just had to provide the proper documentation. And after that I came back to America and I was like, 'wow, it's really bad over here.'

We really don't treat our students well. We really need to start changing the mindset that students are just sources of income. We are the future and this debt is preventing us from taking this nation forward. How are we supposed to spend money in our stores, and help improve the economy if we're paying this debt we acquired when we were 18, and didn't know any better, you know?

Alberto: One thing I wish going forward is that, for all schools, the idea won't be, 'you have to go to school so that you can go on to college and get a job.' I feel like that idea has to be abolished. I think that we should remove the idea of relating education to getting a job. Or to making money. Education is not for that only.

You becoming a more educated individual makes you contribute more to society. You take whatever is taught to you and interpret that however your mind sees, and however you want to. Go out there and study philosophy. Go out there and study economics. Go out there and study business. Go out there and study whatever you want.

I think a lot of us fall into the idea of "yeah I'm going to study this, because I want to be that"…No, if you're going to study bio, make sure it's because you enjoy it profoundly, you know? If you're *going to study philosophy, make sure that you want to read all these philosophical things and just enjoy the experience of sitting in that classroom and taking it all in. If what you're interested in is finance, go out there and learn all those numbers. Don't go into finance because you want to work on Wall Street. If this is something that you're very interested in, learn about that, and take it in as a learning experience. As something that's going to be a part of you, not because you want to go get a 9-to-5, you know?*

Living in the Real World

How do you know when you've become an adult? For a few of us, life during our teenage years was like a video game where the goal was to find the secret codes that allowed you to skip all the middle levels and jump right to the last level called Grown. We were not sure, but from what we'd heard, the Grown level was full of hearts, points, bonus lives, and wonderful previously-locked worlds!

Some of us constructed our teenage lives like the recipe for a perfect meal. We started with a fresh G.P.A., added a few extracurricular activities, sprinkled in some profound community service summer trips, dropped in some recommendation letters, and topped things off with a dash of 'started from the bottom'. We were not sure, but from what we'd heard, if we just followed all the steps, everything would turn out perfectly!

Many of us spent our teenage years like travelers standing on an airport moving walkway. We stood patiently as the walkway of time moved us through puberty, through school, and dropped us off safely at Gate 18. We were not sure, but from what we'd heard, at Gate 18 we would board a flight headed to Life.

For others of us, that whole period from 13 to 19 was like streaming a video on a phone with a bad Wi-Fi connection. There were sections that ran smoothly, but for the most part those were days filled with pixilated images, stalled scenes behind a buffering circle, and endless restarts. We were not sure, and it was hard to hear much, but we had hopes that once we had full control over our lives, the picture would get clearer.

We spend our youth existing in the tension between the distress caused by our insecurities, the lack of full control over the affairs of our lives, the awareness that there is a finish line to our childhoods, and the hope that even if things don't turn out exactly as we planned, we will find a way and be okay in the end.

That youthful faith, the ability to imagine ourselves in a better situation at some point in the future, can sustain us when the waves of reality come crashing in on the shores of our childhood dreams.

LIFE AFTER COLLEGE

Felice: *After I graduated, I had a little bit of a downtime between trying to find work. People would try to tell me, "Just apply for anything. Just go anywhere." In my head I was like, 'no, I have a goal. I have a plan. I've worked that plan.' I had to learn how to ignore people who were trying to tell me how I was supposed to live my life, and define that for myself, and do it the way I felt was possible.*

Janelle: *I wouldn't say hate - I guess hate is a strong word - but I do not like the conversation where some people, as soon as they see me, it's like, "Oh, you're about to graduate soon! What are you about to do?" Please, I don't want to talk about that right now! I should just post a YouTube video like, "Hey everyone, just to answer all of your questions..."*

It's complicated. I'm optimistic/realistic in a way. Sometimes I can think about my future and just be like, 'I'm ready to take it on! I'm ready! Nothing's about to stop me from being a playwright/screenwriter/novelist and all that.' I'm not really pessimistic, because I'm sort of a person who lives in the moment...But realistically, I'm like 'okay, I need to go to grad school at some point and I know I need this type of degree and this type of experience.' So right now, I'm just thinking, okay I'm still going to do what I want to do, and it's still going to happen, but I need to think realistically about how I'm about to make it happen.

Silver: *I definitely think that this is what I want to do, and because of that, it is going to happen, you know? I really do want to work in the animation industry. I have a notebook where I just write down goals. One of the goals that I wrote down was that I want to work in television. So, I have to work [towards] that. I am a very realistic person. I do understand that I might not make it, and that the chances aren't too high. But, I do also understand that the harder you work, the luckier you end up being. So, if you just keep going at it, trying to find work, or just getting to where you need to be in order to be at the level where you can work, then it will happen.*

Quaneesha: *I'm grabbing a lot. It's like, I'm doing acting. I'm working. I also need to go back to doing my master's in psychology. So, all those things are just flying around in my head, [wondering] about when I am going to have time to add that on.*

I took a year off from school. I had plans that once I graduated from college, I was just going to go straight into my master's. [I thought], 'I don't want to take a break, because if I do I'll probably get too distracted and not want to go back.' The only thing that made me take that break to explore was acting... I was like, "Okay, I'm going to give myself a year off from school to dive into the world of acting; but by the [following] spring I need to either be in my master's program or trying to get into the master's program." I know that acting isn't always guaranteed, and that I need to have a backup plan. And psy-

chology is my backup plan. People really didn't give me that 'be practical' speech. Funny, I didn't really get that speech.

Raven: *I think those people who are able to adjust are gonna be the people who ultimately succeed in the end...nobody got to where they are in a straight line. My friend [asked me]: "Well, what are you going to do after graduation?" I hate that question, because I always have to tell people "I don't know." And they're just like, "What do you mean you don't know?! You're not worried?!" No, because honestly, I'm in business. And especially the way business is changing, the way technology is changing business, my job probably isn't created [yet]. The last job that I'm going to have probably doesn't exist at this point. Or the job that I will be creating, probably doesn't exist [yet].*

You gotta kind of...I don't want to say 'go with the flow', because sometimes that can end in complacency...but you can't worry about the minor details of where you're ultimately going to be. You kinda have to let life take its course, continue to be the best you that you are, and make sure that you're always striving for something. Have a goal, but don't think that because you didn't reach this ultimate thing, that you're any worse of a person. It's just that it wasn't meant for you, or that something greater was in store. That's what I have taken with me on this journey: everything isn't meant for me. And the things that I didn't get, I wasn't supposed to...Sometimes you can't sweat the small stuff. As long as you keep on that path of hustling, always making sure that you are on your Ps and Qs, always being hungry, always being ready for the next opportunity, it will come to you, ultimately.

Stephanie: *When I say [I'm] all over the place, I mean in school, and if I'm not in school I'm going to be taking classes for something else. I am most likely to just get into everything. I'm still at an age where I just want to absorb everything. Whether it's with books, whether it's just with life, whether it's with classes and my career...I do so much stuff that it's even hard to pinpoint me. I don't really specialize in anything, so I'm most likely to have a little bit of everything.*

Whenever I did something, for instance I may have painted my sister's nails or something or washed my sister's hair, my mom was like, "You should go to cosmetology school." And then I would tell her that I talked with somebody and we had a real heart-to-heart and I felt like they had a breakthrough, and she's like, "You should be a social worker." You clean blood off of somebody and she's like, "You need to be a nurse!" So, I blame part of that on her!

Krystal: *I just graduated college in May and I literally started working. Well, I had an interview two weeks after graduation. But when they asked for my diploma, I was literally like, "Uh, I just walked across the stage. I don't even think they've printed it yet!" I started work like the very beginning of July so that's all I've been doing, is just like adjusting to being a grown-up...how much fun...yay. Basically, just getting adjusted to working, and then getting adjusted to bills, and now it's getting adjusted to college loans! That's my life right now.*

Jasmine: *On summer breaks from high school, I didn't have to do anything. I was still living at home with my parents. My summer break was my summer break. I could go out with my friends all day, I could lay around the house all day. I did virtually whatever I wanted to do. Summer breaks in college were a little different, but they weren't really that bad. I worked, but I still had time to hang out with my friends because I didn't 'have' to work. I did work because I wanted to, because again, I was still living at home with my parents.*

But now, this is the adult world where you have to work because you have bills to pay. I remember the summers where I could do whatever, and I was actually trying to find things to do. But now it's like, 'ugh, I have to go to work.' To me, an eventful day is to just go to the movies, go out to eat...the things that excited me back then, don't really excite me now. I'm just happy when I get some free time to do a puzzle or read a book. It's nothing like I expected. I remember being young like, "Oh, I can't wait to grow up! I can't wait to do all this!" And now that I'm grown up, I just want to be a kid again. I just want to have no responsibilities and just be free.

Patrick: *Honestly, once you get married, you don't spend as much time with friends. Some of the things that they want to do, you obviously can't do anymore because you have certain responsibilities. Staying out late, you can't do that anymore. You have to come home and make sure everything is good in the household. I wouldn't say that I've distanced myself from my friends, but I would say that I don't hang out with them as much.*

Sometimes when I think about it, it's like, 'man, I wish I was out there, having fun' but there's a certain joy that you get from having a wife and having a son, and knowing that you can go out with your wife and have fun. You can always find a babysitter so you can spend time [together]. It doesn't affect your social life, it's just our responsibility [to take on]. It took me a while to realize that even though I'm married, you still gotta have fun because I have someone who's a partner. So, I don't have to be sitting in the house all day sulking because I'm married and have a kid.

...Honestly, when I first got married it was like, "Man, do I really want to do this?" And I went ahead and did it...Marriage honestly isn't for everyone, because it's a lot of work. But once you get the hang of it, understand it, and know how to maneuver through it, you can always find the joy. I understand that people my age don't want to do it, they don't want to have a family and kid at this age. But, there's gonna come a time when you are going to do it. There's gonna

come a time when you've got to stop the clubbing, and living the lavish life, and understand that there are going to be a lot of responsibilities. You know, having a family teaches you those responsibilities at an early age...It kinda lets you look at yourself in a whole other light. I would say yes, go ahead and have your fun, but understand that it's gonna come to...not an end...but it's going to come to a time when you're going to have to be more responsible with the fun that you have.

WORKING

Krystal: *I actually had an argument with an intern because he kept calling me Miss Turner and I'm like, "Can you please call me Krystal?! Like please, I can't take it!" So that was like one of the biggest things, accepting that, 'you know what? You are a respectable person, and people are going to respect you for the title that you have.' You don't have to sit there like, 'oh, I'm young, I don't know anything.' Because you have a lot to offer, no matter what [your] age. And I think that's why people show the respect that they do.*

Devin: *If I had the power to, and the team, I would create hardware that would be user-infallible. I'm going to [borrow] this quote: "If something is man-made, then it can be man-destroyed." That applies to working with computers because if someone builds something that looks very nice, like the Apple iOS - the operating system on iPhones - for example. It looks nice. It's easy to go through. Everything has a picture. It's user-friendly. Someone will still come to me with questions like, "How do I check my email?" or "How do I add my email?" Even though it literally takes one or two presses on the screen to achieve that.*

User-infallibility would be taking that to the extreme. It would pretty much include everything that the user needs right there on the screen, so that they wouldn't have to click anywhere or go anywhere, everything is just right there. But the reason why that's a pipe dream is that someone would still have questions and try to work something out on their own. There's always something.

Khalid: *I want to go to school for [something] medical. Or law enforcement, because I have a background in law enforcement. But I would like to do medical because I do my homework, and the medical field is projected to be the highest job growth field because all the baby boomers are retiring. So, there's a good market for that. I would either like to be a nurse or a doctor. My mom always said that I had the bearing of somebody who was really protective, so maybe that's why I did the Marines, and maybe why I want to do nursing or something in the medical field, because I'm like a very protective person. Going to the Marines has given me a stronger sense of purpose and discipline, but it's not like I'm always this hard-charger, [screaming] type of guy! I'm still me.*

Patrick: *Being in the military...[when] a lot of people see me, that's the first thing they want to talk about. A lot of people identify me as the military guy. I don't like starting out with the whole, 'oh, I'm military' thing, because that's not who I am. Eventually, when I'm in conversations, I will put out the fact that, yes, I am married and I have a son. I will brag about my wife and my son a lot so people can come off of the fact that I am in the military, and separate me from the stereotype that military personnel only have one mindset.*

People say that a lot of people in the military are always focused on the mission. We have personal lives. We like to have fun. I would say my identity now is, "Yes, I am Patrick the husband, the dad, who's happy to serve my country, and I enjoy it." I think the biggest misconception that people have about us in the military is that we make a lot of money! We get paid, and we get good benefits. We make enough money to ensure that our bills get paid and we're able to have fun. But I have people who think we're making big money, and when we come home they're trying to ask for money like, "You're in the military, you got all this money!" I'm like, "No I don't!" I've got bills and responsibilities. All that money, once it hits the bank account, comes right back out.

DETOURS

Erin: *My procrastination really deals with not pushing myself, you know? I'll have something to do, and then I'll be like, "I'll do it last minute." And it's backfired on me for a while, [but] I always used to brush it off like, 'oh, it's not me.' That ties in with me taking responsibility for my own actions as well. It's time for me to grow up.*

Honestly it happened in February [2015]. I stopped working. I stopped going to school. I was losing a lot of people in my life, and I just really hit rock bottom. And I used to brush it off like, "Things will get good." I used to be spoon-fed my entire life and I still am, low-key, but we're not going to get into that! But my parents put me in a situation where I had to grow up. So, it was like, I would ask them for advice, and they wouldn't tell me anything. They just told me, "Figure it out for yourself." So, I've taken some time off from reality, which is bananas! I'm blessed that I could do that. I really got to know myself in a matter of like, a few months. And it was challenging. Very challenging. I had my lows, I had my highs, I had my mediums, you know? I think that's very important, to like really get to know yourself. Actually, love yourself and mean it.

Christina: *It started off with wanting to get to the point where I'm satisfied with what I do and really go for my goals. I went to college, I finished college...and I had an idea of what I wanted to do. Ever since I was younger I said I wanted to be a doctor. I always wanted to be a doctor, and it kinda just stuck with me. I knew I wanted to be in the medical profession. When I graduated, I'd had this great experience at an HBCU, I'd majored in psychology and minored in chemistry. And I was like, 'okay, I'm going to apply to medical school.'*

...I took the [MCAT] test. I didn't do well on it. I think I took it like two or three times and I just...like I would study for it, I took classes, and I just wouldn't do well. So, I was at that point of, "What am I going to do?" I got into education, and did that after college for seven years. I left, and moved to New Orleans to do a master's program. I said, "This is going to be my transition from my psychology degree into the medical field. I'm going to be able to do this, and this is going to put me at a different level so I can apply to medical school." And while I was [in New Orleans], I did an internship at a hospital and I was really introduced to the field of nursing, which I had never had any experience with. For me, it was always, medical field = doctor.

So, I got introduced to the nursing field, and to the profession of nurse practitioner. It's a profession where you're able to see patients, you're able to treat patients, diagnose, [and] take care of their well-ness. If they're sick, [you can] provide medication and refer them to specialists. I was like, 'this is more of a fit for me.' So, I applied to a nurse practitioner program, I got in, and I've been doing that.

Joshua Jackson: *With the personality that I have, I've always been a bubbly person with a great personality, so I always got along with people and built a rapport with strangers like no other. I would say the breaking point of my success started in 2008.*

In 2008, I was laid off. When I got laid off, I didn't know what I was going to do because I was at a job that was paying for my tuition for my master's program. I was getting all these great benefits and that was around the time when it was really bad with the economy. So, in 2009...I'll never forget...I applied for this job. And I never called jobs, but I'm so glad I did that day. There was a woman on the other end. I remember hearing her voice [and thinking], 'well, her voice sounds familiar, but I'm just going to keep talking.' So, I told her that I applied for this position at the company, and that I was looking forward to hearing back from them about an interview, etc. And she stopped me in my tracks and said, "Joshua Jackson?!" And I said, "Uh...yes." And then she told me who she was, and said "oh hey! How is everything?!" And we just started talking like we were good old friends from high school. The end of that story is that she went ahead and vouched for me for the job I was applying for. They hired me within three weeks.

Maya: *I got my degree in communications - broadcast media - and I thought I wanted to do that. I had an internship...and I realized that this was cool, I liked it because every day is different and you can interact with a lot of different people. But being a city girl [I thought], 'I'm a newbie. I don't want to spend multiple years of my life in the middle of nowhere giving the news!' I just knew in my heart of hearts that I could not do that. I flipped out when I got to college and went to the mall and they had not heard of Aldo, so I knew that I wasn't ready for that! So, then I decided, 'maybe I'll do nonprofit communication' and I didn't know what I was going to do with that, so I ended up doing AmeriCorps for a couple of years which kind of allowed me to dip my toe into the nonprofit world. It is certainly its own world and the people who inhabit it are very interesting. Then I thought, 'I'm going to make a change. I'm going to do something.' And I struck out! And then I was kinda just floating, trying to do something, and then I got back in. And now I'm back to the thought of, 'is nonprofit the place that I want to be?' I think I just need to give it up for good. I keep trying to make it happen, and there just have to be so many things that have to be right for it to really, really work in a suc-*

cessful way for me. So, I think right now I'm re-evaluating, and trying to get out of the nonprofit circle, maybe.

Courtney: *I think I was just a lot more artistic. I was a lot more creative. I wanted everybody to be creative. I pushed everybody to be artistic and creative, and that's what I wanted to do. I was very entrepreneurial. I was always coming up with business ideas and business plans, and writing drafts of things, and going to people with ideas. I always wanted to foster a group that would touch all the different cultural areas: music, art, events. I was just so into being in the young Black and minority culture in Chicago.*

I think now I'm still true to who I was back then, but there's a different shade, a different tone. The creativity and the artistic passions are definitely on the backburner, but I also realize now that so many things that I kind of dreamed about or fantasized about back then...I wanted them and I always said that they were a goal, but I guess I didn't see it as being as feasible. And now I'm in that moment as it relates to family and kids, and being a career woman. It's just in a different shade than what I thought.

I never thought I'd be working for a community college, and I've been there for four years. I've been promoted three times; I'm doing very well there. I never thought that would be my scope of work at all. I never thought I would be the mom that wakes up and takes the kids to school, and works, and comes home and cooks dinner. My best thing is sitting on the couch with my husband and catching up on primetime TV, and being asleep by ten o'clock. That wasn't the life I sought for 30-year old Courtney seven years ago. It comes full circle, you know?

Bernadette: *It's not even in the deep way of trying to prioritize your savings and things. I'm not there yet. It's just the simple things like, if I want a new pair of shoes, I refuse to pay full price. I will shop around and I will research to save. I get what I want, and if I can't find it on sale - or preferably on clearance - I'm not going to get it, because it's not meant to be. But sometimes...the Lord blesses you and [the item] comes back when the store told me it was gone and sold out! So, I go back, and it's just sitting there at 75% off!*

When I lived at home and didn't have bills - just my cell phone bill and my car insurance - I didn't care if I blew $200 on something. It didn't matter. Then, during my first real job after college, I got laid off. I had just moved out to an apartment, I refused to go back home. After a whole bunch of back and forth, I finally got on unemployment. It was like, 'this was my first real job. I'm not going back home. I have to pay my rent, but I still want to be able to enjoy things.' So, I started doing things like thrifting, which is very fun if you know how to do it right. You can find really good things; I look for certain labels of different things that I like. I started couponing, though I don't really do it as much as I used to. I started looking for different promotions of things through Goldstar and Groupon, because I still wanted to be able to live life and do things that I enjoy, but I didn't have the resources to pay for them like I did before. So, I found a smarter way. So then when life picked up and I started working again, and I started to have the resources to enjoy those things, I wasn't going to go back to paying full price!...You can do it the smart way. It takes time, but people do it.

BE BETTER, DO BETTER

Aquillia: *There are a lot of things that I'm not afraid of doing any-more that I might have been hesitant to do before. Things that I've wanted to learn how to do that I would love to do now, and I put my-self in those positions. And I think that I'm constantly trying to learn new things, or start new things, or discuss new things. Before I was in a very small box and now I'm willing to do a lot more, so I'm constantly learning more about myself and reinventing as I go.*

Amadu: *Some people are just walking around unconscious. And by unconscious, I mean they're going through behavioral patterns day-by-day. Like, "Oh yeah, you know, I just gotta get up and go to work." [They] go to work, come back, watch some movie, eat, go to sleep, do it all over [again]. Versus waking up like, "Ahhh, today is a whole new day." You could have died yesterday, but you didn't. Luckily. There are a bunch of people who died today, you weren't one of them. Now it's like: What can I do? What do I want in life? Beyond just the generic, 'oh, I wanna get rich.' What do you want? What are you passionate about? Find out what [makes you] passionate and go for it. Don't get scared like, 'I want this, but that's not really possible.' A lot of people do that and it almost seems innate, like how do you not think of that? No, you don't have to think of constraints. Sometimes you just have to have a dream, and be able to take one step towards it.*

Stephanie: *I was told by a good friend of the family, who I actually keep in contact with on a regular basis, [that] when you're in the room with a group of people, and you are the smartest person in the room, you need to get out. And a lot of the time, we become very comfortable with where we're at, and when you get comfortable that's when you're in trouble.*

For me, I do my best to network. And I network with people who are where I want to be. That's my driving force. Like okay, I see them, and they have a smile on their face. They make their own schedules. They don't complain about their lives. They don't pity themselves. And you can tell, their whole energy is different, their aura is different. They're not tired. They tend to be - I hate to say it - but they tend to be physically active. They like to work out. They enjoy life and you can tell. They may have their ups and downs, but a lot these people [are] already accomplished. Like one of my good friends who I talk to now, she has her doctorate in nursing. She has her Ph.D., and she does research for [the University of Illinois at Chicago]. She and I talk on a regular basis, and I talk to her about the problems that I have. I don't look for her to give me an answer, but I talk to her about my problems, and I tell her what I think could be a solution and she goes, "You know what? I think that's a good idea. That's something I would have thought of." And that's how I know, 'okay I can keep doing this'....and it will always keep you going. It never fails. You may have days when you might feel beat up, you may have days when you feel discouraged. But you talk to that person…and then you keep going. You keep going.

Kasim: *You know, I'm not even going to lie, 2015 was really a big year for me. I feel like before that point, I was really laid back. I was someone who wanted to do [big] things, but wouldn't put in the work to do it.*

In 2015, I made this simple move and joined this program. They took us to different corporate settings where we get to talk to CEOs. And these CEOs are getting paid millions, but when they talk about their lives, they would tell us how they started from the bottom for real and the stuff they would do. And the reaction is the same every time, like "Whoa! You did that?!" And you think about yourself like, 'wow, I could do that too, but I'd probably think that was stupid because it's humiliating or whatever.' Through talking to these CEOs and seeing what they did - I talked to a CEO who was a janitor at one point - you start to know that this position they have now, it didn't just happen out of nowhere. You gotta work up to that, and going to this program made me more aware. It made me content to be like, 'it's okay to do whatever you've got to do to get to the point you're trying to [reach].' It was kind of inspiring.

Jonel: *I feel like...life is short, you know? People say that all the time, but life is really short, and certain opportunities you just can't get when you're older. If an opportunity presents itself to me, then I have to do it. Don't be afraid to try new things is what I'm getting at. I almost never came to Japan, because I was afraid...of just being here for four months. I did go away for college, but I could have [come] back home anytime I wanted to. I always had that option. Going to a different country, I don't have that option of, "Oh, let me go home for the weekend."*

Salihah: *Taking risks...that's kind of what I've been trying to do as of late. I think it's a combination of things. It's stepping outside of my comfort zone, and sometimes doing things that might scare me but also might have a really good payout. It's confronting my fears a little bit, stepping outside of my insecurities and doing things that I know I'm capable of, and just embracing that there are a lot of things I know I can do, that in the past I kind of held myself back from.*

I think I'd always been pretty safe, didn't really do too many things that were too challenging, or that made me feel uncomfortable. Safety and comfort, that's the ideal. That sounds great. But you'll never experience anything different if you're always doing the same thing. I found that I was very complacent and I didn't like that feeling, so I started doing things differently.

James: *I try to go back each day and think about what went wrong and how I can change it. Did I have a bad attitude? Did something get under my skin that probably shouldn't have? Is there some way I can do this better when I get up tomorrow? Is there something I can do differently? I live my life one day at a time. I keep pushing [out] one better day after the next and before you know it, you've had a perfect month, and didn't even realize it.*

Like when I'm riding home, and I got my earphones in and my mind is focused, I'm thinking about, 'how did this day go? Was it a good day? Was it bad?' At the end of the day, the only thing you really want is to be proud of who you are. You want to be able to like who you are. When you like who you are, other people see that. What I've read - which is a good thing - is that a better you, attracts better people. So, if you're constantly evolving and growing, you're going to attract the people you probably want to be around. You're not going to get those people who want to use you, talk about you, make you feel bad, or bring you down to their level. At the end of the day, as long as you are happy with who you are, that's the whole goal. So, it doesn't matter what you do.

Ebonee: *Success means...living comfortably. In this day and age, a lot of people live check-to-check, and they're not able to live comfortably. I don't want to have to worry about where my next meal is coming from, or when it's coming. I want to live comfortably. I don't want to have to live paycheck-to-paycheck...Success to me is having a good job, having a good family structure, you know? Of course, you have your daily struggles that you worry about, but I don't want to worry. I don't want to be worried. I don't want to be stressed. My daughter is five now, so probably about five years ago is when I kinda smartened up a little bit. I was never dumb, I was always a smart kid. And now it's like, becoming a parent and caring about somebody else, and having another life that you have to worry about...there's more to life than fancy stuff.*

Ethan: *Day-to-day, I spend my days doing what I believe to be the most important and crucial thing to do at this point in my life: learning and laughing. In that order, and sometimes interchangeably. Birthday to birthday, I like to assess how far I've gotten, or the goals I've achieved. For this year of being 20, I decided that this is the year I need to learn everything that I need to learn. The laughing thing came secondary. I realized that you have to take life with a grain of salt, and being able to see the humor in everything really opened my eyes to a lot of things.*

The thing is, I have life goals set by age years. For example, by the time I'm like 25, I want to have my first feature [film] in the theaters. In today's climate in the film world, most young guys are not doing that. No one young - like below the age of 30 - is really directing movies and getting their vision out in that way. I have to be ahead of everybody and everything. And film isn't the only thing I want to do, so that makes it even more crucial to be on my Ps and Qs.

Leodus: I feel like to become rich, in my opinion, the blueprint if you had a few books to read as the go-to manuals are: Rich Dad, Poor Dad , Real Estate Riches, and A Little Red Book of Selling. Those three books, if you just went and bought those three books, you should be able to come up with something. Those books are what got me ahead in terms of building the assets to run themselves so that I don't have to necessarily be there to make money. And you can make really good money if you're creative.

FRIENDS & ACQUAINTANCES

Casey: I would definitely say that I was just like, "Networking? I don't really know about that! I'm kind of here doing my own thing. I'm not really a networking type of person. I don't want to go out of my way and bother people, or have people bother me, so that we can talk about things like my future and their future." I think I've changed a lot in terms of that perspective that I used to hold towards networking, where now I don't mind it. I think it's actually a very important thing that you should do as a college student, which I've always been told. I just didn't realize it until now.

Katie: *As far as I'm concerned, you have a blank slate with me and hopefully I have a blank slate with you. And we have to cultivate and see what comes from that. I think it takes a little bit for me to warm up to people and actually call them a friend, but after I've interacted with you and watched you, and I've determined that you seem like quality person, I have no problem making that decision of being like, 'okay we're cool. I like hanging around with you.' Or just being like, 'alright, not so cool...I'm not going to hang around you.' [Then] I try not to put myself in situations where I have to see you...not everyone is completely receptive to that!*

I honestly do have people who I don't like, and they don't like me. It's coming to terms with that too, and just being fine with that. Not everyone is for you, and you are not for everyone. I think people get discouraged a lot like, 'oh, such-and-such doesn't like me' and it's easier said than done, because I want everyone to like me. And I want to like everyone. But that's just not how the world is built....that's not how things function. It's not always easy, people are not always receptive, and that's how I know that we're not meant to be. It's kinda just like, "alright, well you go along and live your best life, and I'm gonna go along and life my best life, and you know...hopefully our paths shall never meet again!"

Shanai: *My friends are all such different people in their own ways...and I have different relationships with all of them. It could be stimulating conversation, or maybe it's that friend that I can do outdoor or new things with. Maybe it's the experiences that we have, the moods that I experience with that person. So, I try to rely more heavily on my relationship with that person, more than whether we're the same on paper. Because we could be completely different, but it's the relationship I gravitate to.*

As I get older, my social circle definitely gets smaller. That also changes with how busy our schedules are. I've been friends with a lot of the same people for a very long time, and I've always had a smaller social circle. Though it's small, it's very consistent. I just think that there's something beautiful that comes from a relationship that you've had for so long. Not to say that you can't be great friends with people who you've met recently, but I cherish my relationship with my family – including my friends, because they're like the family I chose.

Parent Life

Nearly anyone can become a parent. We would like everyone to be a great parent. We expect everyone to be at least a decent parent. We concede that someone will be a bad parent. We condemn someone who is a terrible parent.

We judge a person's performance as a parent above nearly every other aspect of their life. For example, is there anything you could put at the beginning of the following sentence to lessen its blow: "(S)he _____, but (s)he is a terrible parent." None of our typically prized traits - beauty, youth, wealth, fame, and power - are quite enough to overcome the sting of the latter half of that sentence.

On the other hand, you can probably think of many more ways to begin this sentence that present an acceptable trade-off: "Sure, (s)he was a terrible _____, but (s)he is a great parent." If you are perceived to be a good parent, you get a societal pass on a wide variety of personal weaknesses, shortcomings, and limitations.

Since very few people enter into this new role in their lives planning not to be good at it, and nearly everyone would love to be an awesome parent, how do you learn what makes a good parent? Do you ask your own parent(s)? Do you ask the people who you thought of as great parents when you were a child? Do you ask the friends, coworkers, and neighbors whom you believe are good parents now? Do you sign up for a class? Do you buy a book? Do you search on the internet?

These may seem like strange questions, but what is truly strange is that although we live in a country where - in nearly every aspect of human endeavor - we invest a lot of time and resources into identifying who is the best, creating spaces where the best can display their brilliance, and rewarding those who are deemed to be "the best of the best"; we have no such system for parenting.

We don't know who the five-star parents are. There are no Olympics for the people who are the best in the world at any of the many aspects of parenting. We don't have a professional parenting league, where large sums of money are paid to people who display extraordinary parental abilities. There is no Ivy League parent university where we select a group of promising young people to develop their talents and go on to become world-renowned parents.

We work with what we have. We do the best that we can.

HOW I PLANNED IT

Aquillia: *Well, working with kids makes me see what I want to do and what I don't want to do with my kids. I feel like working with kids in this age, I want to be super old-fashioned. Like we're not going to have cell phones...that may be another conversation, because that's just not going to happen!*

Being around kids on a daily basis, I began to see that I really liked this part of this kid in my first period class; and this kid in my fourth period class?...maybe he needs more attention. Will my kids need more attention when I get older? What would that look like, doing that on a daily basis? I think having that, and looking at what my mom did for me and my sister, and how she chose to be around for us.

And my grandma too. And my dad. They had a whole dream team, and they were really on us at all times, you couldn't get away with anything! They made it their mission to hone in on us, like we were the most important things in their lives, regardless of what was going on. And I just wanted to have that same kind of mindset. I want that, and I'm trying to build towards that now.

Courtney: *Yeah, the baby fever is very deceiving! People see pictures of North West - you know, Kim and Kanye's daughter - and they're like, "oh my gosh! I'm ready for one!" Yeah...it's more than that. It's hectic.*

That's how I describe it...it's hectic. You think you have one thing handled, and another thing jumps at you. Kids are always growing and developing, more than I think we even understand, more than we can even comprehend. Their minds are growing so quickly, they're soaking everything in and sometimes they rush to burst it out as they're learning it because they're so excited. It can be exhausting for the parent, but it can be really special and exciting too. But it's just so busy. My daughter is four years old, my son is almost two, so it's kind of like once we thought we had the baby thing mastered and we were entering into the toddler stage, we got blessed with another one! So, it's a learning curve, but I wouldn't trade it for anything in the world. There is nothing like saying you're responsible for shaping a young mind. But that is a huge responsibility at the same time.

Bernadette: *My husband and I were expecting our first child. She would have been a year old this August, based on her due date. And our daughter was stillborn.*

I was that person when we got married who was like, "We're going to have a baby and we're going to do this..." We had names picked out before we even got married. It was planned. You get married, you have children, you have a house. Everything was planned out. For it to happen so suddenly, for there not to be any complications and to just have to go through delivering a child who has passed away...it was a big 'not now'.

Everyone in our inner circle has children. Our friends who don't have children - within the last year - they're either pregnant right now or they have had [a child] since I delivered our daughter early. That was a huge 'not now'. At first, I took it as a 'no'. I took the whole situation as, "Why me? We did everything right. People are out here doing who-knows-what, and have three, four, and five kids! Like, we have jobs, we have the space, we have all these things planned out, there's family support...why not?" So, there was a lot of anger there. April made it a year since she was born, so my perspective on her birthday - her 'angel-versary' as we call it - is kind of like, 'don't allow that situation to be a cover over my life.' So how can I take this horrible experience and not just stay in the [mindset] of, "Something's wrong. Everybody has this, why can't I have it?"

Accepting that 'not now' is hard. Especially when you see other people getting it. Other people who didn't want it are getting it...and it hurts...It takes time and patience. Some days, you're going to have your days when you're motivated like, "Okay, I understand, it's not right now. I have to keep working towards this. I have to keep praying about this. I have to keep encouraging myself that it's going to happen when it's supposed to happen." Other days you're going to be like, "Forget that! I'm doing this, I'm doing that, I want it now! Why isn't it happening now?!" So, you're going to teeter back and forth. There's not always going to be an answer someone can give you that's going to be a philosophical light bulb moment of, "Here's the reason why, and this is encouragement you need to keep going." But that fire that you get when you're angry and you're like, 'why isn't it happening? I want it!' That fire is going to fuel you to keep believing that it's going to happen.

WHAT MATTERS NOW

Ebonee: *Most of my days I spend with my kids. I'm not outside chillin' with the homies. It's just me and my kids, riding out together by ourselves...when I take my kids to the park, that's when I gain my peace of mind, you know? Let them run around and tire themselves out, and I just sit. I look at the sky. I look at the trees, and I enjoy nature. And I enjoy hearing my kids laugh. Being a parent is tiring, but you've got to find time for yourself. You've got to find time for your peace of mind. Because then you take it out on your kids, and nobody wants to be a mean mom.*

Faith: *I'm a mom, I'm working, I'm sort of independent in the sense that it's all on me now, and I have a young son looking up to me now. Now my focus has shifted, and it's even more intense because I'm raising someone and it's not just me anymore. It's about someone else, and someone else who's even more important. Having my son, I feel like I have an obligation to have that focus and have that drive, because I'm leading the way and I'm making a legacy for my son to carry. It's not [about] self anymore. It's completely about getting to my goal, getting to my ultimate career, making sure that my son is good, and that he's raised the way I feel God would want me to raise him.*

Neiko: *Growing up, I was a foster child. I stayed with my uncle, so my parents were never really around. And when I did see them, it was more of a "Hey, how ya doin'?" or "What you want from the store?" or something like that. So, as I grew up, I always said that if I ever had kids, I want them to have the best of the best. No matter what I had.*

I think with me being in the military for those few years, I got to splurge and ball out and 'turn up', as they say. I got to do everything.

But when my kids came, it was more, 'now [you have] a family, you can't have this anymore.' I can if I want to, but I just choose not to. Only because my kids and my wife are my first priority....I guess when I was growing up I was all about the hottest fashion, the newest things out, the materialistic things. Since I've had kids, that materialistic outlook has subsided a lot. I really don't too much care about myself in that sense. I just want to make sure that my kids and my family are right. Me, I can go without, you know what I'm sayin? I'm always in a uniform anyway. But as long as my kids are right, I'm cool with it.

Phillip: *Every morning when I wake up, I'm reminded that it's not about me anymore. It's not about me being a man anymore. It's about me being a dad, it's about me being a husband. It's about me being a Christian. It's humbling. When my girlfriend at the time said that she was pregnant...I took myself out of the equation of being successful, as sad as that sounds. I didn't know what to do.*

Through the eyes of my children now, through their love, their endurance, their courage, their strength...when they say "Daddy" and their confidence that they know they are loved gave me love, and made me remember that this is important...I know how important it is for a man to be in a kid's life, boy or girl. Obviously, for the mother to be in the children's life, it's powerful. But together, under God, and you have good friends and family around you, that's unbreakable. That's when you have respect, that's when you have certain expectations that family needs to meet. You know education is not going to leave this house. That's our priority.

Christina: *A lot of things have changed. I guess my biggest thing would just be having a child, someone who depends on you. It kind of causes you to work a little harder, because I want her - and she's only six - but I want her to be proud of her mom. I want her to be stable and be able to go to college. So, I guess that has really switched from when it was just me, and I wanted to come home and hang out with friends. Now it's more focused on her and making sure that I get to where I'm getting, so that I can be able to provide for her and her fu-ture, the way that I was blessed to have my parents work out things for me and do the same for me by making sacrifices.*

WHAT MY KIDS HAVE GIVEN ME

Kevin: *[Raising children] means a lot. It gives you direction. I'm not going to say I didn't have purpose before my children, but it magni-fies that purpose and maybe even adds more to it.*

It's great. My girl is about to be two in a couple of months. My son is six, about to be seven. You may have heard about the 'daddy's girl/momma's boy' type. I'm coming to find that to be true, because that little girl...I love her so much. I love my son, but she has me wrapped around her little finger. But man, it means so much. I come in the house, and instead of going to my girlfriend to give her a kiss, I go straight to my kids! She gets jealous at that, but it's just a wonder-ful feeling...they just give me a whole new level of motivation. Like when they're complaining about, "Aww, I don't want to share this room!" Now I'm motivated, I gotta get a bigger house. Buy a house, that's the next new step. Those types of things. My car is a put-put. I can't have this car, I've got kids now. What if my car stops on the side of the road with my kids in the back seat?

Little things like that, they're so simple, but it goes further. It goes beyond the surface. Not even thinking about the money or the materi-al [aspect], it's just that you have to provide and protect your chil-dren. Before I had them, yes, I would still try to provide for myself, but it's a whole different level [now]. You have to magnify whatever you were doing because you have kids. If you were doing something wrong, you better stop if you love your kids and you want to be there.

Jared: [My kids] are my motivation. They're the reason why I woke up on that hard mat. I was stabbed twice in the penitentiary. They're the reasons why I didn't get flown out of there on a [medical] helicopter. [They're] why I kept breathing.

...They love you no matter what you do. They might look at you a little differently, but their unconditional love is unconditional love. My kids would write me, draw me pictures. No matter what darkness I was in, in [prison] or in the streets, they made my heart beat. They make me keep wanting to fight, keep wanting to breathe, keep wanting to give more of my effort. And I'm honest with my kids...I don't try to dodge any of that, and my wife sometimes gets upset with me but I'm a firm believer [that even though] they're young, they need to hear the real. And my kids know I'm imperfect. My kids know some of my personal struggles, but they also know Daddy loves them to death, and Daddy will do his best to provide, and Daddy will do his best to protect. That's what's made my transition home a lot easier than a lot of guys.

[Some guys] try to hide or lie about where [they were]...you know some guys, their wives or baby mamas will tell their kids, "Oh, they're just at work" or "they're at college." No, your dad made a mistake and your dad is behind bars. And if you choose to make a similar mistake, they've got a bed for you. I believe that type of talk with your kids is either going to change something for the better, or they're going to do what you did; but I got to be honest.

My son wants to be a cardiac surgeon. How many 10-year olds say that?! That's what I want for my son. Whatever he wants, whatever he's working for, that's what I want for him. And he's not going to be denied because of where his father was, you know? He just won't. I don't know if it's in his blood to keep fighting or what the case may be, but he's going to be one of the best of the best.

WHAT I WANT FOR MY KIDS

Patrick: *Honestly, I think it was just the way I was raised. My parents always taught me to care about the things you do and the image that you put forth to people. I always want to show people that I'm doing what I need to do, I care about how I look in people's eyes as far as the responsibility of being a husband, the responsibility of being a dad. I see a lot of people in the military who have had kids, and it's so sad, but the father was not around for their kids. Being a father is a very big responsibility, and I couldn't see myself walking away from that.*

I had the opportunity and was fortunate to grow up with my father in the house with my mom, and I want to give my son the same experience. I want to be there for my son. I always say - and he doesn't understand it now - that I want him to be better than me. Outdo what I've done. Get better grades than me in school. Go to college and get a degree. Enjoy growing up. When I'm old, I want to be able to look at my son and say, "You are now more successful than me. You're able to stand on your own." I think now as a father, I can see how my father wished that for me. That's the greatest thing from a dad, or from any parent. You always want your child to do better than how you're doing. Not saying my life is terrible or anything, I'm at a good place in my life, but I want my son to be better. I want my son to not have to worry about anything. I want my son, when his family comes around, to be a better dad than I am, to be a better husband that I am. I want him to do better than me.

Neiko: *With kids nowadays - because there's a different breed of kids out here - you have to instill in them the positives. You gotta let them know, "If you need anything ask me. I'm here for you. I'll get it. Don't steal. Don't lie. Talk to me." Truth be told, if we were raised the way some of the older people were raised back in the day, I think we wouldn't have that many issues...It does take a village to raise kids you know? And I don't see that now. Picking up my son, going with my wife, I hear the way some of these kids talk to their parents. And I'm just like, man, this is what happened. This is the start of this kid's destructive life. Because if the parents don't say, "John/Billy, you don't talk to me like that. I'm your parent" and do something about it, they're going to continue to do it because they see nothing's going to happen. And then that's how they're going to go through life, talking to people any type of way.*

IT'S THE LITTLE THINGS

Ebonee: *I thought [my daughter] would be the sweetest little girl that I would ever meet in my life. No, no she is not! She is not the sweetest kid I ever met in my life! But I love her regardless, because she is me. She is me now. She is the person I have grown to be. She is an example of what I should change, because a lot of the stuff she mimics...you know, children are human tape recorders. A lot of things that she mimics - that I do - make me want to change as a person. My daughter makes me want to change...My daughter knew how to spell her name and write her name before she got to pre-[kindergarten], and I was so proud. I was the proudest parent in the world. I felt like I did that, without [her going to] school. ABCs, 123s...I did that. And that's stuff that I like to do. I enjoy that.*

Steven: *The most important person that's following me right now is my son. He's seven months old. I realized with little boys, they never follow your words; they only follow your actions. I know at a certain age he's either going to look up to me as his hero or look at me as just another man. So, I'm very careful about the things that I do, and the type of roads that I want to go down. Because when my son grows up and looks at his father, I want him to be able to say, "He's my hero."*

...The kind of knowledge [that needs to be passed down] is the unfiltered story of our history. How many parents do you know who try to hide who they were to their kids? And when their kids find out, that's when their kids go off the rails. 'This is the person I am. This is how I became that person.' So, you teach your kid that transition so they learn through your story. They learn through your experiences. That way they can skip the problem, and get straight to the wisdom.

Stephanie: *I think the biggest thing right now is just personality, because typically when a child is born you can look at them and you can say, "Oh, he's got his mom's eyes. He's got his dad's nose, he's got his dad's color." For me, my son doesn't really have any of my attributes. He's literally a spitting image of his father. When his personality came into play, it's like, "Where did you get this from?!" So now, I've got somebody who says, "Momma I want juice, go get it for me in the kitchen!" It's like, "Who are you talking to?!" So, I've got that.*

Seeing some of the things he's interested in is really unique. For instance, I know when I was younger - about his age - I was into dance and I liked to run around. My son likes to run around, but he's really into technology. If it's not the phone, it's the tablet. If it's not the tablet, it's the computer. And I mean, the fact that he navigates the way that he does...I remember my mom was in shock when she saw me typing on a keyboard when I was younger, because they had given us computer classes. And the fact that my son knows how to find an app, push the app, go to the search link, find a picture that looks like something he's interested in, click on it, and be able to find all the stories, or all the videos that I posted about trains, it just amazes me. They say two-year olds are all over the place. They are, but when he gets that tablet, to see him actually focus...you can see your child's potential. It's really interesting.

Courtney: *I'm still figuring that out, 'cuz I'm still figuring out myself. Outside of the fact that I know there are several things that I just won't allow her to do until she's an adult - I just know I don't have a tolerance for certain things - [my goal is] just keeping open conversation flowing. It's really a priority to develop the type of relationship where, when she sees things, she can funnel them through me and we can have a conversation. She can funnel them through my girls if she doesn't feel comfortable talking to me. She has a 'ti-ti' [who] she can go to and talk to and figure out her own voice.*

On one end of the spectrum, I feel old. I feel very old and very removed. But on the other end of the spectrum, I feel young and I still don't have this stuff figured out for myself, you know?

What Really Matters

YOLO – You Only Live Once - is the 21st century iteration of *carpe diem*, and was nearly ubiquitous in popular youth culture for several years during the early part of this relatively young century. YOLO can be a rallying cry, an explanation, or an apology. YOLO can be the introduction to an epic story, or the epilogue to a tragic one. YOLO is easy to say, easy to understand, and easy to mock. It has been one of the most useful catch phrases this current generation of young adults has given to the world.

The idea of YOLO is rooted in a few core beliefs about life. First, that each of our lives will come to an end at some point. Second, that we do not know when that end point will arrive. Third, that life should be enjoyed as much as possible. Fourth, that even if we are privileged enough to live a long life, there is a relatively short amount of time where we will have the freedom, time, and energy to enjoy it. Last, and most important, the statement reaffirms the inherent value of each human life. You are a unique combination of your personality traits, your life experiences, your cultural heritage, your physical location, and your location in the timeline of human history. While many people have some of these things in common with you, no one has all of them in common with you.

The fundamental principle of YOLO is that we each have a responsibility to maximize the life we have. Which leads to one of the essential ongoing questions of life as an adult: *What does it mean to maximize my life?* Although your answer will undoubtedly change as you progress through life, there are some key elements of a maximized life:

1) Priorities - What *must* be a part of your life? Which parts of your life matter more than others? Which parts of life don't really matter? Does the way you spend your time, energy, and money reflect the level of importance you place on the different parts of your life?

2) Release - What are you carrying through life? Why? Who are you carrying through life? Why? With all that you carry, what are you not carrying well? What should you stop carrying all together?

3) Self-care - What (or who) do you need to survive? Who (or what) do you need to flourish? How do you know that you are doing well? How do you know that you *are* well? When do you take time to check on yourself?

The myth is that YOLO is an excuse to not engage these questions. The reality is that engaging these questions is the natural extension of YOLO.

Live once, live well.

GRATITUDE

Raven: *I didn't get here alone. That's one thing that I can always say...[I had] people who invested their time. People who invested their effort, who helped me fill out this application, or that [one]. A lot of people have invested their time, their energy, and of course their money, into me. And it's not like they're looking for a return on that time, money, or energy. They just did it because they knew I could be something. And at this point, I still don't know what I can be, or what I should be, that can even make up for all the things people have invested.*

Haniyyah: *I think I valued people in my life before they were important. I think that's one thing that kind of like stayed the same, but I didn't understand the value of it until I got older, until now. And I'm like, wow, all of these people in my life were put there for a reason. All the things that my mother was saying to me, she said to me for a reason.*

...My mentors that I have, my teachers...were very important then, as they are now. My professors are very close to me and I value those relationships. And because I was in that close-knit environment in high school, and then college, and now in my [grad school] program, I'm valuing having those mentors and those people close to me so they can kind of still lead me along the way. Because I don't feel like you ever really grow up. You always have somebody wiser or smarter than you to help you along [in] life.

SELF-LOVE

Ethan: *I don't take things personally, and I think that was one of the very big steps in my growth. I feel that's a big part of anyone's growth. Once you understand that the actions, choices, and thoughts of other people have nothing to do with you personally...that ultimately it is their choice...Once you've established that, consistently established that in your mind and in your everyday life, oh, will it do wonders for you. That was one of the very key things [for me].*

Malika: *I feel like the standard [when comparing] what was important then with what is not now is the validation of other people, and that acceptance. It's like, you don't have to like me, but I still de-*

mand respect. Which was a philosophy that I didn't really follow before. I was just like willing to do anything, even if that meant degrading myself, to make someone else like me.

...Something that was also very important to me then, was kind of being submissive in an instance where I was facing authority or a person that I visualized as an authoritative figure. And it's not only when it comes to let's say, teacher-student, but [also] male-female relations, and other situations, where I kind of held back in order to avoid conflict. Now...nope...all that's out the door!

Leodus: People liking me...I used to care about that to a degree. I used to really want people to like me or whatever. [Now], if you're buying from me, I don't really care if you like me. As long as that credit card is clearing! I learned that you only have about five good friends in your life anyway...actually, it was something I realized.

The way I grew up, I grew up differently from the way a lot of people did. I didn't think it was different, but a lot of people did. I realized why there would be people who didn't like me, who didn't necessarily know me. There are people now who don't know me - who don't know me at all - but they don't necessarily like me. Because they think I'm arrogant or standoffish. First of all, I'm introverted anyway, so I'm not going to make it my business to get to know you. It's not personal...it's just not my strongest point! I realized that a lot of people were jealous because of stuff that I had that I was born with, and people didn't like me for that reason. And I realized that and I was like, "You know what? I'm not going to be sorry for what I was blessed with. So, if you don't like me, then you just don't like me. Do me a favor and stay away from me." And that's it.

Jonel: I would say I care less about what other people are doing in the sense that I won't let it hold me back. Like, 'oh, someone else is doing this, so I can't do what I want to do' kind of thing. I think I care less *about that now than I used to. I felt like I always wanted to be a part of a group, and fit in, and just do what everyone else was doing. Even if it might not have been what I wanted, you know? Now that I've gotten older, I see that is less important to me.*

PLAYING WELL WITH OTHERS

Kevin: *Just a small example: I'm the guy at work, [when] a person doesn't have a car and we get off at nine o'clock [at night], instead of having them wait for a bus until 9:45, I might take them home.*

Or let's say the bum on the corner...I don't judge. Some people say, "Oh, I'm not going to give him my money. They're just going to use it to buy anything." I might be that person - if I'm eating some food and I'm sitting at a stop light - and I know that I could go buy another six-dollar meal, and this person says he's hungry, I might give that person my food. And throw him a couple of bucks. That's the type of thing that I would do. I've always tried to help, but I think over the years [with] me being able to do a little more...I guess [it comes] with age, and maturing, and having a little more money or whatever it may be. I couldn't do that back then, even though my first mindset [was] to say, "Okay, I'm gonna do that." At 12, we're not thinking about that. As children or teenagers, we kind of have that us-against-the-world [mentality] and it's 'me, me, me, me.'

I've had some years where...it hasn't been great. I've been through hard times and I guess from those experiences I feel like, man if I can help somebody, it not only helps them, it helps me feel better about myself; that I was able to do something and I did it, instead of just turning my head. It's just the direction in life that I think we should [take]. I'm not saying that "I'm alpha and omega, do what I do," but I believe if everyone else had that type of mentality...at least try to help. You may not be able to buy that extra meal, but if you're riding past someone who needs a jump on the side of the highway, do it, if you're not fearing for your safety. I feel like nowadays we're all concerned with ourselves. Not everyone, there are a lot of people out there who give a helping hand and are out to help others.

Daphne: *I feel like everybody walking this Earth has a story. Whether they're rich, whether they're poor, whether they're wearing the latest Jordans...whatever that person is, and wherever that person is going, they have a story. And in their story, there's something that you can take from it. It could be a lesson, it could be a name, it could be anything that you can use as a resource.*

Many people run to the celebrities and say, "That's the most important person I'm following." Honestly, everyone around me has something to offer me. Every single person walking this Earth has something to offer me. The homeless person on the corner in front of the bodega, [or] wherever he is, he has a story and he has something I can learn from. Whether he can offer me something or not, he has a story, and that story will benefit me somewhere down the line. It might not be today, but it might be ten years from now and I could be like, 'oh I remember I had a conversation with this homeless person and this is what he said, or this is how he handled the situation, or this is what he went through.' I feel like that makes you a more well-rounded person and it broadens your horizons.

Krystal: *I would say always remaining humble and being appreciative, as well as being loyal to those who have been there for you when you didn't have anything, [and] didn't know what you were going to do. Those are the same people who are cheering you on and pushing you to do better. Those are the people who you have to appreciate. I feel like that's one of the worst things to see; people who you saw start from nothing and they had the greatest support system and everyone pushed them. And as soon as they feel like they're reaching their goal it's like, "Deuces! That's it, I don't need you as a friend anymore! I don't have to talk to you anymore, like, you're not on my pay grade."* It's ridiculous.

Quaneesha: *I'm not into not being myself, I'm still a blunt person. I am always truthful with everything. [Now] I probably hold my tongue [more]. That's something that's probably changed. Before I would be more vocal. I didn't care about how you felt if I told you something. I felt like I was just being real, and [that] you had to take what I had to say, so I didn't really care if you liked it or not. But now I'm more like, 'okay, I think this might hurt this person's feelings.' So, I try to go about it differently. Sometimes it may not come out as I expect it to, but I try to change that.*

People always said, "Oh my god, you're so mean! You're so harsh!" I used to get that a lot. Growing up it was like, "Oh, she's the mean twin. She's the mean one." I would always say, "I'm not mean, I just tell you how it is. I don't like to sugarcoat it." And I guess people took that the wrong way, so now I try...I try...I don't have it down pat. Probably not even close to having it down pat. I'm working on it; I'm a work in progress with the caring part. I think I hurt so many people's feelings with my bluntness that I take a step back and I try. I try.

TIME AND MONEY

Maryka: *I feel like my independence right now is an obligation. Becoming financially intelligent as well, so I can know how to handle my money and not run to mommy and daddy for money, 'cuz they don't have it. Family has also become very important to me as I grow up. I learned that nothing is permanent but the love in your heart. Its energy, and the flow of it, is indeed necessary in today's time. I didn't get along with my mom back then, but I've been learning about consciousness and being more present, and being less petty. I don't have to get my point across to my mom all the time, it's an ego thing. Getting closer to my family and realizing that they won't be here for a very long time...is something that has become important to me as I grow older.*

Shanai: *I would say time matters more to me...I would say the time that I have with my friends and family, I definitely appreciate it more...Just the difference [between] when I was young and I could have easily slept my days away if I wasn't in school. Or being with friends and time flies by so fast. Now you're almost fighting for a moment of free time as an adult, that's when it comes into consideration for me...I would say that money means more to me. You know when you're a child, even if you're working when you're in high school, expenses and money don't really...at least I didn't have the same appreciation as I do now that I'm working. The idea of how much someone makes in an hour, and how quickly you spend that. I would say that I have a much better appreciation for education and bettering yourself in any way. School isn't necessarily the only way a person can do that.*

Amanda: *I think that when you're 14 and you only have like an 8th grade education, I think that what mattered to you, those things are a little bit more superficial because you don't have priorities. You are allowed to be as naive and ignorant as you want, because you're 14. Like your brain isn't even developed yet.*

But I think that once you start to get into your 20s, and your brain is developed, and you do have bills to pay, I think that education becomes a necessity. There are just things that are for your own good, it's almost like a life and death situation. Just knowing how to open a bank account, how to budget myself, how to pay for books, how to learn to study, how to de-stress, how to set an alarm. For me, it was about those priority things becoming more important, and those su-

perficial things becoming less important. Am I going to ask my mom for money [to buy] a dress, or am I going to ask for money for a textbook? I think that as you grow up, life has a way of slapping you in the face, and there are certain things that you just have to know to be able to recover from that slap.

WAKING UP

Joshua: *I've been really into politics, but I've also been getting into social justice type of stuff too. For example, transgender rights. I never really thought about it as a kid in high school, 'cuz I'm a male. I identify as a man. So, I don't know how it feels to be born as a male but know inside I'm a female.*

That's not something I identify with, but I would go online and I would see these suicides from these transgender teens growing up in conservative households. Being rejected by their families or being sent to conversion therapy, which doesn't work. In my opinion, it's abuse. So, I would see these things, and I just felt like this is something I really need to look into and get educated on...This is something that transgender teens are going through that the media doesn't really talk about until something like a suicide happens...Lately, these past couple of years, the conversation has been had and is starting to gain momentum.

Tobi: *I actually have a picture of myself in a car going to primary (elementary) school. So, I'm sitting there in the car, and I see loads of other kids on the street, hawking, or trying to wipe the [car windshield], or just doing some trade with their parents. And I couldn't really understand - apart from the fact that they couldn't afford it - why that was the case. Why you had those children there, and I was the one in the car going to school.*

As I grew older, and got to know more about the country that I lived in, I could not understand why we had so much oil and so many resources, yet there was just nothing to show for it with the common people. So that made me think a lot. It started a lot of things within me. Before I moved, I had a year...and I did my A-levels (college pre-requisite courses) in nine months, as opposed to [the usual] two years. That period was super-intense...at that point, most of what I had was my books. And I realized how much I had learned in those nine months beyond the curriculum, beyond what I had to know for my exam. The time that I spent with my tutors, asking questions and actually having the opportunity to have those questions answered, I know how much that changed the way I thought and the way I sought to do things.

After that, I knew I was going to leave Nigeria, so I said, "Hey, I've got so many books around me. I know what these books did for me, why not just give them to other people who would need them?" So, I randomly got up one day, and went to an orphanage around the corner, and I just spent time with them. I had a book with me, and I was just trying to read what I had to them. Putting those things together, I was like, 'okay, you know what? Why not try and put it towards people who wouldn't usually have the opportunity to have these resources, but I know that - in some way - it would help them.' So, I donated all the books that I had. I gave them to someone who works with schools in the disadvantaged communities. I was like, "Hey, help me get this across to people."

As I studied more, learned more, and got more involved, I got to learn that one of the things that reduces the chances of people going to [take college entrance exams] is actually not being able to afford the books. It honestly shatters me...what you would see in the statistics over the past few years is that performance is dropping, in terms of success rates in school and the number of people going to school. And this is one of the reasons, because they don't have these materials available to them...For children in disadvantaged communities, it is quite a burden on their parents. Education, unfortunately, is not as much of a priority for their parents as it is for those who are privileged...because there are other things the funds need to go to. [I realized] that if getting more books to them would increase their rates of going to [sit for college entrance exams], then let's try to do that.

Rima: *[Back then], I don't think I cared much about anything. Especially when I lived abroad. I was like, 'I'm carefree! I have no worries. There's nothing to worry about.' But now, I guess I care more about what's going on around me. Just in the world in general, all the issues that we're dealing with here in the States as far as race, religion, feminism, sexism, misogyny, and so forth and so on. All those things play a bigger role now for me.*

Kevin: *Back then what was important to me was having fun, [and] making good money so that I could have fun. I still want to make good money now, but it's more so for my children.*

One of my goals in the next five to seven years, is starting a nonprofit organization, whether it be for young men, whether it's just for young minorities. That's something that you have to have money to do. There are grants and things that the state could give, but you have to put some of your own into it. Back then, my goal would be [to] have fun, you know, go to parties and get a couple of 'trophies' and say, "look at this trophy"...not in a literal sense...but that was my [mindset], that's what I was aiming for. But now I would like to do something for us. Us being young men, young Black men, young Hispanic men, young White men.

CHANGING MY PRIORITIES

Krystal: *One of the biggest things is just accepting yourself for who you are, and understanding who you are. I'm not trying to pretend like I found myself, because...no, not at all. I'm 22. Clearly, I'm not who I want to be! I can get it together today, but that doesn't mean I'm going to be the same person next year, or the year after that. It's understanding that you are going to evolve into a different person as time goes on. That's just something you have to accept. The things you liked in high school, you don't like in college. The things you liked in college, they're irrelevant by the time you get to be 25, you know what I mean? There are different life goals and different things going on.*

Joshua Jackson: *Back then, I had on my vision board that I wanted a Mercedes-Benz. And I got it three years after I did the vision board. Now I'm like, 'okay, I got it and that was fun, but now I don't really need it.' I can use the technology of today - Uber, Lyft, Sidecar - or public transit to get around in L.A. because I can work anywhere...I realized that the material things that I obtained through the success that I've achieved, they were really for other people. It wasn't really for me. If you think about it, why did I need that nice Mercedes-Benz? So, people could know that I'm successful. Now that wasn't why I got the car. I really got the car because it was a personal goal of mine. However, subconsciously, it was really for others to know that I've arrived.*

Sometimes you have to rethink why there are certain things that are material possessions that you just absolutely feel like you need to have...and that's what I really had to ask myself. Is me having this house that's over $2,000 a month to rent, me having this car note and this nice Mercedes-Benz, are these helping me out with becoming a motivational speaker and a better writer and all those goals that I *want to achieve? No, not really. If anything, it's holding me back. And so, I had to start changing my perspective on things and saying, "Okay, let me become more of a minimalist so that I can achieve everything I want to do."*

Safiya: *I remember that throughout middle school and high school...well, more so in high school...the most important thing - I'm telling you - was what you were wearing. Nothing else mattered. Whatever you were wearing made you cool. I thought that was my way in. That all I had to do was just wear something nice and everyone was going to talk to me and know my name and stuff like that. That's what I thought was important. Obviously, it isn't in most cases, but when I moved on to college I realized that it wasn't important. Now that I'm at a commuter college, and I'm kind of technically out in the real world, but on a trial basis...I realize that it is not important at all.*

[Another] thing that I used to think was important, was the people you hung out with, your clique and everything. These days I don't feel like that's the most important thing. But having an established network based on what you want to pursue in life, that's important. But that's not the same thing as your clique of friends, you know?

James: *I used to like drama. I used to surround myself with people who liked to talk too much, and just liked to gossip all the time. I'm even sad to admit that today, [but] I was a drama queen. I used to like drama. Drama used to follow me, I used to chase after it. I was always in the middle of something. But now, I don't do any of that anymore. I'll say it like this, I took pride in what it means to be a man.*

Jared: *One thing I struggled with that got me in a lot of trouble is social acceptance. So, what I try to do now, whether it's dressing, drinking, eating, what sports I like, what I like to talk about...I let my circle of friends know who I am, what I'm going through, what I want to be, and if they accept it, great. If they don't, they're not my friends. I used to get confused with acquaintances and friends. So now one of my things is, I want to be surrounded by friends. I want to be surrounded by loved ones because I need love. Everybody needs love, you know? I'm the first to admit I need a circle of good guys around me. I need my wife to be in tune with me. Social circles are no longer important to me if it's not meaningful and it's not genuine.*

Kasim: *Before, I used to put myself first. I used to be lazy. I used to just wait for opportunities to come my way; I wasn't really the type to be a go-getter. But eventually, I matured and saw people out here grindin' and doing their thing. I wanted to gain their lifestyle, but I wasn't putting in the work.*

Sometimes you gotta do things you don't like to get to the point you want to [reach]. I've been through that a few times and you realize when you get that end result that you were craving... and it could be anything, it doesn't even have to be a long-term goal. It could be something short-term. I'm pretty sure everybody's been through that before. You've just got to associate it with a long-term goal and trust that you will see the same result. You wanna be rich? That's a long-term goal, but you know you gotta do all this stuff that you don't like to get to that point.

What's satisfying is that when you get to that point, you're going to look back and be like, 'all that work that I put in was crazy. I did stuff that I didn't even like, but I did it the right way and I got the type of lifestyle I want to live right now and that's all that matters.' Then you just look back and laugh. You start to appreciate it, and you realize that it was all worth it. That's what I did. I just connected some really short-term things that I work at...and when you see results in your short-term goals you [start] to see that, 'if I want to get at this long-term goal, I'm going to have to do stuff that I don't neces-

sarily want to do, but I know that I have to do.' Just do it, and then when that end goal becomes a reality, that's going to be the satisfying part. You're going to look back and be like, "It was all worth it."

Daphne: *I give, and I give, and I give, and I give...a lot now. Whereas when I was younger, I was very selfish. But over the years I've learned that the more you give into this world, the more you will get back. And many people don't understand that statement, and they won't agree with that statement. But I believe that if you give into this world, and you give it with love and you give it with passion, that is going to [boomerang] back at you; and you won't even be able to catch it because it will be so much. So much goodness coming in abundance for you, and you won't know what to do with it.*

Learning to Love Myself

Take a good look in the mirror. This would seem to be the worst bit of advice to offer to this generation. Although being enamored with one's youth and beauty has been a staple of human behavior for all of recorded history, previous generations of young people could never have dreamed of the tools that have been made available to millennials. The camera has only been around for 200 years. The television was invented less than 100 years ago. For that matter, even the standard type of mirror we use every day has been around for less than 200 years.

For the overwhelming majority of human history, the way we saw ourselves and understood our place in the world was influenced by a relatively small number of other humans. Only a small percentage of people ventured beyond the region in which they were born. With the exception of merchants, missionaries, and mercenaries, most people only encountered humans outside of their tribe when they migrated. Even with the proliferation of encyclopedias, magazines, and television during the 20th century, the way people saw themselves was still primarily influenced by the other humans they encountered in real life.

There are more ways to see yourself - and to be seen by others - than the human species has ever known. More importantly, these powerful capabilities have been distributed across regions, races, and religions in a manner unrivaled by any system of government that has been devised thus far. There are areas on our planet where it is easier to get an Instagram filter than it is to get a clean glass of water, a consistent source of electricity, a doctor, a job, a school, a year without bombs, and so on.

One of the side effects of this new reality is that, for many of us, the way we see ourselves - literally and figuratively - is filtered through the collective lens of millions of other people around the world. As our wizards of technology occasionally remind us, our brains are just beginning to evolve to adapt to this new environment. What are the psychological effects of consuming thousands of images everyday through mediums that are designed to rate and rank them? What are the psychological effects of producing images of yourself for other people's consumption on platforms where their responses will rate and rank you?

Can I still see myself? When can I see myself? Where can I see myself? How do I see myself? What do I see in myself?

A reflection, on our self-reflections.

ACCEPT

Daphne: *Every day you wake up, you wash your face, and you look at that person in the mirror. That's something that I think everybody does, or should do. After high school, I would look at myself in the mirror and I'd just be like, "Do I love this girl? Am I in love with myself?"*

When you look at yourself in the mirror and you start picking apart things that you don't like about yourself, that's the first step in knowing that you don't love yourself. I have to look in the mirror and I have to say, "You know what? I do love the freckles on the side of my eyes that nobody sees or people think is a tattoo. I do love my full lips. I love that I'm smart. I have scars on my legs, but I've accepted it and I love that. I suffer from psoriasis but I love that." It's okay for you to love yourself and not penalize yourself because of what society wants you to believe is okay, or what your friends want you to believe is beautiful.

I had to realize, 'Dafna, you're okay girl. You're going to be okay regardless of what anybody else says. You have to love you, because if you don't love you, nobody's going to love you.' So, I had to isolate myself. I isolated myself from everybody and I went into tunnel vision. I made a few vision boards...I don't even think I was talking to friends. I was so focused on finding who I was and building on that. It might not work for everybody, because some people can't be by themselves for too long...but that's what worked for me.

Atisha: *The biggest difference is being aware of my cultural identity. It's also being aware of my beauty. I feel like a lot of young Black girls have had the same experience as me or something similar, where they didn't feel beautiful. Or the things around them, or the people around them, didn't make them feel beautiful. Or they felt beautiful, but felt like they weren't allowed to feel beautiful. [Like] they didn't have a right to feel beautiful. That was a big part of my childhood growing up, learning to accept and to embrace this whole [range] of emotions that I've now come to grips with.*

[Even] talking to some of my friends now, some of them still have those same sorts of insecurities and those same sorts of traumatic experiences from childhood that they bring with them. And it spills over into other aspects of life like relationships, not just romantic relationships - but relationships with people in general.

Noor: *I think I used to look nice because I wanted people to tell me I look nice. Right now, I know that I look nice, so I don't really care whether people tell me that or not. Every woman likes to hear com-*

plimentary or flattering words, but I would not rely on someone to tell me that I look beautiful before I start to believe I'm beautiful.

Before, I used to be that person. I guess every teenager goes through that. I believe beauty comes from within. Half of the beauty of women is when they believe that they are beautiful. So, when she walks in a room, and she knows that she is beautiful, and she is confident that she is beautiful, and she doesn't compare her beauty to the other women in that room...she is so beautiful.

...I do believe that the word beauty doesn't really mean physical beauty only. There are lots of people who other people would look at and say, according to the standards of fashion or modeling, that this person is not beautiful because of their eyes, because of their nose, because of their hair, because of their ears, because of their size, whatever. But even if they have a flaw in their features, that doesn't affect [their beauty]. When I say beautiful, I do believe that all women really like to hear the word beautiful...there are also other adjectives to describe women - like 'smart' - but the word beautiful is very important. Just as the word 'ego' is [important] to men, the word 'beautiful' is to women. [The word] is that big, and that powerful.

Courtney: *I'm natural. Actually, I've been natural since I was pregnant with my daughter. I've been natural for five years now...and I'm not natural because I'm political. I'm not natural because I'm like "pro-Black everything...yada, yada, yada." I'm not a vegan. I'm not a hippie.*

Everyone who goes natural does not take amazing care of their hair. My hair is probably in a worse state now than it was when I was wearing all the weaves and all the perms. I'm natural because it was convenient, because I'm busy. I balance it out. You know people stop me all the time and talk about how beautiful my hair is, and it's a compliment, and I encourage them when they go on their own natural hair journey. But I'm not passionate about it like that.

In the same token, with obsessing over body type and stuff...I'm a plus-sized woman. I'm heavy-set. Heavier now than I've ever been, after the kids. I've had insecurities about my body type and I've had periods where I obsess over the plus-size movement and the curvy movement, and bodycon for big women, and all that type of stuff. And that's huge on Instagram right now...and I go through periods where I obsess over that. And I then also go through periods like I did when I spent six months going through an intake process to get gastric by-pass surgery, so that I could become half of my size right now. I'm still figuring it out, so I can't be overly critical.

One thing I never want to be for my daughter, is a hypocrite. It's very important that she sees in me truly what I say I stand for and that she sees somebody who is honest and open. And so, I don't want to harshly try to impress upon her my own opinions, or limit her own assessment of herself or her preferences. So outside of her coming to me at 16 and saying that she wants to get a boob job, I mean I'm go-ing to be pretty open to having those conversations. But it's my re-sponsibility as a parent to put her around strong cultural representations, and appropriate groups of people, and try for her to have a broad, open mind...I definitely don't have all the answers, but I don't want her to be limited. I don't want her to be sheltered. I don't want her to feel a bias from me in any way.

Erin: *I feel like girls who strive for that [look], going as far as doing the plastic surgery and making sure they're up with the trends...I try not to judge them because of that. If you look at me, I don't have [big] hips, you know? At the end of the day, I know that I'm good with my-self. I'm going to be beautiful no matter what I look like. I could walk outside dressed in a plastic bag, and I'm still going to be happy with who I am as a person. A lot of people are not there yet. They're look-ing at this big booty on TV, and videos, and all that, and that's what they want. But it's not what they need, and until they figure that out...*

You know what irks me? Well, not irks me, but you know what's sad is: Why do you have to compare yourself to me? Why? Who am I to you that you have to compare me to you? I'm not your god. You don't look up to me. Be yourself. At the end of the day, I'm gonna wake up looking the way that I am, going to sleep the way I am. I'm not changing, [regardless] of what you say to me. Whether it's a compliment or you're trying to compare yourself to me and dog me out, I'm still going to sleep as Erin, and I'm waking up as Erin. And I'm content with that. I'm happy with that. You're not happy with yourself if you feel like you have to talk about the way I look. Who does that?! Love yourself.

Before my grandmother died last year, every time I would see her - since I was little, and I am blessed to have had her in my life - I'd be like, "I love you grandma." As long as I can remember, she would be like, "Love yourself." And I used to take it as a joke. I used to get offended like, "Gran-Gran, you don't love me?!" She used to look at me and be like, "Love yourself." And it took me a minute to be like, 'okay I see what she's doing. I see what she's doing.'

Katie: *People's opinions of me and how I present myself to the world [mean less to me now]. I think it's taken me a very long time to just realize this is who I am, this is me, and I'm not going to change for anyone. Especially parts of myself that I like. Just realizing that this is who I am, this is how I view the world, this is how I talk, this is my name...it's just like, this is it!*

Not that people's opinions don't matter to me, but people's opinions that are just silly and superficial and just coming at things that, at this point I'm just like, "this is very much who I am, and this is embedded in me and you know...welp...sorry that you feel that way."

Ashley: [Back then], I probably would have followed all the popular people, because that's what I was doing in my social space. I was a follower. I wanted to fit in with the group of people that I knew. And I wasn't really being myself, because I didn't know who I was. I hadn't gotten to that place where I had found myself, so to speak. And I got to the point where I was by myself. I didn't have anyone I could call and process with, or get their opinion on my outfit or my hair. I didn't have any of that. I was by myself. I had my family, and me. And I was able to really dig deep, and find out who I really was for the first time in my life and say, "Okay, I like x, y, and z and I'm un-apologetic about it. If you're going to be in my life from this point on, you have to deal with that. Because this is who I am. I'm not chang-ing for anyone."

Raven: [Thinking about] my version of perfectionism, I've always had this problem [because] I am a people-pleaser. I want everyone to think I'm perfect. I guess my issue is that I don't allow myself to [just] be normal. I'm slowing learning to say, "Forget everyone's ex-pectations as long as I'm satisfied with the person I'm becoming, and the person I am currently, that's all that really matters."

For a very long time I pressured myself to be perfect, and to make it so that everyone thought that I was perfect and had it together. And a lot of times that wasn't the case, and that's when I had to learn that it's okay for me not to be perfect. It's okay for me to not live up to eve-ryone's expectations, and to be who I want to be.

Especially in college, I was so dead set on being an accountant, be-cause I thought that's what people wanted me to be. But I didn't like it, and it took me a very long time to figure out that it's okay to not like something, because at the end of the day you're living this life for you. But I still feel that pressure sometimes to be perfect, because I feel like so many people invested in me, and there's nothing worse than investing in something and not seeing it come through.

Jonel: *I would say just live your life, and if those people who are around you aren't supportive of your dreams and your ideas, then you don't need to be around them. The world is so much bigger than that, and there are so many other people who will be receptive to you and support you. I think when you're younger, you [look at] the people around you like that's it. When you get older, you realize that you can make new friends, you can start a new life, and you can find a community that fits you. I think younger people just don't see that right now, but eventually they will.*

VALUE

Maya: *You know, I'm still trying to figure it out. I'm gonna stay positive and keep looking up and keep pushing ahead and realizing that I am valuable as a person. And that value is not attached to a job, or friends, or followers, or anything like that. It literally is just me as a human being, as someone who is trying to be the best me, who's trying to really learn who I am, so I can be the best me. But then, also, doing things that are helpful and encouraging for others, for those around me. That's where I'm at right now, really just trying to understand my value as a human being, apart from anything else that's going on: the clothes I wear, where I'm eating...any of it. Just really appreciating my value as a person on this Earth.*

Krystal: *So, you basically have to just accept who you are, and understand that you have to value yourself. I would say that you have to learn to value yourself before you value anyone or anything else, honestly. Until you feel comfortable and get comfortable in that, you're going to struggle. No matter what, you're going to struggle until you're like, "You know what? This is me." You can't change for people, you can only change for yourself and hope for the best and that's it. You don't like me? That's fine, move on to other things.*

I was a big people-pleaser. Oh, I wanted everybody to like me. I didn't want problems with anyone, like I just wanted to be that girl who everyone gets along with and says, "oh, you act so nice." No, sometimes you don't have to be that person. It's really getting over that. And the only way you can get over that is validating yourself. You don't need anyone else to validate you.

Felice: *To be kinda cliché, as a young girl I was more obsessed with how people perceived and thought of me. I was always trying to bend over backwards sometimes to make friends...a lot of people deal with that, where sometimes you kind of put yourself on the shelf, or take a back seat to what you want and what you see because you want to make sure that your friend isn't upset with you.*

As I got older, I started to get into situations where I realized that I was putting my feelings and what I wanted on the back seat to make sure my friends were happy and weren't upset with me. But then they would come to me and do something to me that hurt my feelings, without caring...or taking into account how it would affect me. So it was like, 'okay, now I kinda have to be more selfish with what I want, because obviously these people are going for what they want and doing what they want, regardless of how it's affecting me. And I'm over here changing my life around.'

RESPECT

Aquillia: *Respect has always been important to me. Mutual respect. From anybody and anything. People always say to give and to get it, but [for me it was] learning how to give it; even when it seems as if people don't deserve it. And also learning how to receive it when I came to be a person in authority. That it's okay to also demand respect from people, especially when you give it...and I think it was important to me [back] then even though I was feeling - at some points -*

down that I wasn't more well-known and more popular. It's always been important to me to have authenticity in my friendships. Which is why, even in high school, I still only had five or six people that I really talked to, who really knew me on a daily basis and who I still talk to now. That's really important, making sure the people who are in your life are there for real.

Maya: *Some of the things that have made me as reflective as I am now are the relationships I've been in. I was in a relationship for nearly three years, and when I got out of that relationship - when it ended - I was like, 'oh no! I can't! I just don't know what's happening! I thought this was it.' And the further I got away from it, I was like, 'no, I should not have been in this relationship for a long time.' And once I was able to get away from that, I was able to acknowledge that it wasn't the right relationship for me.*

There were just things that I [would] never stand for now, because I know I should be validated as a woman. That if I say something as a woman, that it is valuable...because I know...because I am a woman. Just as when a man says something as a man, that it is valuable, because he is a man. There were just a lot of things that happened where I was being quiet...just holding on to things I shouldn't have been holding on to. Things that should have been put out, and discussed, and nipped in the bud much sooner than they were. Sometimes in life, you just have to go through it for yourself. There are some things where you can learn the lesson through someone else and see the prototype. But then there are some things you have to go through on your own so that you can have that experience and that journey. For me, that's what it was. Not that it was all bad - the relationship wasn't terrible - but in my heart of hearts when I looked at it, it wasn't what it should have been. And that allowed me to really re-evaluate: 'What is important to me? Who am I? What is my voice?' And to know that I should not have to stifle that.

LISTEN

Faith: *When something's not for me, I just feel it. There could be 10 million people, and I would just feel like I'm by myself. I can just kind of sense it, and I feel it, and that's just how I catch it. I'm more spiritual in a sense, so sometimes I feel like God is tapping me on my shoulder like, "You're about to feel real lonely right now, because you know this is not for you." Everybody has to find their niche and find what's for them and what's not for them, but I know when something's not for me, it's all over me.*

Erin: *Before, I thought I was just Erin and everybody loves me. [I thought], 'everything will work out, I have this great life, I'm good, I'm blessed and highly favored.' But when I went through the process [of self-reflection] it was like, 'you're blessed? Why? What do you have to show for it? What do you do for yourself that shows you're blessed, you know what I'm saying?' And that was me before, naive Erin who just got everything that she wanted.*

But I really had to sit down and say, "If I was to strip away everything that I have right now...I'm blessed to live in a great house with a great family. But if all of that was taken away, and I had to stand on my own two feet, what would I be thankful for, right then and there, without all these gifts?" Then I had to really sit back and actually be like, 'I'm worth anything that I want, you know? I deserve everything that I want and I need in life, just by standing on my own two feet. And I have to work for it, because I can do it, without having to fall back on anything.' I had to know that I could stand on my own. Before, I didn't know that. I was like, "Oh, my parents got me, they'll pay for it." But now it's like, 'God forbid everybody is gone tomorrow, what do you have to show for it? What is your imprint on this world?'

Toshawna: *My parents have a big role...they see so much in me, and they express that all the time. So, it's not like something I don't hear often. But at the same time, they're not with me on this journey...they're not physically there with me to see what's going on. Of course, they're there supporting emotionally and mentally, and whatnot. I guess with everything that I was exposed to, via friends, and reading, and movies, and just everything; I just started not caring anymore. It got to that point where it's like, 'it's my life, and I mean what's the point of caring what other people think when they're not living it?' It's not nonchalance in the sense that I disregard people's opinions, but it's nonchalance in the sense that I'm the one who is more important than other people's opinions.*

PERSEVERE

Tobi: *One thing that I'm so confident about, is that my journey is definitely not the same as anyone else's. Like I might not be where I want to be, or moving at the pace that I want to be moving at, but I know that if there's something that I'm doing, or if there's a dream or a thought...I truly believe that God put that thought, idea, or dream in [my mind], and is faithful enough to see me through. That is what keeps me going...I've had so many good and bad experiences over the last year, which have made me stronger and taught me the principles that I abide by today...It didn't happen in a day, it happened over the years. Falling, learning that I always had to pick myself up, seeing the bigger picture.*

Chelsea: *For me, it was accepting that failure is not the end of it, you know? Of course, failure is not enjoyable, but it's all part of the process. I think whenever someone goes through something, it's preparing you for the next thing.*

So, I'm not saying that when you're facing adversity, or going through troubled times, [to be like], "oh my god I'm so happy that it's here." But do embrace it, and make sure to pick up whatever lesson it's trying to teach you. Just accept the fact that there will be failure, there will be hard times, but it is ultimately preparing you for what is to come. I think it was when I got to the point where I accepted like, 'hey, everything isn't going to be perfect. I am going to mess up, but I need to forgive myself and move forward,' but to make sure whatever lesson it is that I am supposed to learn, I take it with me as well.

Also [being] welcoming...like I remember at some point, if something were to happen, I would either act as if it's not bothering me, or I would just ignore it. Whereas now, if something happens...it's not like I do so much yoga [that] I never cry. I definitely do get hurt, but in that moment, I'm accepting of the fact that "Things are not okay right now. I am hurt. I am crying. But that is okay." It's when you're fully just immersed in that, that you can actually really move forward. But if you're kind of just pushing it away and ignoring it, that would probably only make things worse.

Social Media

You have to love yourself before you should expect anyone else to. It is not a coincidence that the chapter about self-reflection and self-love precedes the chapter about social media. It is not a coincidence that the chapters about our experiences in our families, in our schools, in our minds, and in our daily lives precede the chapter about social media.

I find it ironic that millennials – who are so frequently studied, questioned, and/or ridiculed for their use of digital technologies – are often reduced to two-dimensional avatars by the people commenting on their behavior. We come to our computers, phones, and tablets as multi-dimensional human beings. In this regard, turning on a device and logging onto a publicly shared digital space is not much different than walking out of a home and entering a publicly shared physical space.

There is no single narrative about the young people whose coming of age journey has paralleled the rise of social media. In the same way different people come to parks and beaches at different times for different reasons, people who enter social media spaces represent the full range of life perspectives and personality types. So, for the purposes of this book, the goal is not to map out the vast expanse of virtual land that is social media. Instead, I'm interested in how the identities we carry from the areas of life discussed in the first seven chapters impact what we do on social media, and how we do it.

HOW I MOVE

Maya: I follow a few friends. Mostly a lot of acquaintances from college. I mean, I just follow a lot of foolishness. It keeps me hip, I will say that. Shout out to Instagram which has no chill, which keeps me young and youthful, even though I'm totally not in that world! And I'm thankful, because with Instagram I can understand when I should say something is 'on fleek' and when it's not! I know when something's wack because Black Twitter and all of Instagram have memed it to death! Although I am getting old-er, I am not old! So, it is important that I keep up with those sorts of things.

Steven: Social media I think - at its core - is supposed to be for you. I post some things that I like. I post some things that I wanna go back to. I post some things that I've enjoyed. I'm not really posting it for an audience. I post things that I find enjoyable.

I'm really careful about the things that I do because I know that the things I do now are going to lead to the type of person I'm going to become. If I don't sometimes have that out-of-body experience where I'm putting the breadcrumb trails of my life together and seeing how it's going to shape up, and being really specific in the things that I do…if I'm not looking in the mirror at the person I am, I may lose sight of the image.

Haniyyah: I think it got to the point where you start hearing, "Oh, you millennials, you're always posting such-and-such on Facebook!" So, then you start getting kind of like, worried, about what you're posting. So, you're like, 'maybe I shouldn't post this until I have something valid to say. Should I be saying this? Maybe not. Maybe I'll just listen and sit this one out.' So, I think that's the approach that I take with things…That's just what people say, you know? "Be very careful about the things you post on social media, because you can't necessarily erase it." So, you're like, 'okay let me pay very close attention to the things that I post.' And when you see that you're like, 'okay, well this is going on. Do I need to talk about it right now because you know it's going to get a lot of likes? Or do I need to just take a pause real quick, and think about what's going on?' Because I feel like a lot of times, things happen so quickly that we're very quick to respond based on our emotions instead of actually thinking about what is going on. So, I think just by taking a second and reading and seeing what everybody else has to say, and processing it, taking their thoughts...I still do post, don't get me wrong, I post! I post on my Instagram. I post on my Facebook. I still do those things, but I'm very mindful about the things that I do.

Dante: *I'm not a too big user of social media, but in real life I follow my business partners, my co-founders. I follow them every day in a very tangible way, and they follow me. It's amazing, so they are the number one people I follow. If they weren't my business partners, I'd be following them anyway; that's how I got to be in business with them. I got into business with them because I follow them to begin with. I trust them.*

Ashley: *I do not follow anyone on social media. I don't think people are real on social media, and I do not want to follow fake, fictional characters...and that's all I feel [I see] on social media. I do use social media to keep in touch with family - my family is spread out across the country, so I keep up with them - but it's not following anyone, per se.*

If I were to say I'm following anyone in real life, it's the people around me who are beyond happy, they are content. They are in a place in their lives where they are totally satisfied and they want for nothing. That doesn't mean that they're wealthy, it means that they are satisfied with where they are in life. And there's this joy that ex-

udes from them. And I follow them because that's where I want to be. So, these people are my mentors. I talk with them on a regular basis and say, "How did you get to this point? And how can I get there?"

Kasim: *On Facebook, I maybe have like 500-600 friends. I don't hang out with 500-600 people. I've probably met those people, or encountered them once in my life, but maybe like a good 450 of them I wouldn't say I claim them as [friends] I would hang out with like that. The types of friends I hang out with are people who I feel I've built a bond with, in a way. I feel like they could push me to the next level. They can make me better, I can make them better, you know? There are just certain people you rock with, people you hang out with more than others, people you just have a better relationship with. It's not everybody.*

Shantel: *My Tumblr is dedicated to God, scripture, and Christian-related things. I don't really post anything else, I don't really follow anything else. That's kind of my source of encouragement during the day.*

Twitter...I don't really tweet that much anymore. And that [account] is kind of locked anyway, because I don't really care for everyone to follow me, or know any of my thoughts. My Instagram & Facebook are locked as well...I realize that my clients have my full name...maybe my clients might go Google me...like, I don't need them to find me at all! Everything is locked. Everything is hidden. Not that I'm doing anything that is going to be very obscene, but I just don't need you to know that. If you don't know me one-on-one, and we haven't met...you don't need to follow me. I don't really need to follow you.

Amanda: *I would say I tend to connect more with people I have a face-to-face [relationship] with. Just because I'm very clear on...well,* sometimes it may not seem like it…but I'm very clear on what I want for my life and my goals. So, things that don't add up to my goals just sort of go under my radar. Like fashion is not one of my goals. Social media is not really one of my goals.

So, for me, if I'm following someone, it really has more to do with what I want out of my life. If I share something, it has something to do with who I am and where I'm trying to be. I mean, I might see a *Cosmopolitan* article about something like makeup and I might check it out and scan it, but it's not like I'm just 'oh my god, did this person upload something?!'

Quaneesha: *For some reason, I don't like to follow people who I really do not know. If I do not know you, I will not follow you. It's weird. You know Facebook is still a great way to connect with other people and actors. If I find someone who's trying to add me, and I don't know you from anywhere and we don't have any mutual friends, I will write you like, "How do you know me?! How did you find me?! Why are you trying to add me?!"*

Someone told me that since I was getting into the acting world, I should be okay with certain people following me. I'm kinda not okay, because if we don't have any mutual friends, how did you find me? It's like a privacy thing. I think everyone is so used to random people following you, and they think that's the norm. I just kind of find it creepy. I feel like if I was to have people follow me and it's dealing with something [related to] acting, I need to have a separate account based solely for acting…If I was to do that…and people started following because of that, I would most likely accept it. But my personal…no. It's one of those things where I want to have [a lot of] followers, but it's kind of weird and creepy to me at the same time.

…I do not put my personal life on Facebook as much. Before, when I first started with Facebook, I used to put everything up. 'Going to the store. Going here, going there.' As you grow up, you see that all

that is not useful. Everybody does not have to know your every move. Now, I don't want people who are not really in my life to really feel like they're a part of my life. I think people are just so used to the norm of like, "oh yeah, everybody knows her. She's doing this, she's doing that." It's like why can't you do things...not secretly, but [keeping it] to yourself and then share it with the people you personally know?

Katie: So, I'm going to start off with the fam. I was raised by a lot of great people. [I use social media] to see what my parents are doing, and my sisters...we're all super-close and we're always in and out of each other's lives. And they're always super-inspiring. Just to see them and all that they do, it's really cool. No slackers in the family! As far as friends, I think a lot of my friends are just doing some really cool things and so that's always really cool to see...I honestly haven't had to cut that many people off. I really have been blessed that I've just kind of fallen into these great friend groups.

I feel like there are definitely stretches where people are just not living their best life, and I think that's when you especially need to be there for them. You know, everyone's not going to be 100% every single day, or every single month, or every single year. People are going to go through hard times, but I think that is when you have to come around them and support them...'Cuz I've definitely been there. There have definitely been stretches where I've been like, 'I have absolutely no idea what I'm doing!' And people kind of came around, and encouraged, and challenged me as well, so that's always been really helpful.

WHO I FOLLOW

Krystal: I feel like the things that celebrities put up on social media and stuff like that, it's very superficial. A jar of new makeup...blah,

blah, blah...it's nothing like, substantial. I actually value what people I know, and regular people that I follow, say with their posts on life and their perspectives of things more than I value someone with thousands of followers like these big celebrities...I feel like no matter what, when you talk about social media and celebrities, they go hand in hand. So, when speaking in that perspective, I feel like you can't not mention celebrities, because that started this phase. People no matter what, whoever you follow, you follow at least one celebrity.

Joshua: *I follow a lot of people. On Instagram I follow some celebrities, but that's just because it's Instagram. You have to follow them because that's like the unspoken rule, you know? I follow Kim Kardashian...I don't know why I do, I don't even watch the show! It's like, 'here's who you have to follow,' and Kim's there.*

I follow Beyoncé, the really famous celebrities like that. But that's just to follow, just to say I'm following them. But there are other people I follow too. I've been really into politics lately, so on YouTube I follow The Young Turks. They're a progressive news site, and they're solely online. I feel like the cable news networks, because they're financed by large corporations, they're very limited in what they can say or who they can be critical of, so I go to online news sites to get alternative views. There's Secular Talk and The David Pakman Show. They all identify as progressive, but they're not afraid to be critical of [President] Obama. He's not perfect, so even if you're a Democrat, you have to be critical of Obama as well.

Also, on Twitter and on Instagram, I follow an individual [named] Laverne Cox. She is a transgender woman and she's an activist as well. She's also on this show called Orange Is The New Black. I also follow Franchesca Ramsey on YouTube; she's known for making...really funny videos that kind of open your eyes in a fun sort of way. She makes really good videos on why it's important that we

can't stop talking about race, or on being an ally. Really good, in-
formative videos on those sorts of things.

Maryka: *The most important people I follow are my favorite celebri-*
ties such as Beyoncé, Usher, Nicki Minaj, Drake, and Big Sean. I fol-
low them because [seeing] them posting pics of their lives brings me
inner motivation. I see the vacations they're going on, the cars they're
driving, and just how happy they appear to be. And subconsciously, it
pushes me. I want the finer things in life as well. So, it's kinda like,
when I look at their pictures, I have access to their lives and I can see
what they're doing and what I'm not, it pushes me to want to work
just as much as they are.
*   ...Initially when I joined Instagram, I just followed celebrities be-*
cause that's what people did. People just followed celebrities. They
wanted to see who Chris Brown was arguing with today, or what
Rihanna was wearing today, what joke is Drake talking about, or
Tracee Ellis Ross...what's she rapping about? I guess we all want the
finer things, and we all kind of chase this one thing, and celebrities
kind of give off the image that they're already there in that limelight
that you want to be in. Eventually, the more celebrities I followed - as
well as the experiences I've had in real life encounters with big celeb-
rities and stars - it just makes me motivated when I follow them. They
post a lot of inspiring quotes and I feel like I can learn...it's a learning
thing.
*   But I don't just follow them, they're not the most important people*
I tend to follow. I'm also on a path to consciousness and enlighten-
ment. So, I follow a lot of spiritual leaders such as Eckhart Tolle,
Oprah, and Iyanla Vanzant. And I follow their Facebook pages, and
their YouTube channels...for my personal spiritual growth.

Faith: *I'm very intentional about who I follow. I'm not just randomly*
like 'Accept, Accept.' I look into who I'm following. I follow Iyanla

Vanzant because she definitely displays a lot of positive qualities, and gets across a lot of things to young women and men. [Even with] the famous people I'm following, everyone has impacted me or said something positive along the way in their posts to make me follow them. So, everyone that I'm following is important, and I have to keep them in my circle as far as social networking.

Mikal: *The most important person I follow?...I think that would probably be Childish Gambino, even though he doesn't post anything. I think that he's mastered social media to the point where it causes his audience to react to him, as opposed to him having to react to the climate of the world. So, when he's ready to work on an album or anything, then he has complete control over the masses, and he can just put something out and everybody is going to direct their attention to him. Just because of the fact that he hasn't been saying anything, and it's been boiling for all of us to know what he's thinking of.*

Ethan: *On social media, the only person I [actively] follow is this Instagram comedian called [Lorenzo Cromwell]. I follow him because he's different from the rest of the comedians. He's like...genuinely funny. He's the only one where I can look at every video and for the most part be in tears! He's original. And that's something a lot of these [other comedy videos] lack. It's fresh. It's along the lines of sketch/situational, and the thing is, he doesn't say much. Like he says a little, opens it with a basic premise of what the video is, and in the skit, he says a little bit and the rest...it's just comedy based on his delivery and his setup of the situation.*

This is one of the things that I've been trying to master, the creativity. Creativity is like the mastery of simplicity. I love that about his videos, 'cuz a lot of other internet guys...they do all these drawn out skits that are in this spot, with this many people and all this. This guy was in his room with a camera just on him, and he is creating entire scenarios. You get the sense of everything just from his room. I feel like that's dope, because he's really acknowledging the fact that we don't need all this extra. We just need this...He's a dude I've really got to meet someday, that's the only time I've ever felt that way about anyone off of the internet.

Steven: *I am a father and a husband, so I have to say the most important person I follow on my Instagram is my wife. As far as successful celebrities who I've really been following and seeing their lives unfold, I would say Kevin Hart. I think that the things he's doing right now as a person, he is just passionate about being him and passionate about his future...When I think about Kevin Hart, and I think about myself and how you have to lay that groundwork in the beginning before you can start getting that traction towards your success...he's being more than just his core of standup comedy. He's really growing into himself, and he's laying down his entire blueprint to his success in his social media. Like he's telling you, "Guys I'm working hard on being me." And that's something that you don't see.*

Noor: *So many people I follow on social media are interesting to me. Some of them are people who I've met in real life. Some of them I'm still waiting to meet. Number one to me, and the person who really influenced my life with his books and writings, is Paulo Coelho. He is a Brazilian writer, and started to write like 25 or 30 years ago. He was not famous at first, but he became famous. His best-selling book is The Alchemist, and it's a life-changing book for so many people, including myself.*

I do [also] follow a lot of people [who are not artists]. Some of them are famous and have lots of followers, some of them are not. There's one Kuwaiti blogger who I really like because she is so open about her relationship with her husband. Her name is Marwa. She's a blogger, which means she writes, and I do have respect for people who write.

She writes on a weekly basis, and she's so open about marriage and about relationships, and what women and men should do. I really like that. I like the openness in her articles and blog posts. It's really interesting to look at what she posts.

Courtney: *Right now, I would say the most important people I follow – because it's really ridiculous, the blend of people who I follow is very interesting – are a young couple from Atlanta. They're actually pastors. I started following them when they had just gotten married, and the wife was really an activist for celibacy and for purity and saving yourself for marriage and whatnot. She hadn't lived that lifestyle until she met her husband and they were dating under an extreme sense of purity.*

I actually started following her when I was single. I was a single mom; I was living at home with my parents, and I was kind of in an interesting place in my own life. I started following her and reading her blog, and then I started following her husband. So now, almost four years later, I'm still following them. Their ministry has grown tremendously; it's insane. When I first started following them, they were living in a little apartment with no kids, the husband had just quit his job because God told him to go into ministry full time. Then they started a church. They have a huge following, they do conferences...

My upbringing and my life were very different from both of theirs. So, I can't say that I relate to them, but something about them really resonates with me. The honesty of their ministry and their approach, they don't mince words. They speak very candidly to this generation, and to their social media community about keeping an open eye and an honest lens towards everything that you're viewing. They always have very appropriate Bible verses to post pertaining to what's going on. They're very keyed in with God. I don't know, they touch me. They're very inspiring. And they're not like super frugal walking around with like corduroys and loafers; they're cute. They're just dope, and they resonate with me on a different level.

Kevin: *As far as social media, I recently became friends with Dr. Umar Johnson on Facebook. I mean, I love his message and what he's trying to do with the rebuilding of young Black men...and just young men period, not to just limit it to race. I think he's very powerful as far as his message. I really do support his message. The thing is, I'm not familiar with a lot of these people's names. I just see them as public figures, and I go see something that they post, and then I'll go on their page and maybe add them.*

Leodus: *The main people who I'm following on social media? I'm following Mark Cuban, Bob Johnson, Tim Ferriss, Jeff Gitomer...but I also use [social media] to share a lot of stuff. My Facebook is not all serious all the time. Since I read all the time, I come across these people.*

Some of these authors are people who my mom might have recommended, or people I just stumbled upon. I looked them up online; I'm online all day so I try to read up on updates they have. They have skill [development tools], things you can do to make yourself better. I'm a student of the game, so I'm always trying to make myself better. There's no reason to reinvent the wheel. If somebody is doing what you want to do, then you should probably do what they do on a daily basis.

...I look at things like this, you know Mark Zuckerberg is my age. He started Facebook when I was in college. He has 30 billion dollars. He's a smart guy, but I don't think he's that much smarter than I am in terms of mental [capacity]. 10% of what he has is 3 billion, right? Okay and so 1% of what he has would be 300 million, right? Okay. So, I'm like, 'Hey, I'm not 1% of this dude?! I can't get 100 million?!

I can't get 50 million?! I can't get that?!' No, I don't believe that. I think I can do it. And I think that you can do it…Why not?!

Aquillia: *The most important people I follow - on Instagram because I don't have a Facebook account - are small, Black businesses. They are all people who have either started their businesses because they want to see improvement in the Black community and they said, "Hey, if we recycle these Black dollars in our communities, we can see a massive growth." Or people who just have awesome ideas and are really going forth with their dreams, and they want to sell their products and just be noticed, which is also cool. Those are the most important people...and a couple of other pages that highlight these Black businesses too. They have a whole list of Black businesses to support; they have their own communities that are uplifting people who are doing what it takes to make our community feel good, look good, and just have more money.*

Tobi: *The people who I follow on social media, I either follow them because they're doing...not exactly the same thing, but we're working towards the same goal: which is probably inclusive development or increasing economic opportunities. It's not only about that, it could also be about them just following their dreams and breaking boundaries. Living beyond their comfort zone, and living beyond themselves.*

Those are the people I tend to follow on social media because - let's be honest - there are days when we get up and actually just don't want to deal with the day. Then you open up Instagram and you see this person doing this, you see this person doing that, and you're just like, 'wow, I need to get up and get myself together and do what I need to do, regardless of how I feel.'

...I also tend to follow platforms like She Leads Africa, which is kinda like an online community which motivates women across Africa to get up and be bosses! On Twitter, I follow a lot of activists, po-

litical influencers, politicians, and news forums. So, it's usually people or things that motivate me, remind me of where I'm going, or are working towards the same goal...and obviously a few friends!

Devin: *As far as social media is concerned, I still have a couple of my buddies from high school. That network of people that I gained from high school and the time that I spent in college...they pretty much keep me posted on everything, so all I have to do is look at my Facebook feed. As for the people following me...just to be fair, all my people who follow me are as important to me as anyone [else]. The clients of my side web design business, my fans for gaming...everyone's important.*

Shantel: *On social media, I do follow my friends and some of my family, and - especially for family [members] who have moved away or for cousins who are like 20 years older than me and already have families established - it's nice to see what's going on with them and connect.*

Also on social media, I follow people who post a lot of different scriptures and encouragement from the Bible. Another account I follow, that isn't Biblically related at all, is Humans of New York. I really like them on Instagram. [Their page has] a lot of individuals from New York, and little snippets from their lives, and what's going on with them. It kind of makes you realize how we're all connected, how we're all going through the same struggles. And mostly everyone's comments [on their page] are positive and encouraging, so sometimes it's nice to see that when you hear so much negativity in the world.

Daphne: *I think right now the most important people who I follow are people in my age group, and people who are a little bit older than me as well. I follow a lot of people with visions, a lot of people who are dreamers, people who are doing things. I call it, 'the visionaries, the dreamers, and the doers'. I follow a lot of people who are really pas-*

sionate about their dreams, and they are doing everything that they have to do to achieve those dreams.

I also follow people who have a story. They came up from something; it wasn't just handed to them on a silver platter. They [may be] really struggling to get to where they want to get, but nothing is stopping them. They're on a mission, and they're going to get whatever they desire. I love watching these people post on Instagram or on Facebook that they met this person today, that they signed this new contract, or that they designed this new sneaker. That motivates me to do what I have to do as well.

THE GOOD OL' DAYS

Aquillia: *I started out loving social media. When it first came out, I was all about it. I had all of the apps on my phone, except Snapchat, I don't understand what Snapchat does or is! I don't know, maybe that might have been a little too new for me! Facebook I had the most, and I thought it was cool. I was able to update all these thought-provoking statuses and it was great, and I had these pictures and it was awesome.*

Then after a while, I realized that Facebook came out in 2007. It is 2015, I have 1,000 friends and I only talk to six of them. These are not people who actually know me in real life, and I'm not interested in knowing them in real life either...unless I see them in real life. If I don't see you, I have no desire to connect with you on this fake level that we're doing. And I was like, 'well, I'm not just going to sit here and just do what people do every year: the yearly purge.' Like, "If you don't see me, you know why" statuses. Nothing like that. I was just like, 'you know what? I'm just going to deactivate it and that's going to be that.' Which...you cannot delete your Facebook, you can only deactivate it...you can never get away. I don't know, it's crazy. It's insane.

With Instagram, I had two pages. One was my personal and one was for Rebrand [Chicago], but I don't even use my personal anymore. I have more authentic people there who I actually know and stuff, but sometimes what you see on a daily basis...sometimes I just don't care about seeing it. Like, 'what is the point of this?' And if I have to ask...then I don't really want to be involved with it.

Malika: *I've had Twitter since '09 and I've seen a lot of stuff on that site! It's crazy...but I started getting really tired of the things I was seeing. There's a lot of disrespect, especially about the topic of feminism. There were a lot of misogynistic people I was following. People who were creating negative vibes for me, and could not create a space where I could speak my mind freely without feeling like I was judged.*

So little by little, I started unfollowing them and blocking those who I felt were the most irrelevant. I just starting filtering out, and when I started using some of the hashtags and having the global conversations with people, I gained a lot of access to people who were having the same conversations. There were some topics that I didn't even think people cared about and I started reading about them on my Twitter, so I'm like, 'I need to do this.' So, I started doing that with every one of my social networks. I started talking more to my friends, and they created their own environments, so we networked between that. I felt like I needed more substance to what I was consuming.

Faith: *That's the reason I'm not on Twitter right now...I only did it because I was watching a show and they needed [the audience] to vote, and I voted through Twitter. But other than that, Twitter was one of those things - especially when I was in high school - that was like, "Oh, everybody follow me."*

They would write their Twitter names on the [school] bathroom, and pass papers around like love notes...like, "Here's my Twitter." It's crazy, and I was like, "What is going on?!" And the things that came from Twitter...It was completely ridiculous. There were so many fights and things going on because of Twitter. And I was like, 'oh my goodness, let me get off because I don't want anybody to look [at] what I said on Twitter and it's a problem.' So, I just put Twitter on the backburner. I didn't even understand certain things like how to post and how to respond to people, I didn't even get it, so I was like, 'forget it, I'm not even interested.'

Shantel: *I just want to let everyone know, in my spirit of semi-hipsterness, that I was on Twitter...at the beginning of Twitter. By myself...no one else! And the rapper that followed me was Chip the Ripper, a rapper from Ohio! I feel like I was in the first class [of Twitter users], because none of my friends, none of my siblings, and none of these people who I know are now on Twitter [were on it then].*

I was on there by myself one summer in 2009; no one was else was on with me. Then months later, everybody came and I was like, "Oh, so now I have to go get it again!" [Back then] there were mostly a lot of famous people on there. So, you could find famous people or famous organizations to follow. For me, I wasn't going to follow some random person named 'Jonathan'! Like I don't know who Jonathan is, and Jonathan lives in Kentucky...I don't need to follow you on Twitter. But you didn't feel the need to have your account locked; it was open. Anyone could follow you, and you could follow them. There were a lot of ghost accounts, people who wanted to follow you and [when] you clicked on their [profile], you were like, 'who is this? They're not tweeting anything. Why are they following me?'

Kevin: *I don't even have a Twitter. I'm not going to even lie. I'm a 30-year old man without a Twitter. I'm not the person who says, "I don't do social media." I do get on it from time to time, but I take it with a grain of salt.*

[For] some people, it's all of their life. It's crazy how you get in an elevator at work and [there's] no interaction like:

"Hello?"

"Sorry, I was on my phone."

You gotta remind them, "Hey, I just said hello." It's like, 'you're not important because I'm on my phone and I was just posting my Facebook status.'

...I think a lot of social media is being used for acceptance. I think it came out with a different purpose. Like when I first got into Face-book, it wasn't even open to the general public. It was something for college kids. Back in...[it was] maybe 2005, I would say, [when] I joined Facebook. And only college students could get on...I forgot what the requirements were back then, but it was definitely linked to only college kids. Back then I was like, 'oh this'll be cool.'

Because I was going to school in Mississippi, being from Chicago, [I thought], 'it'll be cool once I leave here to interact with people who I went to school with.' I thought it would just be something for recon-necting: "Hey, how's it going? I haven't seen you in five years. How are your children? Look, I have two kids now" type of thing. Nah, now it's like, "Hey I'm getting ready to go to the mall. I just bought me some new Jordans. Look, I just posted a picture of these new Jordans." Or, "Keisha just got into a fight. Look at it, it's on Facebook Live. I just recorded it, so I'm cool. Gimme your likes. I WANT YOUR LIKES!"

Jasmine: *You know how Facebook started to do that thing where [they]...remind you what you did on this day five years ago, or this day six years ago? It's just amazing when you see a picture from six years ago and you're like, "Wow, I haven't talked to that person in years!" And it can go either way, like "Ugh, thank gosh I haven't talked to that person in years!" Or it's like, "Oh man, I haven't talked to that person in years. I kinda miss them." And then you go back and reflect on how much fun you had. And you reflect on how great your friendship was, and you wonder what happened...but you know everything happens for a reason. But I just would appreciate it if Facebook only reminded us of the good memories, and not the bad memories!*

TABLES IN THE CAFETERIA

Krystal: *I try to keep a mixture of different people on my news feeds and timelines and stuff like that. Only because it's so amazing to me to see other people's perspective on things. Because most of the times, you think like your friends, or you agree with the people that you know, or [with] your family. You were all raised with the same tradition, so basically everyone is agreeing. But when you see people say things and it is their regular life, you're like 'wow.' To you it's so radical, but that's really normal for them. And sometimes they post stuff and I'm tempted to just delete them or just say, "No, you know what? I don't need to see this anymore." But then sometimes I'm like, 'I need to force myself to be exposed to how other people see, and how other people think.' Especially when I went to college, that's what I learned; 'cuz that was the shift from having all Black friends to meeting White people. And I'm like, 'whoa, Facebook is totally different after you diversify!'*

Jason: *There's a cultural divide in social media, 'cuz it's just a reflection of the larger society. Society is grouped into segments...so I wouldn't put that past social media. If social media is a reflection of the larger society, I would say of course social media has different segments. Black Twitter for example. In Black Twitter alone, there are the conscious and the unconscious. There are people who would rather just have entertainment and laugh, who essentially have no interest - whether on purpose or not - to learn about themselves, to*

*learn about African people, or to learn about where they come from. I
understand that. Some people just want to have fun and that's under-
standable.*

*But I would argue the reason why people are not interested, the
reason why everybody is not on the conscious side of Black Twitter or
Black Instagram, is because we haven't been taught in schools. We've
been socialized not to. The culture that we live in has socialized us not
to value African history, not to value ourselves. And I think as more
and more people become conscious, as more and more people continue
to spread information, all of a sudden, you're going to see change.*

MIGHT JUST LEARN SOMETHING

Phillip: *I see the power of social media. Something can become viral
whether it's entertaining, whether it's conscious or not conscious. If a
person is believable and it can attract people, the human life still has a
soul to it. The human voice still has a soul to it, so people are attracted to realness, to things that they can identify with.*

Jason: *I think [due to] recent events in America, there's been a shift
in consciousness. I think people are becoming more conscious and
aware of the continuing social ills in America. I think that's a positive
thing. I think it was inevitable after the onslaught of social media.
Social media has been essentially the medium for that movement, that
change in consciousness. Facebook, Twitter - Instagram especially -
these things awaken people. It just provides information in snippets,
but it's powerful information.*

Maya: *On my Facebook, I will say, that's a bit more mature. Because
it is longer form, I just get to learn a bit more about people and what
they stand for. I also get to share things that are important to me. I do
a lot of article sharing. I'm at a point in my life where I am using Fa-*

cebook to kind of enlighten people. Not to say I'm some kind of guru, but I'm more doing it to put things up that are interesting to me and to keep them up there so I can remember that I've liked these things, that I've read these things, without having to have a billion bookmarks. But also, to share with people and to be able to give people something else to think about, so I like that.

Malika: *A lot of what I read or follow is coming straight from Twitter. I follow people who are very instrumental in the protests that have been occurring since [2014], and in the vigils. They have gotten people more motivated to participate in fighting the social injustices that affect us. I look more towards those sources, those outside sources, because the conversation with my family can be extremely limiting and different perspectives on social issues can be easily dismissed. But these individuals, they're contributing to it, they're having these conversations. They're understanding the viewpoint of the Black body. And me being bi-racial, that's something that's important to me, because a lot of the individuals on my Puerto Rican side don't get that.*

Dante: *As for social media [and the topic of] following vs. leadership, it's interesting because in [a] sense I definitely follow it. For instance, the march that occurred in the wake of Eric Garner's death, and the decision on that, you know I was part of that...it was one of the most amazing experiences I've ever taken part in. And in truth, I don't read the news. I really don't. I don't read it on a daily basis...but that day I physically followed the news.*

The news I was following was through social media channels. People were announcing on Twitter, and announcing on Instagram where we were going to be, and what was happening. I had followed that case, but what I was physically following were [social media posts stating], "We're going to be at...everybody come here, to this place." And I found out about it through Facebook, and all the directions for the night went [out] through social media. So, I was second-order following. Someone tells me in person, "Hey, let's do this. This is what's going on," and I move with it...That night, I wasn't the leader of the movement. I was a follower of the movement. And I accept that.

To tell the truth, that's why I don't feel inclined to be on social media as much as my peers are, because I have things I have to take the leadership role in, and I expect that with other things, other leaders will emerge and they will give me the opportunity to follow them.

Mikal: *One thing that I do see with this generation is a huge push of social media, and a great use of it to connect [with] each other and be more socially aware. I don't know if you've had a chance to go to any of the rallies...the few that I've gone to, I didn't see anything about it outside or talking to anybody face-to-face about it. It's just like, you see it on Tumblr, and you know that everybody's going to be there. And you know that it's going to be a peaceful thing because you have a good connection with the people who are blogging about it, and you know they're all about the peace. That's a great thing that I've taken from this generation, that connection with social media and the ability to use it to connect the culture.*

Haniyyah: *You know everybody's important in their own way. I really feel that way. No matter what type of opinion they have, I feel like it's very valid. Whether they agree or disagree with me, I still think that they have a really good point. So most of the time - especially with social media - scrolling through my feed on a day-to-day basis, I see what everybody has to say about the most prevalent issues.*

Alberto: *I learn things on a regular basis from my Facebook. I learn about different things on Instagram. I learn about different things on*

Snapchat and Twitter. It's not that we're just wasting our time, it's just that maybe somebody should go out there and teach these people to do other things, or more productive things with social media. I don't think there's something wrong with it. It's a tool. I feel like I hear a lot of that, "Young people, all they want to do is just be at home or just chillin' on the block." No, it's not that. Maybe...no, it's not maybe. It's a fact...people just don't know any better, you know?

I remember I saw Oprah on a video, and she was talking about Maya Angelou...Oprah shared with her one day that sometimes she reminisces about her past errors and stuff like that. And Maya Angelou, to paraphrase, told her to not worry about those things because she did what she thought was best, because she didn't know any better. And that's what everybody does. You can't blame somebody for doing something if they really don't know any better. Whatever they know now, that's what they're going to use to make a decision. And if they don't know much, then guess what? They're not going to make a very good decision.

Felice: I feel like they're missing the revolution that we're trying to bring about. I kinda feel like they're missing that Public Enemy, KRS-One type of thing we're trying to do here with social media. I think they're missing the goals that we're using social media [for]. A lot of the things that we know about [come] through social media. I'll never forget that I was on Tumblr and found out about Trayvon Martin months before the trial started.

I feel like they've got to give our generation a little bit more credit for that. We're using social media, or we're always stuck on our phones, but that doesn't necessarily mean that we're using it for frivolous means. We're using our social media to educate each other, educate the nation, and kind of bring about the change that I feel like they were fighting for in the '50s and '60s. It's kinda like now it's getting passed on to us. [Now] that we're getting exposed to the politicians *[who] bring out the people who are like, "We really don't like y'all too much."...We've got to figure out a way to [say], "You don't have to like us, but we're not going to accept this and that. And you're not going to put us in the same kind of box that you put our people in before."*

BELIEVE HALF OF WHAT YOU SEE

Maya: *It can be a bit much. Even when you know that everybody on Instagram is not doing everything on Instagram that it looks like...you just gotta take a step back. Sometimes I just take those social media breaks and step back so that I can just be with my own thoughts and not have all of my thoughts filled with, 'I saw such-and-such on Instagram doing this or that. Maybe I should be doing this.' Or even thinking, 'how did they get there and I'm still here?!'*

Shanai: *I think that everyone is inspired in their own different way, but for me, that whole social media force is detached. You don't really know who those people are. Especially for the kids and the younger people I come in contact with, they need something that is more tangible than a picture on their phone, you know?*

Shantel: *Look at a celebrity's account. All you see is pictures of their faces. Some of them do show pictures of food, but it's usually always their face, always their clothes. So, everyone wants to emulate that, and they do. Basically, people are trying to use social media to make you be envious of what's going on in their lives like, "Look how I'm living and how glamorous this is!" Like famous people wise, yeah you are wearing those shoes. You might have rented them, or you might have bought them, who knows? Or had them given to you for free. But all of us common people? It's like, "You can't afford that, I've seen what you drive! I see where you live, what are you buying those Louis Vuitton shoes for?! You can't afford them, come on, chill out."*

Courtney: *Yeah, because everyone's so insecure. Social media has created a huge level of insecurity because everything is so visible, so you're constantly comparing yourself to other people. So, you feel like you've got to show and prove, you gotta floss out...and I can't be overly critical because I've done it. I mean I'm not really in that frame of mind right now, but everybody does it.*

Even if you're posting a selfie, how many poses do you actually go through?! How many photos do you actually take before you find your selfie? And then once you find it, how many filters are applied? How many apps do you use to adjust the photo before you actually post it? And then how long does it take to think of a caption to put under it, you know?!...But that's what people do! It is what it is.

It's funny, but you have to remember in your moment of insecurity or your moment of comparing [yourself] to others, you have to remember that it's just not realistic. I definitely have moments when I get down on myself about things that I'm seeing. I may not be at a place in my life in a certain area, and I log onto Instagram at that moment and everybody is doing it or whatever and I'm just like, "Ugh, what's going on with my life?!" But you have to check yourself, because we don't know how accurate that is. And honestly, 10 years ago, before all of this nonsense, we were only comparing ourselves to our immediate peers that we were in contact with - not to say that was even healthy - but the fact that in 10 years we've gone from comparing ourselves to...like 50 people. Maybe a broader scale at college, but still...we've gone from that to being able to compare yourself to thousands of people in a matter of seconds because it's all at your fingertips. It's very powerful. And I think what people don't talk about often is the insecurity that comes along with that.

Katie: *Social media has perpetuated that, because now it's so easy to get your ideas and your thoughts out, and everything is connected. Like I put something on Twitter, and I can also share it on Facebook instantly, you know? So, there are definitely more avenues to get your thoughts and ideas out there, which has produced some beautiful things, and which has produced some not-quite-so-great things. People are so quick to point to our generation and be like, "Oh my gosh! You guys are ruining everything!" And it's like, no, people have always talked about other people since the beginning of time. Now it's just easier to see.*

And like I said, sometimes it's great and people are held accountable on things that they should be held accountable for, and sometimes it's too much. You just have to find that balance and, once again, whatever works best for you.

...You know, I don't follow a lot of celebrities [on social media]. Just because it's so easy to fall down that rabbit hole. It's so easy to just look at pictures like, "Oh my goodness, Beyoncé, your life is just great! My goodness, what am I doing over here?!" But that's not the path that's for me, you know? And it's so easy to get a perfect picture, and to make everything seem like it's great. But you don't know the backstory. You don't really know what's going on in people's lives. So, I have to be very strategic in who I follow and what I do, so I don't spiral out of control.

Faith: *I think it's all within the individual person and it definitely relates to our experiences in life away from the social network. We tend to bring whatever we've learned throughout life to the social network.*

Growing up, I was always around old-school people like my grandmother. I grew up in a beauty shop. I was around a lot of wisdom...and I feel like everybody's environment is somehow attached to them and that's what they bring to social media. And a lot of times, their background is completely different and they pose [as] this person on social networks to impress people or to hide something that they may lack...that's the downside to social media and social networking. And TV, and all of these outlets.

We have the power to change the outlets that we use either to better or degrade each other. We have the power to change it and alter things like that. But I feel like we haven't gotten there yet, where we realize that we have that power to say 'yay' or 'nay' to what's going on with social media and our social lives.

My Black Life

O nce you add black, you can never go back. Most of us are familiar with the saying; *a picture is worth a thousand words*. Well, there is a corollary to that idiom, which is: *one word is worth a thousand pictures*. Of all the words in the English language, there are few more potent than the word *black*, particularly when used in reference to one or more human beings.

A significant factor in the history of at least four continents over the past nearly 600 years is rooted in the responses to the questions that arose from this use of the word.

What does it mean to call a human being black?
What does it mean to be called black?
If a being has been called black, are they still human?
Who is black?
Who gets to decide who gets to be black?
If one is indeed black, when and how are they notified?
Where does one go to confirm that they are black?

In the context of the United States, a culture that is perpetually looking to the future and focused on what is new, the word *black* is constantly reminding us of the past and refuses to forget what is old. The word is like a birthmark on the body of American English. Our reaction to the word is inextricably linked to our reaction to the people who inhabit the label.

For example, what images come to mind when you read the following sentences?

I am acting.	I am acting black.
The children are playing.	The black children are playing.
I live in a decent neighborhood.	I live in a decent black neighborhood.
They go to a great school.	They go to a great black school.
Each life is precious.	Each black life is precious.

How does your set of mental images change when *black* is added? Does the word add clarity to the initial sentence, or complexity? Does the word evoke a sense of pride, disgust, indifference, or shame? Do you feel included when the word is added, or excluded? Did adding the word make you want to read more, or less?

Wrestling with any one of these questions could take up an entire discussion, documentary, or dissertation. Or it could be just another day in your life.

MY HERITAGE

Malika: *My identity has been something that I've been kind of trying to make sense of for years. I'm turning 22 and it's like, I'm still just right in-between figuring out what being bi-racial really means. And it's something that I've always been very sensitive to. Because phenotypically, I look Black. It's like I also have another culture, but people have always been very dismissive when it came to that. My mother and my sister are both fair-skinned and those are the people that I lived with for most of my life, and whenever the question of my father came around, even when they were together, [other people] would question it like:*

"Oh, does she have the same father?"

"Was she adopted?"

"Oh, she's a friend."

And so, I was always categorized as the other, and never really a part of the family. It was definitely very frustrating.

When it came to dealing with other people, I had a blatant kind of discrimination against me because my sister would be treated so highly, like people put her on a pedestal, and then when it came to me it was like "Ugh...ew...okay." I had people call out my sister on the street and then when I looked around because I thought they were people that I knew, they were like, "Not you blackie. You're ugly," and stuff like that. In one of the most diverse places I've ever grown up in...it was ridiculous.

I spent a lot of my years believing that Blackness was ugly and wishing that one day I could have like...I don't know...I could realize that I just had a really dark tan and it would fade away and I would get lighter. It created a hatred towards my Blackness to where I even blamed my father at a point. It's like one of those things that I couldn't really help. And it was only until my junior year of college - this was last year - that I was able to stand in front of the mirror and tell myself that I loved myself. I made it a daily habit of mine to the point where I started feeling it. Because of that bi-racial identity, that inner conflict...Trying to figure out the aspect of myself that was real...so yeah, identity...it's been a lot of trying to understand and better myself.

Jason: *Living in the Caribbean for eight and a half years, the first eight years of my life essentially, I think it molded a different viewpoint. When I came back to the states...I'm an American citizen, but I was learning how to be American. So, I'm absorbing all this information about American culture, much more so than the average American... I was a person growing up in Brooklyn trying to [first] understand the social ills in Brooklyn. 'Why do Black people do drugs? Why do Black people do this? Why do Black people do that? Why do we eat this? Why do we eat that?'*

It's constantly just these negative images of Black people. Black people doing harm to me. Black people doing harm to each other. And you want to question it. You want to know, "Why do I have to live in a circumstance like this? Why do my people have to continue to suffer? Why? Why? Why?" And growing up in [an] environment where knowledge is foremost, it's the most important thing. "If you don't have any knowledge - especially as a Black person - you're not getting anywhere." You hear this constantly over your life. So, I'm going to try to absorb this knowledge. I'm going to try to seek it out. That's what I did. I tried to find answers to my questions: "Why do my people have to continue to live like this? And who were we before we ended up in this situation?"

Daphne: *I remember the food, I remember the ambiance, the family...being around such vivid culture. Haiti was just so beautiful. Whereas in New York, basically you're just hustling, hustling, hustling. Back there, it was about culture. It was about family. It was more so about [getting] to enjoy life for what it was. Whereas here, you're trying to make a living, you're trying to do everything, and trying to be who you need to be. Back home, it's not as pressured, I would say it's more relaxing.*

Chelsea: *I am from Haiti. I was actually born in Haiti. I came to the United States when I was three-years old...The last time I went to Haiti was about three years ago, so it was definitely after the earthquake. And surprisingly enough, I still had an amazing time.*

When I first got there, it was little bit scary, because even the White House (National Palace) in Haiti was still divided in half. You know the part that was super cool was that when I got there I ex-

pected everyone to kind of still be depressed from what happened, but the children were just amazing. So resilient and happy to see me. And it's interesting because whenever I'm in Haiti, I feel more comfortable than I am here. Like I can literally wake up and go pick a mango off of the tree and not worry about where it's actually coming from.

You know, honestly, I believe that Haiti is just like any other place. For instance, in Brooklyn or New York City in general, there are some places where you'll see homeless people lying in the streets, whereas when you go to 42nd street it's beautiful and lights are everywhere. So, Haiti is kind of the same way. There are certain parts where...um...it's a bit saddening to see people just lying on the floor asking for food, [and] garbage is in the streets. And there are other parts where it's like paradise. I guess it all depends on what part of Haiti you decide to go to...but in terms of the whole image that everyone has of Haiti, like it's the poorest country. Like literally any article you will read will begin with "the poorest country..." And yes, there is poverty in Haiti, of course. But that's not all there is to it.

Tobi: I'm Nigerian. A lot of people tend not to believe that when they see me or hear me speak...[but] definitely not in Nigeria. I mean, you do have those odd people who are trying to be funny and they're like, "Where are you really from?!"

When you're home, you just switch to an automatic...how do I put it? There's no Nigerian accent, I hate when people say that...but you switch to a very authentic accent. In other places...I get asked [questions], or people are surprised to hear [my accent] because...apparently, I don't look Nigerian. I have no clue what that means! I've had people say to me, "Oh you look like you're from North Africa" or "You look like you're from East Africa." And it's like, "Do I, really?"

I remember [one time when] I was traveling from Dubai to London, and I had two women from Ethiopia ask me if I was from Ethio-

pia too. And I'm like, "I cannot look like...I mean, I could probably look 'not Nigerian', but so much that I look like your sister?! Like sister-sister from the same country?!"

MY HISTORY

Jared: *I'm an African-American adopted by a White family, so I've never known my roots. I've never known where I came from. I've never known my medical history, or what my [birth] parents did for a living, or how I was adopted.*

My adopted family was great. They instilled a foundation in me. My father was a doctor, my mother was a social worker, so I had a good life. But I still had to go out there and find out what makes me tick. What brought me back was the foundation they instilled in me. They instilled good qualities, good morals, and good character in me. So, when I was out there bumping my head, I knew that [life] wasn't meant for me...my [birth] mother carried me at the age of 12 and birthed me at the age of 13. And anybody at that age is not capable of raising a child, I believe. I was adopted into a better situation. [My adopted parents] were stable financially, emotionally, relationship-wise with each other when they adopted me. So, my situation enhanced.

However, it also left a void. I've been in counseling and seeing therapists my whole life. The whole not knowing, it's leaked out...sexually, academically, [in] any type of avenue of life...it's leaked out. I've gotten better at covering it in certain situations and certain areas. But I mean, it leaves a child with a void. Either they find it out, or they neglect it and deal with it later in life. And I've been searching. Since I've been in the fourth or fifth grade, I've been on the hunt. That's why I say I've bumped my head so many times. A lot of people try to cover it up and act like nothing's wrong, and deal with it when they're 30 or 40, and that's just not my personality.

And again, I got adopted by a whole other race. So, at that age, when I became conscious and was like, "My hair is not like theirs, or my skin is not like theirs...my friend's parents are cooking different meals than they're cooking, or I'm dressing different..." That put me on a desperate search. I was like, 'something's not normal' - I wasn't necessarily saying it was wrong - but I just said something's not normal about this situation. And I took it into my own hands, which I [maybe] should not have done, but I took it into my own hands to figure out.

Kasim: *When I was younger I was like a goody-two-shoes. I was just really innocent, like seriously innocent. It was all about grades. I used to just hang out with like, the smart people. Seriously, when I saw someone who looked remotely bad I was like, "No, no, no, I'm staying away from them!" I was not playing no games, I was in the crib as soon as school was done! I ran home.*

As I grew older, I [became] open to anybody, to the point that I would hear you out. When I hear you out, automatically I can tell whether I can rock with you or not. I guess when I was younger, I would just see something and I was like, 'nah.' I wouldn't even hear you out or try to have a conversation. I guess that was just a young me, like I said, I was innocent...it was something I claimed proudly at a young age, around the age of 11/12 and under. It was really when I started high school that stuff started changing.

I dubbed myself as innocent, and other people saw the way I moved, and saw me as innocent. Innocent just means that you're the perfect child for your parent, you know what I mean? Whatever your parent wants you to do, you just abide by it and try to do more. That's what I mean by innocent, [that] you're not the type to just fall into peer pressure because it's cool, you just follow whatever your parents say. So, if your parents say not to do this, and your friend is telling you, "Nah just do this, it's no big deal man." You're like,

"No! My mother told me to do this and I will do it!" You're just following the rules all the way. That's what I mean by innocent, there's
nothing wrong, you just don't want to get in trouble and you're
scared, so you want to be innocent!

Khalid: *During boot camp...there would be days when we would be
out in the field, which is called 'being in the woods', and you
[couldn't] go to the bathroom unless you had someone with you. The
bathroom would be like down the block, and let's say it would be two
in the morning, and I would wake up like 'man, I have to pee.' I'd
have to find somebody who was in my group, and wake them up like,
"Hey man, I've gotta go to the bathroom." And the guy would be like,
"Alright, let's go." So, he would get up from his sleep to walk with
me all the way to the bathroom, I'd do my do, and we'd come back!
That's how they train you, to always be together as a team.*

*...when I come back [home], I usually grow out my beard. I usually
let my hair grow because I'm not allowed to have it while I'm on du-
ty. I take off my uniform and everything, so you wouldn't really know
I was in the military unless I broadcast it. Which, when I first started,
that's what I did. Like I went back to my high school in my dress
blues. I walked down the street in my uniform. Now that I've been in
the military for a little bit, I just try to be low-key.*

*...I would say it's like a security blanket in a way. Because when
the protests for Black Lives Matter and everything were going in New
York [City], I was either here [on base] or I was doing training. I was
watching it from a TV screen, and looking back I wish I was actually
there in the protests and everything; because looking at it on the TV
screen you don't feel the same emotions that you do if you were actually there protesting.*

*Being a young Black man in the military, all the generals, all the
higher-ups, all of those people are White. I've probably only seen one
Black higher-up. I've never seen a Black general, or I've never seen a*

Black colonel. I've only seen people who were at my rank or below, or like a lieutenant, which in the officer world is not really that high at all. It's more like a shocking thing, because even in the military there's still racial...not a divide...but it's still there. There are still people higher than you who don't look like you, and then the rest of the people who look like you are the same rank as you or below.

I wish when I see all these things happening, I could call my boss and be like, "Hey, I'm taking a leave of absence to go protest," but I can't do that!...With the [people of other races] here, that doesn't really affect them because it's not something that concerns them, like it would concern someone like me. I see them looking at it like, "oh that sucks" and keep walking. But I see us, people of color, who look and say, "It's 2015, and we still see this." And it's just like, what are we doing to change it? Because being in the military, I can't do anything. I can't show up to work with a black fist raised in the air and stuff. So, it's more like, 'okay, I see it, but what am I doing to change it?' I feel like I'm stuck in this blanket of security and it's just like I want to be more involved with what's going on, but right now I can't do anything...The uniform comes off at the end of the day. They say, "Yes, but you're a Marine."...But I was somebody before I was in the military. I was a young Black man in Brooklyn. And New York [City] is a lot different from Jacksonville, North Carolina. I try to remember who I am, because I won't always be a Marine. Eventually - really soon - I'll be Khalid again. So, I try not to forget who I am and where I came from.

MY INTERESTS

Devin: *I grew up a techie. I always loved having all the gadgets and stuff. Every time a new [Apple] device comes out, even though I might not always have the money for it at the time it launches, I get it maybe six or seven months later and it's still like Christmas. Every time I get a new device, it's sort of like a mini-Christmas for me. I get to see what all the months of hype on the blogs - like Cult of Macs and iMore - was about. I actually get to hold it and see all the work that Apple or Microsoft put in, and see what that work yielded.*

Amanda: *When I hear French I can recognize it, so whenever I hear like a slight [indication] that someone could be speaking French, I just stare at them and listen really hard. I get really excited. So, I'm on the train and these two guys are talking, and it was like maybe three minutes into their conversation and I'm thinking to myself, 'they're definitely speaking French.' And I'm on the train like, 'say something to them. Say something! Say something!' And I never do, and I'm so disappointed in myself. One of these days I'm gonna talk to somebody. It was a lot easier when I was studying abroad, because I had to.*

You know, imagine the conversations that I could have. I'm afraid of embarrassing myself and not pronouncing [words] correctly. I don't know if I would say that I'm fluent. I understand it pretty well. I can have like a simple conversation, depending on how fast the person is speaking, and depending on how [good] their English is. Then we could kind of have a conversation. But I wouldn't say that I'm fluent.

...I'm most fluent in Haitian Kréyol. I don't know a lot about Creole in New Orleans. I thought that was like a completely different Kréyol. I thought that they just stole our name! I haven't even heard anyone speak it. I need to go to New Orleans, obviously. The history sort of speaks for itself. I mean there were Africans - like the whole Atlantic slave trade - that were taken from Africa by French colonizers. They changed their language up, added things, and forced them to speak differently. And I think that's how Kréyol came to be. It was the African dialect, a little bit of Spanish, a little bit of Patois, all these things kind of mixed into one with a heavy French undertone be-

cause that's what the masters spoke. So, the slaves kind of took the language and made it their own.

MY BODY

Atisha: *Seven years ago, I was in middle school and I was always doodling in my notebook. I don't think I was very culturally aware. I was, like a little bit, but not to the extent that I am today.*

I used to recreate other people's drawings...I just remember my art teacher was looking at some of the drawings, and they were pretty good for my age. But she asked me this question, "How come you don't draw any Black people?" I couldn't really answer her question. I was like, "Uh, I don't know." And I tried to find a drawing that looked the most like a Black person!...a drawing with a person whose nose looked like a Black person's nose, like anything! I also remember in high school, I asked one of my close friends to pose for me so I could draw her, and she was like, "I don't know." And I was just like, "Why don't you want me to draw you? I will draw you for free; I just need somebody to pose for me." And she was like, "I don't know if you will draw me well because you don't really know how to draw Black people." She wasn't intending to be mean or rude or anything, but she said that she's never seen me draw any Black people so she's probably not going to come out looking cute! It really...took me back. I had to think about it like, 'Exactly, why am I not drawing Black people?' I couldn't fully grasp it, but I just remember not being as conscious of the mental space of young Black girls or the way society influences us to think about what beauty is...I didn't realize exactly why I was doing it, but you could write a paper on why I was doing it.

Janelle: *I'm a fair-skinned Black girl. Sometimes I do have to check my privilege, because that's also something that I wasn't very aware of when I was younger. I was one of only two girls in my entire mid-dle school who was light-skinned, so I didn't even realize that I really had any privilege until I got little bit older. Even in high school I wasn't really aware of it. But I was more aware of it freshman year when I got [to college] and I didn't even realize how much privilege I had being a fair-skinned Black woman.*

Blackness has always been a thing that hasn't been very...liked, I'll say as a euphemism. The lighter you were, the closer you were to be-ing White. So, people just automatically treated you differently be-cause [they thought], 'oh you're closer to what I am, so you're probably a little smarter than the darker girl.' [This is where those] little videos come in where the little Black girl is pointing at the white doll as being the prettiest and the smartest, and at the darkest doll as being the dumbest and the ugliest...people still make those comments today, which is like ridiculous to me. Like how can you even still have this view? But they always make these comments about 'exotic' girls being pretty and "Black girls this, [Black girls] that, and Black girls don't know how to be in a relationship. They don't know how to keep a man, they got attitudes...blah, blah, blah."

The darker you are, the more they just think 'oh, dark-skinned girls are ugly.' How can you not be attracted to an entire color? I just don't understand that. It doesn't make sense to me. Everybody looks different, but just that whole idea of people automatically somehow internalizing the fact that they treat people who are darker different-ly...more so women, with me it's a little different. I wouldn't consider myself [as someone who] looks 'ambiguous', where someone wouldn't be able to tell I'm Black because clearly by some of my features, I defi-nitely look like I'm mostly Black. So, I could never get away with that, unless someone was really clueless!

Ebonee: *Now that [my daughter] is getting older, she notices the dif-ferences. Especially because she's in school. When you're in the house, or you're around [people in] our community, you see people of color like us. You see people with hair like us. You see people who dress like us.*

When she goes to school, it's diverse. Especially because of gentrification, it's definitely diverse. She goes to my elementary school, [the one] that I went to. When I went to elementary school, a lot of the kids [who] were there were Hispanic, they were of Latin descent. Now, there are more African-American kids, a couple of Caucasian [kids], Asian [kids]...it's very diverse. It's like, "Oh Mommy, Suzy has silky hair. How come my hair isn't like Suzy's?" or "Mommy, Suzy has white skin, how come my skin is brown?" and questions like that. I tell her, "God makes everybody different. God makes everybody different and I want you to be comfortable in your own skin. You don't have hair like Suzy, because God didn't give you hair like Suzy. God gave you hair like Mommy."

There was a point in time when I was wearing weave heavy, and my daughter said, "Mommy I want hair like yours. Mommy, I want a weave." And after that, that day, I didn't wear weave anymore. I'm like, 'no, because my baby has to appreciate her natural hair. She has to appreciate her natural beauty.' There's nothing like being Black. Being Black is beautiful. I love being Black, and I want my daughter to love being Black. I don't want her to feel any different from any other kid.

Maryka: *I embrace my natural hair because it's all me. I'm not doing anything to change the texture of it, or change the curl pattern of it. I'm not trying to conform to America's standard of beauty.*

I realized at a young age when my principal - Mr. Muhammad from Bedford Academy [High School] - would hold history classes and would inform us about our ancestors and things that they went through. And it inspired me and I'm like, "they went through all of that for me and I can't even..." I don't know...I guess it comes down to I don't want to be like anyone else but me. And I felt like [by] perming my hair, I was being someone else. I was sitting under a dryer and getting intense heat damage. Coloring my hair to be conformed to this standard idea of what beauty is. I just learned that I want to be me. I want to be myself. I feel like my hair is unique, and it's beautiful. And I should embrace it by wearing it in its most natural state.

It's not only just been about hair. Being natural, I'm very careful about the products that I put in my hair. Natural oils only, and only natural products that haven't been processed. And I just feel like it turned into a lifestyle change for me as well. What I put into my body is also very important and that's at the forefront of my [mind]. The vegetables I eat, working out, all of those things. It started off with natural hair, but then it just became a natural lifestyle.

Felice: *Being born with a disability comes with its own challenges. Being born with cerebral palsy comes with its own challenges. I feel like people - because I have a disability - are kind of surprised that I am confident. But my parents never really raised me to associate who I am as a person with my disability. It was always, "Your disability makes you who you are, but isn't who you are." So, I was always confident, regardless of it, because I always knew that I'm still smart, I'm still a valuable part of society regardless of my limitations.*

I've always been a confident kid...With my disability, I was always just like, 'okay, it might be different, but I can still get it done.' I think maybe what I would want other differently-abled people to understand is: just because you're different doesn't mean you can't have a normal life. Because that's what I kind of struggled with growing up. I had my struggles in New York. Kids in New York are so mean! Kids can be...yo...I definitely had my fair share of schoolyard unfortunate situations. I guess I got to a point when I was like 12, where I was just like, "Look, I'm not going to take this anymore! Y'all are not going to keep doing this to me, and I'm going to start standing up for myself!" Because I was always one of those sweet and nice kids or whatever. I'm still a sweet and nice person, but it was like one day I was like, "Nah. Go ahead, kick rocks! It's over now!"

After that, people started being nice to me! That was so crazy! Because it's like, I was nice, I was sweet, and people are teasing me. And I'm like, "Just stop! Can you stop?! I'm so nice! Be my friend?!" Then one day I was just like, "I don't care if you are my friend, get away from me! Don't talk to me! I don't need you! Who cares?!" And that was when everyone wanted to be my friend.

It's kinda hard for me to say, growing up with a disability is such a unique experience, but it doesn't feel unique when you're living it, sometimes. Because you live with it every day. Sometimes for me - I guess because it's not as severe - I sometimes forget about it. But then there are certain situations that may happen where I've got to figure out how to do something differently than [other people], or have to accept that I can't do something that I wanted to do because of it. It's like okay, now I have to kind of grapple with this thing. And it's hard because people are always wanting me to say what I would say to someone growing up in my situation. And I don't really know what to always say, because everybody's situation is always different. It's very unfortunate to me when I do meet people with disabilities, and I can tell that they aren't confident. I've met people who are older than me, who I can see in them that they are so self-conscious about themselves. And it's just like, you know, so what that you're different? As I got older, and I kind of built this confidence, people started to want to be around me just because of that alone. Because they can tell that I didn't let the situation make me jaded or angry, and I was comfortable and happy with who I am.

MY PRESENCE

Rima: *I lived in Kaolack, Senegal, which is like a region. I think there are four regions within the country, and Kaolack is its own region. I lived in a small village. I mean it wasn't like scrap huts and things like that, but it was small. I was a kid, so there was this whole freedom thing that at nine-years old you don't have in America. My curfew was 10 o'clock. At night. It was really just a calm environment. There wasn't too much going on, and when something was going on, you'd know. Everyone was talking about it. Word really travels fast!*

...Where I lived, I wasn't exactly cut off from the world, you know? It very much had all kinds and forms of technology. It's not like they were back in the '90s and you were hearing the AOL [dial-up modem] ring thing. We had Wi-Fi! We had an imported goods store, and things you wouldn't generally find in your corner store, you'd find there. It was pretty much the norm. Nothing felt too odd or out of place. I actually felt more odd, and out of place, when I came back [to the U.S.]. I felt like I knew nothing!

One thing in Africa that's kind of different, is the way you handle your problems. So, over there, when you first get there you're automatically going to stand out. You're an American kid, and me who's like incredibly light-skinned, they constantly called me white. You stand out. So there, you'll get picked on, people will curse at you, it's whatever. Until you kind of put your foot down like, "Look, we could go hand-to-hand combat right now!" Like that's the only option! Whereas in the States, if you go hand-to-hand combat with somebody it's like, "Whoa, what's wrong with her?!"

Jonel: *I think here, people are more curious than close-minded. I feel like if you go to Tokyo there are so many foreigners there because it's a big city, people are used to it. But here, there aren't that many foreigners. Not that many tourists come through, so I think every time* someone sees me, they're like "Whoa...what's going on?!" I have a friend here who's from America too, and she says that she loves walking behind me to see people's reactions! 'Cuz I also have my afro going on, so people are like, "What's going on here?!"

I don't know, I just get a lot of stares mostly. I think they're more confused as to why I'm here! They woke up that morning like, 'oh, everything's going to be normal, going to be the same.' And I just came out and ruined their day! I get a lot of stares, but I'm used to it now. And especially if someone hears me speaking Japanese, they're like, "What is going on?! We're not coming back out until she leaves!" Sometimes I [go jogging] around my neighborhood, so I'm just in my mode running, and I see people turning as I'm jogging.

My job here is to assist in teaching English, and I feel like my presence brings curiosity to the language, which makes the kids want to learn more. Which makes me happy. So, my [students] ask me questions all the time about my hair, or the clothes that I wear. Sometimes they write me letters, whether it's in correct English or not, sometimes in Japanese. But I feel like because of my presence, they're more curious about English and learning it.

MY WOMANHOOD

Malika: It's crazy how drastic that change is. A complete 180 [on a subject], from 'I never thought about this before' to 'now it's all I can think about' is Black feminism...Black feminism has been a large focus of mine, and something that I'm still learning about. And along with that are issues of sexual violence.

I realized that when I was younger, I participated in jokes and comments that were made degradingly towards both subjects, and that added more to the perception that these aren't real issues. And once I finally caught that, oh my god, I just gave myself like a verbal lashing. I was so disappointed in myself. And ever since then, I vowed *to change the language that surrounds [those issues]...This is still something that I'm learning, and it's been different every day. When I first heard of feminism, I didn't understand it. I kind of had this thing where I identify myself as a woman of color, but I always thought that race came before my sex, my gender. And so, I always had that as a priority, but I'm both things, so I started focusing on it a lot.*

Feminism in itself, we're women who just feel...not even women...men and women who believe in the equality of both sexes and genders, and everything in between. It's kind of reaching that harmony where we realize like, "Okay, let's talk about the disadvantages that women face in comparison to men. Let's talk about that. Let's try to find a way to fix it." And for some reason that's a threat. When you have issues of let's say, street harassment, where it's like a woman tells a guy 'no' and suddenly she gets shot or hurt because she denied this guy. This is mostly what we're talking about. It's not always protesting this or that. We're trying to get people to face a certain reality that keeps being pushed away and trivialized.

With Black feminism, it goes to a deeper level in the sense that, sometimes the ideals projected by the standard feminism kind of eradicates that part of someone's identity where race also plays a part in it...so Black feminism kind of brings that all into fruition so that we can all have the discussion.

MY MANHOOD

Jared: *I was, and in a sense I am, institutionalized. I would call my cell my home, because of the years of being there and going through it. But to actually come home means to come back to your wife, your kids, your extended family, and your friends that have been waiting on you and rooting for you, writing you and praying for you. And now you have a chance to walk out of those gates and say either: "The time did me," or "I did it."*

So, for me to come home, I had all the cards stacked against me, and I'm still out two years later. And I'm kicking. And I'd like to say I'm making a positive difference in my household and in my social circle. I'm home. I'm going in my refrigerator. I'm getting the [car] tires fixed. I'm filling my car up with gas. I'm buying Christmas [presents] for the family. I'm home. I'm eating Thanksgiving dinner. I'm going to Foot Locker and buying Jordans or Air Maxes. I'm not ordering commissary or New Balance [shoes] off the [commissary] list. I'm able to be out here free with a new chance to stay out.

...I'm six feet, 250 [pounds]. Tattooed from my head to toe, but I love my kids, I love my family, and I break my back for them daily. And I hold doors for ladies and older guys. Everybody is not what you see them as on TV or on the computer. There's a different side, and a different depth to some of them.

James: *I used to be a very big pessimist, and I was always depressed. I [had] very low confidence. At some point, it felt like I was self-loathing. I was just confused all the way around, didn't know what was going on. I wasn't happy with my life, and I was always talking negatively. And I didn't realize I was chasing people away. So, one day, I got up and [said to myself], "Let's say I died in my sleep and didn't wake up. I do not want to be remembered as a person who was always negative." I want to be remembered as somebody [who made people say], "I want to be around this guy. He's fun to be around." I want to be able to get up and say, "I actually like getting up in the morning and going to do what I've got to do."*

It's one of those things...it was a very hard process. Even just as simple as getting up and getting in front of the mirror in the morning and saying three things that I like about myself. Eventually it started to grow. I would constantly do that. When things would go wrong, I would constantly ask myself, 'What do you like about yourself?' And eventually it builds confidence. [My] drive comes from people who saw me during those times and still had more confidence in me than I had in myself ever. Even though I had a lot of people saying, "No, he's not going to be anything," there were still a few people I held on to who knew from the start that, "He's going to be something. Ten years from now, he's going to be something."

Our Black Lives

You cannot give what you do not have. These words from my father were shared during the fairly routine hours-long conversations we had about life during my teenage and young adult years. As with many pieces of sage parental counsel, this sentence resonates more as I get older. It's a statement that provides clarity for relating to other people: *Don't expect someone to give you what they don't have.* However, it is also a statement that provokes self-reflection: *What do I have? What can I give? What do I not have? What can I not give?*

This statement applies to individuals, families, communities, and nations. We cannot give what we do not have. They cannot give what they do not have. This is an acceptable fact of life for most people, because it reminds us that no single person or group of people has everything. It reminds us that other people have capital and capabilities that we don't have. It reminds us that we have resources and revelations that other people don't have. It reminds us that we are members of an interdependent ecosystem of humanity. It reminds us that we need each other.

You need to have something in order to give it. So, what happens when you have nothing?

You have to consent to a transfer in order for your action to be considered a gift. So, what happens when the things you had were transferred without your consent?

In order to be a full member of an ecosystem, there must enough to sustain you and enough of you to sustain others. So, what happens when there is nothing to sustain you, and you are being consumed to sustain others?

The previous chapter raised the question: *What does it mean for an individual to be called black?* This question takes on even more urgency when extended to hundreds of millions of humans around the world. *What does it mean to call a group of people black? What does it mean for a group of people to call themselves black?*

I am not sure that it is possible to measure the amount of human intellect and imagination that have been directed towards those two questions over the past few centuries. Multiple nations, across the world, constructed entire economic, political, and social structures upon the premise that to be Black is to have nothing, and to be nothing. The label was designed not only to excommunicate a group from the family of humanity, but to declare that they were never full members in the first place.

To me, one of the greatest demonstrations of the power of the human will has been the lives of the humans who came to inhabit this label. Riding on the parallel tracks of creationism and evolution, the people who entered the nothingness of Blackness adapted to their environments by speaking life and light into their own existence. They made something out of nothing. They debunked the myth. They exposed the lie. They revealed the truth.

We do have, and we can give.

THE LEGACY

Jason: *Black people in America have been programmed over 400 years to abandon their culture, idealize Eurocentric values, amalgamate themselves, purposely lighten their skin to fit into the dominant group. And all of this stems from a lack of consciousness.*

If Black people - I'll just call them people of African descent - just realized the contributions that their lineage have made towards the advancement of humanity, that information alone will liberate them. Because that information is powerful. Understand that your people built the pyramids. Your people had sophisticated empires and sophisticated civilizations way before the European ever thought to come to Africa. If you only understood, or were aware of the information, that alone is 50% of the task towards liberation. 'Cuz the ultimate goal is always liberation. It's always been liberation. But 50% of the task is understanding it, the other 50% of the task is praying and working towards it. I might be simplifying it, but that's how I view it. That's how I view things.

Massamba: *I spent all my childhood back in Senegal. I came here when I was in the 11th grade, so pretty much the first two decades of my life I spent in Senegal. The experience I saw there is that we are very much involved in our children's lives. Over there, we have much less access to technology, but we have a connection with our brothers and children. They see us as their mentors and role models, rather than artists and movie stars. [Since] they have less access to TV, we have that power to influence their lives instead of [celebrities]. So, when I came here, we didn't have exactly the same culture as I knew [previously], but at home my parents and I are trying to foster that environment.*

Amadu: *Another thing - and this is now going to go up to a different level - speaking of how Black people interact with Africans...it switches so drastically from being in middle school to being in college. In middle school, Africans used to get joked on. You get to college, African people are not the joke. Best believe. They know where they come from, or at least they have more of a stronghold on their history, of-tentimes, they tend to be more on the wealthy side.*

And in fact, they try to separate themselves from African-Americans. Whereas in middle school it's like the exact opposite, like "Ohhh, he's African! Hahaha, laugh at him!" You get to college, no, it's the other way around. Africans do not want to necessarily identi-fy with African-Americans. So that's also a huge problem in my eyes, because what are we doing - and what are they learning - about Afri-can-Americans that seems distasteful so that they don't want to iden-tify with African-Americans, you know? That's sort of an issue.

THE COMMUNITY

Neiko: *Being a young Black male in our world today, you have to be taught things like this, because as you can see, we're having issues all across the globe today. We have young Black males who either have been taught how to handle different things and walk away with it, or they have not been taught because there's no man in their lives. I'm hoping what I can say can help some of these young kids out here who don't have a man in their lives who can correct them when they're wrong, let them know about [women], let them know about anything that they need to know about. And if I can do that just by telling them a little bit about me, then why not?*

Mikal: *With someone like Brother Corbin, he tried his hardest to connect with us. I remember this one night, he brought me out to [the Brooklyn Academy of Music] to do some kind of poetry event...and he would never judge the art that we had. With the span of generations [between] me and Corbin, our art is different, and we speak about dif-ferent things, but he would never look at [our work] like it was less-than. He would always try to take it in, and try to understand it.*

I feel like that's symbolic of what the relationship was, he would try to understand each student and try to connect with them on deeper levels. Even when I was playing basketball, he would come out to games and he used to call me George Gervin. I wasn't good at all, I was really bad, but he would call me George Gervin and he would try to motivate me to come out and do better each game. He would just try to find the level that we could both connect on.

Ebonee: *You know what's wrong with this generation? This new generation, these little 15, 16, and 17-year old kids...they were raised by their grandparents. They weren't raised by their mothers. Their mothers were so busy running the streets being young parents, that [these kids] weren't raised by their mothers. They only had their grandmothers, who are barely able to take care of them. Therefore, they have no real structure.*

They're missing that structure. Structure, structure, structure. You have to build structure in your home. You have to have some type of structure within your home. You have to have some type of discipline, and a lot of these kids lack that. That's why they don't care about anything. They don't have anything to care about. It's like, "My mother doesn't even care about me...My father doesn't care about me. What do I care about? What am I supposed to care about?"

You know, you find your peace within your friends, and these friends ain't really friends. And you grow to learn that as a person, hopefully before it's too late. But for some of these young boys, it's too late. And I can't bring my kids up in that type of environment...there's a certain type of community that you bring your kids up in, and it destroys you. Living in the projects destroys you. It destroys your spirit. You become a product of your environment. I don't want my kids to become a product of their environment. You can teach your kid, but they're always going to choose their own path. I want them to see something different, so that they can want to choose a different path.

Erica: *Right now, I am involved with the young people's ministry at my church. Through the church, I also go out to the juvenile detention center and I talk with kids there as well. So, my biggest goal right now is just to bring them a certain sense of hope and just showing them love, and impacting them in that way. Because there are so many youth out there right now who are lacking love from home, and from their parents, and from certain relationships. So just being that light-bearer, that hope-changer for them in a sense, it's a huge task. It's something that I pray [about] daily, that I need help with, because it can be a bit daunting at times.*

For me, the biggest shocker was the fact that they're all pretty much normal, everyday kids. Most of them you would never even suspect that they did anything that would land them in there. I've met some of the sweetest kids I have met to date in there. So, there's a huge discrepancy between what society tells us, and what the media portrays [about] who's in those detention centers, and who really is.

One thing that I've learned in my year of going, is that what they're lacking is love, essentially. They all just want that love and that comfort. A lot of them have like, certain anger issues and things towards their parents who weren't there for them, and they're just frustrated. They don't really know how to handle and how to deal with that. So, they give in to the wrong things that are in their neighborhoods and around them. They make the wrong decisions with certain friends. Some of them were the only one who got caught...and it was like their first time doing something. So, to hear things like that, it really hurts. Just to see that they're struggling with something, and it really has nothing to do with their action that landed them [in that place], but personally – on a deeper level – it's [about their] home and lacking that love from their parents or guardians or whoever.

Stephanie: *I got into the field of social work, and I started working with teenage girls. They know that I'm older, but I'm still kinda young. I'm 28, so I'm old because I've got a few gray hairs in the front, but it's like, "Oh, your skin is not wrinkled and you look alright. You can wear jeans and your clothes aren't out of date, so you're okay!" The kids will let you know!*

So, I'm talking to them, and at first, they would see me when I'm coming to work. I work overnight...[and] I'm not allowed to come into work in a skirt or a dress or anything like that. So, when they see me, it's kinda like sweatpants and my old running shoes that I've been wearing for a long time. I look really comfortable, there's nothing fashionable about me. Now I had a job interview probably like three weeks ago, and one of the girls saw me getting ready because the interview was at 10am and I don't get off until 8:30 in the morning, because I work overnight.

So, she saw me getting ready. She saw me putting on a dress - it wasn't a scoop neck but it was right by my neck - I put on some stockings and my flats. And she was kind of looking at me and she was like, "Oh my god! I didn't even know you owned clothes like this?!" And I said, "Yes." And she said, "Well, why are you putting on your sweater? It's going to cover how pretty your dress looks." And I said, "I'm putting on my sweater to cover my tattoos." And she goes, "Well, why would you get any tattoos if you're going to cover them?!" And I said, "The tattoos are for me and yes, I do want to show them off, but right now I need to show people that I can be professional. That I can go into a certain space and I don't have to basically throw out any ideas that I have imprinted on my body. I don't have to do that."

...She used to make a joke that she was going to get 'I'm With Stupid' tattooed on her forehead. And that's when I told her, "When you get a tattoo, honey, you need to get a tattoo with meaning." And she was like, "I'm glad you told me that, 'cuz I was gonna go get my boy-

friend's name tattooed on me because I don't see him every day."
That's [when] I was able to tell her. I was like, "Honey, don't do that.
I did that already and it's covered up." I was able to tell her from my
experience and she was like, "Man, Miss Stephanie I didn't know that
you had did that. I didn't even know that you had this tattoo on your
wrist until now." It was one of those moments where I was able to
help her, because you could tell that a light bulb went off.

THE REALITY

Ebonee: *How can I say this? ...When I say that I'm raising an Afri-*
can-American boy and a young African-American girl, it is open sea-
son on these Black young men. These cops are killing everybody for
anything. And these girls are out here, they're going crazy. They
don't have any structure.

And this society does no better with these celebrities. Everybody
glorifies people on social media. You can't do that. You can't. Because
there's nothing like being Black. And a lot of people, they take our
culture, and they try to make it their own. And it's like, "Hey, we did
it first. We did it first." I have to show my daughter that it's okay to
be Black. It's definitely okay to be Black. But you have to know how to
carry yourself [while] being Black. I don't want to have to tell my son,
"You can't go here because the cops are going to be there. You can't
go there because I don't want you doing this, and I don't want you
doing that." I want my child to be free. I want my child to be able to
walk outside and not have to worry about anything. That's what I
want.

Being African-American, you don't have that privilege because
people already have this idea of what you are as a person. You can
come from a great home, you can come from a good family. But they
already have this idea in their heads that you're some gangbanger, or

you're some little hoodrat from the projects. And then you open your mouth and you speak, and it's like, 'oh, you're smart.'

Raven: *One thing I saw when I went abroad was that I kinda won the geographic lottery when it came to being Black, as much of a lottery as you can call it. I had the opportunity - it might not have been the best opportunity - but I had the opportunity to go to school. I had the opportunity to do a lot of things, whereas a lot of the Black people who were in Europe - other than Paris and London - are immigrants coming from Africa. So, there's a big issue with homelessness, with joblessness, and that could have very easily been me if I wasn't born in America.*

When I went to Paris and London, everyone seemed a lot more accepting of everything. In Amsterdam, especially. So, America kinda disappointed me in many ways when I came back, but at the same time I kind of grew an appreciation for America. So now I'm in the awkward place of...I guess...ungratefulness.

One thing that I can say is that to be Black anywhere is to be oppressed. But to be American anywhere is to be privileged. I felt like there were times when my Blackness didn't precede my 'Americanness'. So, no matter where I went, I was always American first...there were plenty of examples where I go into somewhere, and because I was dressed differently from the other people from the Diaspora who had migrated...they would be so respectful and everything. And I'd be right next to someone else and it would be weird. They would act like [the African immigrants] didn't have money to spend in their store too. That's one thing that I've seen, you can't escape racial tension. You can't escape racial issues...you can't just go to Europe and say, "All of my problems will no longer exist."

THE MINDSET

Aquillia: *[Back then], I didn't think it was important to praise Black culture. And by that, I didn't know back then that it was like a big deal to be happy that I was Black. I thought Black was cool. I was happy, I knew my history, I knew all of that. But I didn't know what it meant to really uplift and celebrate and really grieve when our culture hurts or anything like that. I didn't understand that at all. I think I'm at a much better point now, today, to do that and to celebrate our victories and everything at this point.*

I didn't think that was necessary then, for whatever reason. Even though my parents really made it a big deal for us to know our culture, and to celebrate our culture, and our history; I don't know...I didn't internalize it. I think having to define who I am as Black woman in the years after that, showed me that there's a lot that I should be celebrating, and a lot that I should be grieving over, and I was happy to learn that lesson.

Daphne: *I could answer this in two different ways. I see a lack of unity. I see destruction. I see ego, and I see a lot of pride. Especially in the African-American community where my young brothers and sisters...we're not using our power the way we need to. People are not realizing that being Black is a powerful thing. There is so much power and there is so much juice in our melanin that people do not understand that.*

Being an African-American, people should find that to be...riches. It should be considered like money! But people take it, and they manipulate it. They let the system eat them up. And you can't let the system eat you up, because the system has already set out an outline for you to fail. So, don't give into the system and allow the system to eat you up. But that's what many of my young brothers and sisters are doing, and it's sad.

If my African-American brother needed me, you should be okay with helping that person. If my young African-American sister needs me, I'm going to stop what I'm doing and help her. But so many people are focused on them, them, them...them making it to the top. When you make it to the top, are you going to be at the top alone? No, that doesn't make any sense. You want to be at the top and have a table full of people that you can share that million-dollar meal with, not eating by yourself, you know?

Amadu: *I mean after this past year - or even currently - you know the whole Black Lives Matter movement, my own personal experiences through life...right now I have a couple different perspectives. First, just speaking about African-Americans...we have some work [to do]. It's in all aspects. We can't do it in this Western approach, which is to break things down and handle them individually. We can't really do things like that. I don't think that's how we originally operated.*

We have to look at it from a more holistic point of view. So, family structure, teachers, medicine, education, all of this history, this stuff is very important. It's not enough to just teach someone about math and science, or to get them into a top-tier school. You would be surprised how many people can get into a top-tier school and feel lost when they get there. They don't know where they fit in. There's a difference between coming and being nervous about what new friend you may meet/have, and actually feeling lost, like you feel misplaced and you don't have a place.

I don't think that I ever had that happen to me, so I can't speak on that in a sense. I feel like the way me and my brothers were brought up, we were very conscious of African-American heritage. We were conscious of how our people were oppressed. But we were also cognizant of what we would need to do in this system - the way it's set up - to succeed. And that is an aspect that may be lost right now. And there's no blaming...it's simply the fact that the information is not being [disseminated] throughout our communities.

And also, we have a little bit of greed. We're suffering from the same human flaws that any other culture or race is suffering from...The issues that we suffer from are the same exact issues that every other race or ethnicity suffer from: greed, [and] the inability to be compassionate. Those are just two that seriously hinder how a community defines itself. If you don't feel that the brotha' walking down the street is seriously your brother - someone that you feel responsible for - that's not a good community. Just 'cuz you live in the same area does not make it a community.

Atisha: *I like to read a lot, and Facebook is very helpful in my [artistic] practice because it helps me to keep up to date with current events. I can get the gist of it, but then I can go and do my own research into what's happening around the world. The [African] Diaspora is not just about my Guyanese American experience. It's about every Black person. It's about everyone.*

I love this song called "Captured Land" by Chronixx - he's a Jamaican artist - and I feel like we are all living on captured land, and it's important to have the experiences of everyone around me.

THE GOAL

Jason: *I think we should build our own institutions. I think we should fund our own institutions as a collective. Teach our people the information that they need to learn to better themselves. No questions about that. If we are continuing to be oppressed, and we are not seeing the oppressor as the oppressor, I mean when are we going to eventually wake up? It's time that we come together as a collective and do what's best for us at the end of the day. The first law of nature is self-preservation...self-preservation.*

Phillip: *If you kind of look at the world as it is now, we represent a large portion of fashion, a large portion of entertainment, a large portion of civil rights, a portion of history. But in the power struggle, we're not in that industry, in that fabric, in that infrastructure. When you look at all the different industries and advancements, we don't have that touch, that representation.*

When I [talk about being a Black male] I want to say, "Hey, I'm from here. I'm this color. This beautiful color that God chose for me. I don't want to be ostracized. I don't want to be put in a box. I don't want to be categorized as someone that's not you...I just want to say that I'm equal, I'm here to advance the world, to advance my family, to advance life, to make and sustain life." And I feel sometimes - as hypocritical as that sounds - the only way I can do that is to identify my past and the people that came before me as Black males. To make sure that they're aware that we are making contributions, we are here doing good things.

Katie: *I think there's always that struggle of wanting to be the leader. We remember the Dr. Martin Luther Kings and the Malcolm Xs, but that's not everyone's role. And not getting discouraged about not being the face of a movement. That's okay, there are a lot of unknowns [who were] in the Civil Rights Movement - or even today - who we're just not going to know about. Their part isn't any less important, because none of this change would have happened without them. We need everyone. Honestly, we do.*

I always had black Barbie dolls growing up. I know that with a lot of young African-American girls, there's a whole crisis of not looking like people on TV or even [having] toys that don't look like you. So, my parents kind of spearheaded that, and were just very careful about [that]. That's all that I've ever known.

I've always known that Black girls are wonderful and amazing, because that's what I grew up around. I grew up around wonderful, amazing women. And once again, I'm very lucky and very blessed. Of course, media is always going to get in and there's always going to be a little bit of that struggle of not looking like everyone on TV, going into spaces and not looking like everyone there, but just realizing your worth and that your opinions matter.

It's a lesson that I'm still learning today, because naturally I'm not super-outgoing. It doesn't come naturally to me. I can turn it on when necessary, but it still takes me a little bit to speak up sometimes and make my presence known. I think that's a journey that I'm always going to be on, [a journey that] everyone is kind of always on. So, each and every day, just kinda waking up and going into spaces...I think a lot of [people] in society know that already, but sometimes we just have to wake up and we have to do whatever you do to get yourself pumped up. You know, look in the mirror and just be like, "I deserve to be here."

I'm Spiritual

Everybody gets a trophy nowadays. This has been one of the common charges leveled against millennials as they matriculate through young adulthood, delivered at them with a range of intensity levels. Some are playful jabs from their older sibling generations - the Baby Boomers and Gen Xers. Some are rhetorical handwringing from people who are concerned that the saying *they don't make 'em like they used to* extends to assessments of this young generation's strength and resolve. Still others use these charges as a way to silence the voices and dismiss the opinions of millennials who are challenging the prevailing wisdom of the status quo.

Ironically, millennials were not the people who developed the worldview of that all children should receive positive, self-esteem boosting, life-affirming tokens of appreciation. Millennials were not the people who translated this worldview into the participation trophies, certificates, and ribbons which are distributed to schoolchildren across the United States. Millennials' primary role in this chapter of American parenting and education was accepting the praise and the awards of the adults in our society. However, the question of whether or not every single person deserves a trophy is a profoundly useful one.

A trophy is simply a way to confer the value of the trophy giver *to* the trophy recipient. The trophy's value - and, by extension, the value we ascribe to the person receiving it - depends on the individual or institution who presents the trophy.

So, if a child gets a trophy at school, the trophy is important because the society believes the institution of school is important. If a young athlete receives a medal, the medal has value because it reflects the values of a society that believes in rewarding extraordinary achievement in sports. A five-star rating, a championship ring, a magazine cover photo, a series of designatory letters after a name; there are endless ways groups of people in a society recognize and celebrate individuals for reflecting the beliefs of that society.

Perhaps the problem is not with the trophies. Perhaps the problem is with who is giving them. We give them. We humans, with all of our convictions, and all of our contradictions. With our capacity for generosity, and our capacity for evil. With all of our knowledge, and with all of our ignorance. We are beautiful and imperfect beings. We give beautiful and imperfect trophies, which confer the beautiful and imperfect values of our societies onto our children. We do the best we can.

What if there is more beyond our limitations and imperfections? What if our value is not determined by the beliefs of the societies we are raised in? What about that which is beautiful *and* perfect?

I BELIEVE

Salihah: *I think the same things matter. If anything, [now] they just matter more. I'm a pretty simple person. To me, the things that were important were my family, my friends, [and] my relationship with God. The older you get, you realize just how important those things are. As you get older, you start to lose people and people get sick. You're kinda forced to - even if you're not someone who believes in God - in some ways I think you're forced to assess your own spiritual-*

ity. And that just happens because life happens. So, the older I've gotten, the more I think I hold those things close and dear to my heart.

I've always interpreted spirituality to be the way that you interpret and make meaning of the world around you. For a lot of people, like myself, they do that through religion. There are other people who make sense of the world through other things, and that's fine. So, I can definitely understand people who are really empathetic and sympathetic towards other people and different things that are going on, but who may not necessarily align themselves with a specific religious group. And I also think that kind of just having an awareness of other religions, of what other people believe in, and what's important to them is also a part of spirituality. So, I think we're living in a time when people are defining that for themselves and don't want to necessarily hold tight to tradition and certain things that their parents believe and what they grew up believing. I just know for me, that's always made sense.

Aquillia: *Another thing that still is important to me now is my faith. Being a Christian is probably the best choice I ever made. It is the best choice I've ever made. It's helped shape who I am a lot and how I treat other people. In 2007, I was just starting to figure out what my life as a Christian meant and now I'm still figuring it out. The importance of it - the necessity of it - is still very real in my life.*

SEEING THINGS DIFFERENTLY

Maryka: *I was 13...very studious, and a die-hard Christian at the time. But now my experiences, meeting different people and going to different schools, gave me a different perspective and a different way to look at life. I'm not a die-hard religious Christian anymore.*

...I used to throw the Bible up at every situation, like I did not curse and tried to just live the way the Bible said wholeheartedly. But

as I grew up I just did more research, and I learned the root of where Christianity even came from, what my ancestors practiced and how it was beneficial to them, and just the foundation of Christianity, and it just led me to a different route. We all have our own spiritual journey within, and we all have our own demons, and our own addictions and temptations. I learned that you don't go to hell because you didn't follow what this disciple wrote millions of years ago. You're not going to hell because you didn't listen to what the disciple Paul said. It's all about how your heart feels, ultimately.

THIS LITTLE LIGHT OF THEIRS

Amadu: *There's a guy, he's called Sadhguru [Jaggi Vasudev]. After what my parents have taught me, what I've learned myself, and what interested me in school when we spoke about religions and ways of life and cultures...he sort of sums up what I've been trying to express for a long time. He speaks about being able to let go and get rid of emotional attachment to events.*

I have to be very careful in the way that I say this: there's nothing wrong with expressing emotion. The issue, however, is that people are not conscious of the emotions that they're expressing. In fact, people are simply reacting to what is going on around them...If you had the ability to be conscious of how you felt, then you would be able to decide whether or not you want to grow angry or be happy at all times. You can grow sad if you want, it's entirely up to you. The point is to make it conscious, versus an event happening and you immediately have a reaction on your spirit...[on] who you are and how you feel.

Chelsea: *Now, I read so much more. I am obsessed with Eckhart Tolle and Oprah Winfrey. No seriously, like Oprah...oh my goodness...listen, I've literally watched every single interview. Do you know how people sit and binge watch television shows? I sit and* binge watch Oprah interviews, and I think I've heard every single podcast. It's from her that spirituality became super-important to me.

I now know that I am a spiritual being having a human experience. So, it's almost impossible for me to live a fulfilling and righteous life without doing anything to take care of my spirit. So that's kind of my priority right now. As I've grown, my understanding of God has also grown. It's no longer like, 'hey, I need to go to church because that's kinda what I grew up knowing.' I really try to just get a deeper understanding, and now everything that I do, I do knowing that there is a higher being. And I don't do anything without that understanding. Whereas back then, I kind of did everything as I pleased, and just assumed I was in my own will. And now I think with the understanding that there is something more than me, [that] there is something higher than me, I am able to go further.

Massamba: *I follow my religious mentors. The reason why I follow them is because I am totally at peace. They influence my everyday practice. Remember when I said [my daily routine is], 'work, work out, pray, and movies'...they shaped [that routine]. They are the ones who really put this mindset into me, so that's why I say they are the most important, most influential people in my life.*

MINDING MY BLESSINGS

Shantel: *I think I've developed a lot through prayer, and my relationship with God. That's changed my perspective on a lot of different things. Back in '07 I was a sophomore in college. I wanted to [study] pharmacy and I had a breakdown. I was like, "You know, I'm sick of school. I'm done with school. Let me just graduate and go about my business." And when I graduated, I was working at IKEA and I was like, 'I have to do something else with my life.' And basically, that was revealed to me through God. A lot of prayer, a lot of constant,*

"God, what do you want me to be? What do you want me to do? I know your decision will probably be the best thing for me."

And weirdly enough, His decision for me has been one of the most challenging things for me the past couple of months. I really do feel like God showed me that He wanted me to go back to school to get my masters in social work. I did. He really got me through, and blessed me to pass my licensing exam. And He blessed me with this opportunity to work doing case management.

It's been a very challenging time working here. Not that my co-workers aren't great, they're very supportive people. But it is very difficult learning all this information and having so many different personalities from your clients coming at you each day, and having clients who can be so draining. Each time that person calls, it's like, *"They're calling me again?!"* And learning how to have that compassion and that care and that desire to help them in their situation...I'm not going to say God gave me a blessing and a curse, 'cuz He'll never give me a curse, that's not who He is, that's not His character. It's a blessing on top of a blessing that's going to come later, but in the process of [being] molded into the next blessing. It's just really difficult right now in this process.

OPEN MINDS AND EXTENDED HANDS

Noor: *I think, we're all the same. We're all the same. That's what I see. A lot of people can see differences. I can see similarities, and that's important to me. Of course, I can see differences and contrasts, but we do have a lot of similarities.*

As a Muslim, [I recently visited] a church for the first time - I don't know if people will agree with that or not - but even in a church, the talks that we had in there, the questions that people raised, were the same. We have the same questions about beliefs...I had always been curious to go into a church. But not to go inside and look at the building and how beautiful it is. No, no, no...this is not what I wanted to see. I wanted to see people praying. I wanted to hear what they say. I wanted to understand.

It was a whole Sunday session, one hour I guess. So, I went to the church, I prayed with them, I listened to the sermon...it was really interesting. I mean, how did I end up going to the church? It was a Catholic church, and a recommendation from a friend of mine. He told me, "Okay, you know what? You want to go to a church? I used to go to this church. It's good, the people are nice, you won't have any trouble or anything." Being Muslim, I cover my head, so...yeah. Actually, I was really excited. I was a little scared before I went, but the moment I walked in it was really quiet and so peaceful. I wasn't scared at all. People welcomed me. I didn't feel like a stranger, like somebody was looking at me and thinking, 'what is she doing here?' or anything at all. Even the priest, he shook hands with me and he welcomed me to the church. I felt welcomed.

CHARACTER GOALS

Erica: *Two years ago, the most important people I followed were people who just radiated positivity and change and impacting other people's lives in a positive way. And that truly helped to kickstart my self-growth journey.*

Once I made my decision to truly take my relationship with God to another level...when I read the Bible, it's so interesting. Getting to know Him through hearing other people's experiences, just even the example that He set while He was on the Earth, like He was so full of love. And He was so humble and so gentle with everyone that He came across. He drew multitudes of crowds just based on His demeanor...but ultimately, I feel that He was able to grasp them because of the love that He had within Him. I feel like it's so important to just be filled with love. Imagine the world, if we all just loved one another and we loved ourselves. The world would be a completely different place.

Katie: *One of my favorite qualities about the Lord...Jesus - I had to take you to church for a minute! - I've always liked how when He was seen with people in society, like a tax collector or something, and [other people] would say, "No, you can't hang out with them. They're not cool. You know how society feels about them. Don't talk to them. What are you doing?!" And Jesus was always like, "No...I'm gonna...it's fine guys, I've got this! I'm going to interact with them, and it's going to be fun. You're gonna see that this is also a person, they have hopes and dreams and desires just like you. Just because they have this title, they're not defined by it." I think I'm paraphrasing Matthew or something, I don't know! I've always really liked that, and [I have] tried to bring that kind of philosophy to my life.*

GRATITUDE

Chelsea: *For me, yoga is part of my spiritual practice. Whenever I'm doing yoga, that's when I can be present. I do it early in the morning, because it kind of sets the tone for the day for me. When I'm doing it, I'm kind of just...there. I'm centered. I'm allowing myself to just be. I notice that I'm breathing. I'm thankful. It's like one of those things that really keeps me grounded. That's what I go to. If I've had a long day, I'm like, "Okay, you know what? I'm about to do some yoga." It's super-beneficial, [not only] to the physical body, but to my mental health.*

Ashley: *I think happiness is an emotion. It's fleeting. It can be manipulated by anything going on in your environment at the time. So, you could be happy one minute, you stub your toe and you're not happy anymore.*

I think contentment is much deeper than that. It's really a state of mind. A state of being that nothing can impact. I think part of contentment is satisfaction with where you are. Not like satisfaction from food, where you are full but you're going to be hungry again, but [where] you are completely satisfied and nothing can change that. I think that peace comes with contentment. And joy...Nobody can take that away. Nothing. No outside circumstance can change the sense of joy that you have. So, contentment consists of joy, satisfaction, and peace.

I'm A Creative

D o what you love. Love is often considered the purest of motivations. To engage an aspect of life from a place of love is the highest expression of our humanity. Some things we do because we love the outcome. We enjoy seeing that our actions have contributed to improving life on Earth. Some things we do because we love the living entity - a person, an animal, a plant - that benefits from our actions.

Some things we do simply because we love performing the set of behaviors that comprise the activity. We may love doing an activity because it showcases our talent. We may love it because it's our only talent! We may love doing an activity because it comforts us and brings us peace. We may love it because it propels us out of our comfort zone and brings us a rush of adrenaline.

We love activities that inspire our hopes for the future. We love activities that help us recover from the pains of the past. Some activities we love because they allow us to understand and communicate with the world. Some activities we love because they protect us from the negative elements in the world.

We think of creativity that emerges from love differently than creativity that emerges from other aspects of life. Creativity produced by love is not the same as creativity which is the result of necessity, obligation, or desperation. Love-directed creativity reflects the core elements of Safety, Respect, Trust, and Truth - which exist wherever authentic love is present. This is one of the reasons we encourage young people to do what they love, and one of the reasons why we celebrate the ones who are able to.

The default life motto we are all born with is: *Do what you want*. If and when we successfully transition into adulthood, the motto changes to: *Do what you must*. For adults who must acquire the necessities of life, the motto becomes: *Do what pays*. For adults who are able to acquire life's necessities, the motto changes to: *Do what you can*.

While these elements are essential for healthy countries and strong economies, they are insufficient for exceptional societies. Any society that seeks to be exceptional needs people who are dedicated to activities which bring more love into the world, and spread more love throughout the world.

We need people who do what they love, and do it for the love.

WHERE IT CAME FROM

Joshua Jackson: *The writing piece was always in me as a kid. I've always been fascinated with literature. I used to always read books as a kid. I actually got teased by my family members because I used to always read on Friday nights when they would have the whole Friday night lineup [on TV]! It was 'Family Matters' and all those shows that we all love from back in the '90s. And I would be in the room just writing and reading. That's all I wanted to do.*

Malika: *I've always been very outspoken, and I became introduced to spoken word poetry when I was in sixth grade. I was 12 years old, and that's when I started writing spoken word. I had already started writing about things that I didn't fully understand, and poetry was how I grew to understand things, so it was like a learning process. I would always write about my neighborhood. Things that I saw, things that I experienced. It was always very personal, and when I started gaining more of a language for it, it started being directed more towards systemic issues and things that I feel people need to hear.*

Safiya: *To be honest, I'd never really been a popular kid, so all I would spend my time doing when I would be by myself is just writing stories. I have a very vivid imagination; almost to the point where it hurt because I couldn't have other people see what I'm seeing in my head.*

I would create these stories, these movies in my mind, and I was just like, "How can I get other people to see this?" Because I think this is truly amazing and I want other people to see that and under-stand that. I felt like writing was the best way to express that, so I would write stories, and I would be terrible at it. And then I would just practice and practice and get better at it. Basically, what it did was help me cope with being alone so much. It helped me to express my ideas throughout my entire life. It basically became my comfort zone. That's what it did for me throughout my entire life.

Now, I find myself in a better place socially. When it comes to writing, I just want to get people to see what I'm seeing. It's more like I want to put it on the screen. I want books to be written about it. I want movies to be made about it. I want to go further, you know? So, it's not just like a coping mechanism, or something that I do in my free time. It's actually a passion, what I really want to do.

Atisha: *This happened to me over a period of time. There was never a moment that I had an epiphany that I have to draw, or that I have to be an artist...I like to use this anecdote because I remember using it to answer one of the 'Why do you want to be an artist?' questions on my college applications.*

I was in my junior year of high school and I was doing this art show at MoCADA. It was part of a program where teaching artists came into public schools. I made multiple pieces and they were in this show, and a woman came up to me and asked me what I was going to go to school [to study]. And I was like, "Well, I'm going to be a lawyer." Which, I've realized, is a very common thing among a lot of people who do anything creative. They've been like, "Oh, I'm going to do law."

So, I told [the woman] that, and I had my heart set on that because I wanted to make money and I wanted my mother to be proud of me immediately. That's something that will always be in demand. There are always going to be lawyers working. She looked at me and she was like, "Are you serious?" And I was like, "Yeah I'm gonna be a lawyer." And she was like, "What a waste of talent." And she walked away from me. It was dramatic, and it was like a final decision that she made...I remember that like it was yesterday. And my heart sunk because I didn't understand why she was being so rude.

So, I went to my mentor...basically what I got from that [experience], when I sat down and thought about it, was that the woman thought that I was doing a disservice to myself. It wasn't her way of dismissing me and putting me down. It actually opened my eyes a little bit, and I thought to myself, 'maybe I am a waste of talent, like what am I doing trying to be somebody that I'm not?' I just thought that [studying law] wasn't where my heart was, and I was just doing it for all the wrong reasons. I don't wake up every day and think about being a lawyer, or taking the bar exam or whatever. Every day I wake up I think about the drawing I was working on the day before. I dream about it. I dream about what I'm gonna do next.

Silver: *First, I understood that the people who said that to me weren't necessarily trying to dissuade me. They were saying it from a place of love and they actually cared...I listened to what they had to say. I un-*

derstood that they were coming from a place of love, but at the same time I knew what I wanted.

So, I had to make a decision: Do I do they want, or do I do what I want? Essentially, I had to decide that I wanted this for myself. For example, my mother wanted me to be an architect. For her, it seemed like a compromise because it involves drawing and design, but at the same time it was a more practical profession. So, it seemed [to her] like, "Hey why don't you do this instead?" I tried it out for a while...and this didn't seem like something I wanted to do, and I've always lived my life with just one thing in mind. I try to envision myself 10 or 20 years into the future...and I realized that I didn't enjoy seeing myself as an architect. But somehow, I knew that I would never give up on drawing. That if I lost my hands, I'd probably draw with my feet.

LEARN YOUR CRAFT

Ethan: *Art is expression and things of that nature. But art is really based on a rule of thumb. Art is allowing yourself to make mistakes, and when you're good enough, and you've got some experience, you really become an artist and you know which ones to keep. Going to school just teaches you the basics, the foundation of it. Only when you have mastered the basics, can you really be an artist and freely do what you're feeling. You'll know the ins and outs, and how it will affect whatever it is you're trying to do or express. In a lot of ways, learning the basics is essential. School isn't for everybody, and school isn't always the best answer to getting those foundations, but definitely learning those basics and mastering them is essential, no matter what you're doing.*

ONE OF THE COOL KIDS

Silver: *Once I transitioned into college, I was essentially just sur-*
rounded by like-minded people. Animators who wanted the same
thing. We had shared goals, shared aspirations, and the same inter-
ests. So, it was weird going there the first time, because back in one
school where you would kind of get punished or chastised for drawing
in class, you go somewhere where it's expected. It hit me when one of
my first professors was actually upset with us for not drawing while
he was talking. That was so weird to me. At first it was a hard transi-
tion, but over time, I realized it was the place for me and that I was
home.

*   ...With animators specifically, you can usually tell by the way*
they're dressed. That isn't a bad thing. There are certain habits that
you pick up in middle school, like 'oh I like this show' or 'I like this
artist.' So, I'll dress to replicate that. I don't want to sound mean, but
when I was walking around my campus, we have a great variety of
artists. We have photography kids, animation kids, film kids, graphic
design [students]. And an animator really sticks out, because he'll
have on a Pokémon shirt or something like that. At a certain point,
animators are super busy, so for most people - I'm not going to say all
- fashion is kind of secondary.

*   If you look at a film kid, they're always extremely well- dressed.*
It's like, "Okay, this person has a lot more time." It could be a mix
between time and interest, because I do know some pretty dapper kids
from my animation days. They're also really good too, so it's like not
only are they just killing it with the animation, but they also manage
to have the time - or the energy - to put effort into the way they look
every day. Towards the end of my thesis year, I was basically a stain.
I was just deteriorating in front of a computer. It was bad.

MY ART

Atisha: *[My drawings] are basically about this alter ego I created, which represents me, and she's going through life living as a hybrid. She's experiencing certain things that I've experienced. I use that as a premise for the drawings, and most of them are done with pen and ink. I use blue ballpoint pen to make the people, blue is the color of their skin. Most of the rest of the drawing is the environment, so I use mixed media for that. Sometimes I use glitter, or patterns that I've gotten from the internet, or different textiles transferred on as photo transfers. Sometimes I use watercolor paint and different types of materials, but the one thing that remains constant is the blue ballpoint pen.*

Most of the people in the drawings are characters that I have come up with, and they are based off of people who I know or people who I'm familiar with. The environments are places that people would recognize, if you grew up in the Caribbean. The architecture, some of the plants, even certain types of clothing...I really don't know how to talk about them right now, because some of them are still in progress and I've been working on like five drawings at a time, just going back and forth...'cuz I don't just draw. That's the thing that I love to do the most within visual art, but I'm well rounded in a lot of different things like printmaking and sculpture.

NO LABELS PLEASE

Mikal: *I don't really buy into the sub-genres of hip-hop. Whether it's the conscious, or the trap rapper kind of thing. It's all creative art. Some people choose to do it one way and some people choose to do it another way. I don't think being a conscious rapper is better than being from the trap, because they're both spreading a message that people can connect with. The way that the conscious rapper spreads his message, some people may not be able to connect with it as well...I think in music today, it's heavily built off of the internet and it's heavily built off connections. So separating artists kinda kills what the genre is about and what the genre is trying to build, so I don't think rap should be separated like that.*

A FOOT IN THE DOOR

Safiya: *You know what's funny? I'm very passionate about writing, but I'm not passionate about award shows. But I want to be recognized for the work that I do. I want to be recognized for my talent because I believe I'm talented. I still have a long way to go, but I've also come a very long way. I feel like - if I continue the way that I'm going with receiving help and getting advice from people who are higher up on the talent bar than I am - I feel like I'm most likely to win an award of some sort for my writing. I'm sure there's some kind of award!*

I recently went to the Writers' Guild East and spoke to one of the people who work there...and I was expecting her to be like, "Listen, you gotta have a certain amount of merit to even be in this office." Honestly, she was very welcoming. The people who are in charge, they're not what you think they are. How do I say this? It doesn't matter what you're doing, you're always going to find a place where, in order to get higher up, there will be some people you have to talk to. There'll be some people you've got to network with. And it's always a bit intimidating to do so.

That's the kind of feeling I had when I went in to [visit] the Writers' Guild for the first time. I kinda pushed myself to speak to some people - just to get some advice - and they were so welcoming. They all gave me their business cards. They were all just like, "Well, what do you do? How do you do this? Well we can give you opportunities to volunteer anytime!" It was just like, wow, I didn't think it was going to be this easy to just talk to these people. I'll say this, if you feel like you have a talent and you're passionate about it; don't be afraid to walk up to somebody who is your idol, or somebody who is in a position of power who can give you advice, or someone who is just generally higher or above you. Because if you are in a place where you don't have a lot of knowledge, people are willing to give you the knowledge. People are willing to help you out, because they want to see what you become. They actually do care.

Before I went in to [visit] the Writers' Guild, my mindset was that, 'it's probably going to be hard for me to get my foot into the door, because people aren't going to care about little stories that I write at 4 o'clock in the morning. Nobody's going to care about that.' But it turns out, they actually sit with you. They actually help you. I just say all that to say this: Just don't be afraid. Just walk up to them. It's not as big of a deal as you think it is. You'd be surprised at how far you can get by just not psyching yourself out and making yourself nervous about it.

REALITY CHECK

Quaneesha: [The biggest misconception] is that they'll get discovered within a year. The biggest thing is, "Okay, I'm acting. You know what, let me go audition. I know I'ma get that role." It's the expectation of getting a role. Check yourself. Because you will spend so many days sad and thinking twice about what you want to do as far as acting if your only mindset is: you're going to go, you're going to get this role automatically, you're going to become this famous actress that everyone will bow down to, you'll be on red carpets...everything that you think of.

That's where I started. You start picturing yourself on the red carpet, [thinking about] who you're going to take on the red carpet...then you don't get the role and your dreams are shot down, kind of. So, it's *like a reality check. I just think that that if you're coming here [to New York City], it's okay to have goals, but don't get upset if you don't accomplish those goals right away. Because it's so easy to think that just because it's New York and there are so many acting opportunities out there, that you're going to be discovered immediately.*

Shanai: *I'm an artist first, so my life is visual. So, I rely heavily on inspiration...Everything inspires me. It could be the weather. I love walking, being outside, and interacting with what's around me. It could be a visual image. I'm the kind of person who looks for that...My art is my outlet. If I'm in a place that I can't exactly articulate or don't understand, art is how I get those feelings out without having to put it in words.*

That's what I try to help with when I come in contact with children, is giving them that outlet to express themselves in ways that they may not want to articulate. They can know sad feelings, or confused feelings, or happy [ones], whatever they may be; and being able to get it out without having to say it all the time. Everyone has their own outlets, whether they recognize it or not. It may be working out. It may be art. It may be music. It may be the way you do your hair. There are just so many different ways adults are able, but I think we need to rely on those things more as outlets, rather than letting every single feeling build up inside, you know? We all just need more outlets in life.

WHAT I HAVE FIGURED OUT

Ethan: *As you create, what I would say is absolutely necessary is to be excited. I think a lot of people start off that way, and as they're going, they'll lose the excitement.*

And here's the thing about excitement, especially for creatives: Say you're a music producer or an artist, or whatever you're doing...when you're excited about it, and you're dying to show somebody, you know you've got something. You know it's something great. Have you ever seen an interview with an artist, and they're just like talking about, "Yeah, the album is going to come out, whatever, whatever"? They're not too ecstatic about it, then you go listen to it and it's not even that great. Like you know when they're like, "Nah, this is a classic! This is that fire!" When they believe it to that degree, it may not exactly be what they say it is, but there will be something there. There definitely will be. So, I believe excitement is the thing. And [laughing] can help with that, or be part of it. For me, it helps me keep the excitement alive.

...What I find is that people get discouraged a lot, and they're so unsure of themselves. They're always looking for outside validation. Now when it comes to art outside validation is somewhat necessary, but the thing is, it starts with you. 'Cuz art is an emotion. I always tell people this. Art is an emotion. When you start to think about it first, before you go into how you feel about it, that's when it becomes...weird. Like if [the people] don't feel it, they're not going to be able to appreciate it as much as they [could]. That's why certain artists will always reach the people in ways that other artists can't. You feel it, and that's what people want at the end of the day. Despite how intellectual or whatever it is, they want to feel it, that's how we connect.

Hello World

See, and be seen. The rapid pace at which life-changing products have been delivered to the world by our wizards of technology has been matched only by the pace at which people around the world have found innovative uses for those products. Silicon Valley invented products we never knew we needed, and the rest of us invented solutions to problems they never knew we had.

The innovators, investors, and institutions behind the evolution from the static HTML pages of Web 1.0 to the user-generated and shared content of Web 2.0 understood that people wanted the ability to engage with others directly. We were not content with merely being consumers of the images and information packaged for us by the professional media industry. We were frustrated with having the ceiling of our creative expression set by record labels, movie studios, TV networks, and publishing companies. We had an unsatisfied desire to be seen, to be heard, and to be understood.

This is particularly true for many people who live as members of a marginalized and devalued group within a larger society. People who grow up as children in these groups adapt by developing a unique form of sensory compensation, where their imaginations expand to enable them to envision a future for themselves which they cannot see in the current state of their daily surroundings. In fact, their imaginations have to expand so much that they not only can envision themselves in roles they have never seen in real life, they also have to be able to imagine themselves not recreating the stories that have been told about their group.

Many people are able to go out into the world with a blank slate and write their own story. Others enter the world with a slate filled with negative stories about them, and they have to learn how to erase and write at the same time. For these people, the ability to see the world with their own eyes, and to *not* be seen by the world through the eyes of others, is an invaluable gift.

Through the use of social media, millennials in marginalized communities around the world have undertaken the largest rebranding campaign ever. They have not settled for playing cultural defense on social media, limiting their online engagement to the work of explaining their identities, contending for their humanity, and attacking their perceived enemies. Instead, they are playing offense by celebrating their heritages, expressing their creativity, and exploring their curiosities. As a result, even before they board a plane, train, or boat to visit a foreign land, many millennials will have had more exposure to the range of human life in the country they are visiting than any other group of young people in history.

We now have the ability to do better than knowing capital cities, flag designs, famous landmarks, and government leaders. We now have the ability to know other people in their full humanity, and to be known by them in our own.

WHY I WENT

Joshua Jackson: *Jacksonville, Florida just seemed so small to me - no offense to anyone from Jacksonville! That is my hometown. But at that age, at a young age, maybe 9 or 10, I always wanted to see what else was out there other than just my hometown of Jacksonville. So* that's why I ventured out and started taking trips across the U.S. and eventually got my passport. I've been to London, I've been to Paris, and recently I was in Australia for two weeks on vacation for New Years. I love to just go places where I can free my mind, turn off my phone, and not really even listen to music. Sometimes I just want to be by the ocean and just hear the waves as I'm writing in my book near the sand.

Massamba: *It's priceless to travel. I think it's one of the biggest gifts you can have in your life. Each country has their own culture. So sometimes when you travel, you get to see a culture that is totally different. You get to see people who have different mentalities, different routines, different values, and different views of life.*

When you travel more and more, you get to find yourself. For example, sometimes you can have a hard time living in your own culture, but when you travel you see people with different mentalities, you see people who you can fit in with. You just learn a lot by traveling. Even if you don't envy them, just by seeing how they live [and] what their mentality is, you get to grow.

Noor: *A lot of people travel, and they don't really mix with people. Like, they go out, they study, but they only make friends with people of their nationality. They eat the same kind of food, they don't go anywhere except to their college, and then they go back home.*

So not traveling doesn't [just] mean being locked in at home. It could also be travelling physically, but not mentally or spiritually...I have met very few people who are of a similar mind [on this topic]...people who travel to discover themselves, to learn more about the world, to learn more about different cultures and all of that. There are few of these people really. The majority of people travel so that they can let go and just enjoy themselves - which is okay - but to me traveling is all about a whole change and discovering yourself. Discover-

ing at least one part of yourself which you had not found, or did not know existed, before you traveled. For me, when I go back to Saudi Arabia, or wherever I go back to, I always think, 'what did I learn from my trip this time? What did I gain from this trip besides the contacts and people I met?' There has always been a part of myself that I have learned about. This has been the treasure of every trip I take.

WHAT I EXPERIENCED

Joshua: *In the spring semester of 2014, I studied abroad in Strasbourg, France. It's in the eastern region of France right next to Germany. Germany is literally a 10-minute bike ride away, so that was pretty cool. During my breaks, I would visit other countries. I went to Porto, Portugal...Berlin, Germany...London, and Paris. So, I was able to get a good European feel...When I traveled abroad, not only did I get a better sense of Europe, but I also felt like I learned a lot about myself. I'm a shy person, so I learned how much I like to just explore areas by myself. Just take it all in. I also got a better understanding of how people from other countries view Americans.*

Raven: *I think that being abroad restored my sense of adventure. Mainly because it was nice to wake up one day and not be in the same place where you were yesterday. That's kind of what I wanted my life to always be. Not necessarily location, but just [my] mindset. That when I wake up, I'm not the same person I was. I've learned. I've grown. I've aged...unfortunately!*

In my time abroad, I went to eight countries and about 12 cities. This was within a four-month period. So almost every weekend, I would be in a different city or country. I went to Paris. I went to Geneva. I went to London. I went to Berlin and Prague. I went to Amsterdam. I went to Tarragona, Spain. I was in Barcelona for the duration of our program. I went to Seville. I went to Girona. I went to a bunch of places. One thing that I really liked was that every day was a new adventure. So even if I was just in Barcelona for the week, because I had classes, every day was a day to do something new. And that's kind of the approach I've taken with my life now. Every day is a day to do something that you've never done before, or to do something that you have done before...better.

I used to be a couch potato...but [now] on the weekends, I always want to be doing something. I always want to do something that I've never done before. Yoga in the park, going to different places...like, in all my years [living in New York City], I've never gone to Governors Island. There are just different things that you don't even need to have a lot of money - or any money - to do. I had never thought about just looking up stuff [like] 'what to do in New York today' and actually go and do it. Before it would be like, "Oh I'm going home" or "I'm going to chill at a friend's house" or "You wanna go to the movies downtown?" That was what my weekends were. It wasn't anything special. But now I actually want to do stuff. I want to see different things. And I think that's what I enjoyed about being abroad, it restored my sense of adventure.

Massamba: *In my last year of undergrad, I did study abroad in Sweden. In Gothenburg, [about] three hours south of Stockholm. It happened because I was very much dedicated to my major. At my school, we had an exchange program with the college in Gothenburg. So, when I found out that they had an amazing program...when I saw that their program was much better than what my school had, that was the main [reason] I went there. Compared to my school, their program is much more comprehensive. They covered more topics and more areas.*

...[when I got to Sweden], my first thought was that it was actually so similar to the United States. Their culture is similar in a sense.

Not totally, but they have a lot of similarities. The second thing I noticed is that learning English is very good because I was outside speaking to all the people [there] in English. So, I didn't bother learning their language, it was okay to speak English. One thing that I gained from that, is that learning English is very valuable, because now pretty much anywhere you go in the world, if you know some English you will almost be able to get by with just that.

The other thing [I noticed] is that they have different practices in certain areas. For example, here [in the U.S.] if you go into a restaurant to use the bathroom, it's free. But over there, in certain places you have to pay to use the [restaurant's] bathroom. You go to the cashier and pay, and they give you the key. I also noticed that people [there] don't really like sharing rooms. For example, on their college campuses, almost every [student living in dorms] has their own room and their own bathroom. Most of the students...I would say about 85% of the dorm rooms [have their own bathroom also]. It's the expectation, it's their culture...it's not just how the dorms were designed. Even if you go into the classroom buildings on campus, their bathrooms are designed for one person at a time. They are more private in general.

Amanda: *Well I think a lot of Americans seem to have this notion that Europeans are more open, and are just more understanding of race...I think when Americans go to Europe, for whatever reason, they seem to think, 'oh, these people are going to be in all these interracial relationships, and they're just gonna be so excited about Black this and Black that.' For me, it wasn't very different. I wasn't any more Black, or any less Black, when I was in Paris. I was still regular me.*

I remember I actually had a little thing on the train with some police officers. We won't go into it but I remember thinking, 'whoa, these people still see my color before anything.' So that didn't really change. I think - especially when you go to Paris - the difference is that they speak a completely different language. So, for them, it's more [about] who speaks English versus who speaks French versus who speaks Spanish versus who speaks Arabic. It's strange because over there I feel like there are two different types of attitudes, especially in Paris. There's one attitude that's like, "Don't come here if you don't speak French. You're going to be embarrassed." They just don't understand why we would try to go over there and not speak even a little French. And then there's the attitude of loving English speakers, because there are so many English speakers in Paris now that it's bizarre.

Like America...on language...it's just...we suck. I'm sorry. They speak so many different languages over there. I mean, I went over there thinking that no one is going to speak English, and everyone speaks English. Everyone over there speaks English, and you're sitting there and you're trying to say a few words in French, and they're looking at you like "wow..."

I think that if you're an art person, that's where you need to be. If you're a fashion person, that's where you need to be. For me, it wasn't all that serious because I wouldn't identify myself as an artist. But I think for artists, for people who...that's how they make money...going over there would be a completely different thing than for a regular old joe like me who just wants to be a psychologist.

Salihah: *Just recently I was taking a trip to Puerto Rico, and I went with one of my friends. We also went with some of her friends, and I had never met them before, but we had the best time. That might be something that a lot of people are turned off by. Like, 'I'm going on a trip with people I've never met before?! There's no way that's going to happen.' You don't know what the dynamic is, and in your head, you kinda maybe get a little anxious about it, but I was willing to embrace it. I knew my friend, and I trusted her so whoever she brought along, I felt like those were people I could probably vibe with too. There were so many things that were different, but in the best way. It was a really amazing experience, especially for me 'cuz I don't really have the opportunity to travel that much.*

Technically Puerto Rico is a U.S. Territory, but it's not really in the States, so that was really my first time going outside of the States, and I was blessed to have that experience. One of the first things we did when we got there was go to the rainforest, and that was mind-blowing. We hiked one of the trails and it ended in this really beautiful waterfall. We were climbing around the rocks in the waterfall. We were taking pictures in the tower that overlooked the entire rainforest. It was just really, really beautiful and it was nice to be away from the city and to have a chance to be in nature and marvel at it. I don't think people really have the opportunity to do that too often.

Khalid: *When were deployed [in Japan] we had a curfew, so we had to be back on base by midnight. So, we could go out into town and stuff, but we had to be back at a certain time. And they were a lot more strict out there than they are here. Since we were in a foreign country, they always said, "a Marine is held to the highest of standards." So, we really had to watch what we were doing. We couldn't get into fights. We actually had to be on our Ps & Qs, because they weren't playing out there. They were like, "You will be back by midnight, or you will lose your rank. You will conduct yourself in a military manner at all times, or you will lose your rank." They were a lot more strict because we represent the United States of America. It's like, what the townspeople see of us, they think [reflects] what people are like in America. So, it was two-sided. Yes, I was in the military, and yes, I was a young Black man. In Japan, the only Black people there were the military people. There weren't Black men living in Japan with the locals and stuff.*

Jonel: *Actually, right now I'm in Morioka, Japan. I'm about two and a half hours north of Tokyo by train. During my senior year of college, I studied abroad here for four months and I loved it. I loved it so much. While I was here, I did a home stay. I did kind of like an internship where I taught English at a school, I was an assistant. I really loved it, and after, I learned about an opportunity where I could come back and do it full time.*

I've always wanted to visit Japan, which I did when I was in high school. And when I was in college, I studied Japanese and I was like, "Maybe I should study abroad, but I'm not sure. It's so far away, maybe I can just learn the language and be content with that." But then I figured that would be such a waste. So, I was looking at programs that my school had, and my school only has year-long study abroad programs, which I was really, really nervous about. And then my teacher mentioned to me one day, "Hey I know you're really nervous about going to Japan, but I think you should go. There's a shorter program available to you." And that's when I said, "You know what? Just do it. Just do it."

HOW I SEE THINGS NOW

Tobi: *I think traveling has definitely helped me with being more aware of other people's situations. I do look back [and think], 'my bank account really isn't how it could be if I didn't travel!' But I know that it has played a key role in who I am today. I've been able to live with different sets of people as I've traveled, meet different people, and kind of share in their problems and issues. Seeing the way they see the world, and the way they see life. I've been able to take that in, and kind of adjust the way that I deal with people and how I do things.*

Noor: *I think the more I travel, the more I realize that we really are all the same. We have the same concerns, the same problems...almost. The same things that make people happy, like falling in love or meeting someone who is great, or having great food. The same things that make people happy are everywhere. This is something that I'm grateful to know.*

Before I traveled, I always thought that people are so different, and that I would feel like a stranger. But I never, ever felt like a stranger wherever I went. I always belong to any place I go to. Part of why I am a journalist is because I really love to listen to people, and I try to understand why they do the things that they do. It is the same when I travel. I love to listen to people's stories, and then I try to understand their points of view in whatever they're doing. By traveling, you get to see different cultures, different personalities. You deal with people who you don't know and you have to trust, because you have no option but to trust, right? I always say this to my friends before they travel, and I always say this to myself when I'm traveling away from home before I go to sleep: The only GPS I have is not in my phone, but in my heart.

Our Generation

"They don't look like us."
"What are they doing?"
"They have it easier."
"What are they wearing?"
"They'll never know what it was like."
"What are they buying?"
"They think the world owes them something."
"What are they protesting about now?"
"They call that music?!"
"What do they want?"

Abook about this most recent chapter in our cultural history would be incomplete without a Top 10 list. In a list of the *Top 10 Most Annoying Things We Can't Get Enough Of*, Top 10 lists would have to be somewhere in the top three. Like a well-constructed comedy bit or song lyric, an effective Top 10 list expresses an underlying truth of daily life.

As it was for the generations of young adults before them, daily life as a millennial often involves oscillating between the inquiries and the evaluations of the older people in your society. On one hand, we love to observe young people's behavior. We monitor their preferences. We are fascinated by their speech and their style. We inquire about their opinions on the world.

At the same time, we are constantly evaluating and judging the young people in our society. We try to guide and direct their behavior. We spend a considerable amount of time and money attempting to shape their preferences. We are surprised, and occasionally horrified, by the words they use and the clothes they choose. When we discover that their opinions about the world involve changing it, we will use any and all means at our disposal to keep things as they are.

We can do more than talk at or about the young people in our society. If we truly care about the future, we must do more than judge and generalize; because although the possibilities are limitless, the resources are not. Millennials still only have one planet to work with, at least for now. They only have three living generations of elders to call on for support, at least for now. There are no more millennials coming. To paraphrase a popular cultural expression, *"they all they got."*

And now that their entire generation has officially entered adulthood, they collectively inherit that which has been passed down from generation to generation since the beginning of human history: Responsibility.

WHAT'S GOING ON WITH US

Massamba: *What I would like to see is that we come to a common [understanding] that we are claiming to try to build. Meaning that every community, whether it's African-American, White, or other cultures from other parts of the world; that we try to understand each other. And each community tries not to be offended and use their offense as an excuse to [isolate] themselves. That's what I would like to see, but I have doubts whether we will come to a point like that. I notice that the kids don't have that problem, but usually the problems come in when they get old. You know, the kids will become leaders one day.*

For example, I get along with people from other religions, other cultures, [and] other backgrounds. I get along with them fine. The problem is, once we are more responsible adults, now we will see that we have more responsibility. When you're 21-25, we don't have many responsibilities other than our bills really. We don't have any group, community, or a country behind us. When we grow up, we see, 'oh, now I'm representing such-and-such. I'm representing this culture. I'm leading this culture. I'm representing this part of the world.' That's where I see the problems [coming in].

That's what I see actually. I see many of our leaders, whether they're in politics, culture, or religion; sometimes I feel like they don't [reveal their true] selves. Rather, they are controlled by their communities or by their people. So sometimes you see a leader behaving a certain way, not because he wants to, but because he is somewhat forced. His community is expecting him to do so. That's why I say the problem isn't really with people themselves, it's something much bigger.

Neiko: *Well, for my generation and the generations after me, I feel [like] there are no civil rights leaders. We have the older people who've been in the game for a long time who are still out here trying to fight and do what they can for us. But...if we can come together and go out there as one, then I think that's going to do a lot more for us. Because we won't have a civil rights leader. Not a single one in my generation and in the generations to come.*

What [does] leadership look like? To me, a leader would be able to come to Chicago, take a look at what's going on, put a plan together; and try to come up with something that's going to take the kids off the street so they're not out there in the streets selling drugs, robbing people, gang banging, doing all that. Like back in the day, they had recreational places. Let's bring back some of those. Like we used to do at Judson [Baptist Church]. We had the basketball team during the summer, you know what I'm sayin'? We would go on different trips. Just to get us out of our environment. To show us something different. And that's what a lot of these kids out here need. But we don't have anybody to do that nowadays.

Aquillia: I think it's really what you choose to look for. Because in any neighborhood, in any generation, you can choose to see negative things all day and only point out those negative things. But I see my [students], and they have some really positive family stories. They have really authentic things about them that stick with them; and that encourages me, especially with my neighborhood.

But then you hear stories and you see things from our generation and you're just like, "What?! Like what on Earth are you doing?! That's not what we said we were going to do when we were little, like why are you doing that?" So, you kinda have that pendulum effect. But I feel like overall, the authenticity...actually it's something that I have been seeing grow more. I feel like people are really authentically showing how they feel about things. Our generation has gotten really good at being - when you actually speak to them - authentic about how they feel about things that are going on.

And again, not Facebook rants, not anything but actually sitting down and talking to someone and saying, "How do you feel about this thing that you've just heard?" Or, "What do you think we should do about this?" I feel like people have really genuine answers about that. And I feel like people are really forming genuine friendships and relationships because of that, which is a really, really cool thing...and the people who I'm around all the time always have plans for their lives that include other people, and they're setting goals. So, in my mind, I'm looking for positivity in those areas, so I'm seeing positivity. And I think that's how it goes for me.

Toshawna: *I mean, it's always good to be optimistic, but it's also good to be realistic. I'm optimistic [about] the unity [within] my generation, they're coming together. Especially with the inequality and the injustices that have been going on in New York [City], and throughout America for the past couple of months...years now. Seeing all the efforts to come together and to try to get rid of this attitude of hate and racism and all these other negative vibes, you know a lot of people share these values and share this want for equality and peace.*

And we can get there, but they have so many old heads and people who are stuck in their ways that have a say in most things, [since] the people who are trying to have a voice don't have the finances. And we know that money rules everything for the most part. There's a lot of work that needs to be done, but it starts from my generation becoming the leaders of the financial industry. At least those who share the ideas of hope and equality and unity and peace.

Shantel: *I'm hopeful that we will keep it going. That we won't get content and then not really strive for a true change. I know I'm not out there in the forefront with picket signs, yelling and protesting. I applaud those that are. I'm an observer, so I'm in the back. I'm watching, I'm reading the articles. I'm trying to do a little bit of my own digging and research so that when I do post something, when I do say something, I have some accurate information.*

It's easy to jump on the bandwagon of the trend to protest and change the nation, but it's hard to really do your research and get educated before you say something. So, I encourage us to continue, but we've got to really educate ourselves, and get educated on what are the best ways to break down that system. That system that is so negative, and so full of hatred. I know it's going to be a process and it's going to take time, but I hope and I pray that we continue to want to break it down, and not just be in this trending moment of the year to just post something and add a statement here and there. To really take our time, even in our homes, to really research and read true, authentic, articulate articles and gather information regarding how to truly change the system.

Casey: *It's kind of hard to [describe], because some of the people who I know or have come across in my life don't voice their opinions that much. But I wouldn't necessarily classify our whole generation as not being blunt about certain things. In terms of a lot of the issues within the African-American community in the United States, I can go on Facebook at almost any time and see people who I've grown up with, or who I went to high school with, voicing their opinions without holding anything back; and giving the realest portrayal of their emotions and feelings towards the subject matter. Such as the deaths of Eric Garner or Sandra Bland, and a lot of similar situations. So, I guess my generation does have people who prefer to stay back because they don't want to cause any trouble, but we also have a lot of people who seem to be on the front lines and ready to take on any person who is unaware of what's really going on.*

Rima: *I would like to see a level of understanding, because I see [people] being active and I see all that. But you find a lot of times, they think that because this thought is right, [they can] kind of shut down other people who haven't grasped the concept. So, somebody [might] say certain things, but you don't understand that certain situations led up to that. So, it's kind of this slight 'closed-offness' in their minds that kind of causes it to be like, "Yeah, you're right, but also your approach is wrong."*

Atisha: *I would never limit myself to just having Black friends because of whatever reason...[but] the people who want to be cut off from society or just want everything to be sugarcoated to fit into their comfort zone, those are the people I don't want to be friends with. I* can be friends with anyone, just as long as they have a sense of awareness and they don't just want me to censor myself and make everyone feel comfortable.

Nowadays, if you want to talk about issues that Black people are facing, you have to make every White friend feel comfortable and try to not say anything to them that's going to [seem] mean. I'm not here to make someone feel comfortable, and make them always happy with what I have to say and sugarcoat the real issue that I have to talk about...those are the kinds of situations that make me realize the difference between everyone. Not just the difference between Black and White people, the difference between everyone. If you really want to make a change, you will know that it doesn't just take Black people talking, or Black people speaking out about issues.

Casey: I guess some of us have seen enough, but I also think that having seen enough for some of us isn't necessarily enough for all of us. I still think that there are people out there who don't believe that racism exists, or that gun violence is an issue. [With] any social issue or injustice that takes place in America, they kind of just go, "Well that's just one case, we don't really need to move forward from this. It's just one isolated incident, everything will be okay."

And then you have people who are ready to stand up and figuratively go to war for their opinions and what they believe is right. Which is a good thing, but I don't think there are enough people like that yet. There are a huge amount of people on that side of the spectrum, but I don't think there are enough of them to create a widespread change yet. It's unfortunate to say, but I think it will take more incidents to take place before everyone gets on board. I don't even know if everyone will ever be on board, but hopefully they will be.

...I don't think there's been a unification of all these people. There are a bunch of people who are behind this movement or who are part *of this collective, but the collective hasn't gelled together yet. The other side - the hater side of the argument - they kind of springboard off of one another like a well-oiled machine. They come together very well, and they are successful in shutting down numerous arguments because they all unite. Whereas [the movement] side are together in smaller groups, but not yet all together the way that the haters are.*

Dante: *I think what happens more often is that people come together in large moments, and there appears to be a massive 'we'. But there are still sub-tribes, and there are still sub-communities and sub-networks that exist in every system, and in every country. I think social media is obviously a platform through which people are creating more passageways for information between their groups, and forming new groups too. The internet has always been that, but I think people have a naturally tendency to live in small groups and to operate in small groups during the majority of their time. But people mobilize too, you know? People mobilize to do big things at once, together.*

Katie: *I spent some time in AmeriCorps NCCC, and so that kind of started this journey of wanting to volunteer, and wanting to get others to volunteer. I think it's just such a lovely and wonderful experience. It definitely opens your eyes to other people and what they're going through.*

Every single time I'm at an event, some of the feedback that I get is that [the volunteers] want more interaction with the people they're helping. And I think that's just wonderful because they want to see the people they're helping, they want to interact with them, and that just causes kind of like a chain reaction of them caring about the people and their community and the situation that they're in. It's like, you can't just remain blind to what is going on, when you've actually seen people's faces. It causes an empathy that I think sometimes people lack.

Kiana: *This world is just yearning for a great change. Like it needs it. And I feel like with the heart that I have, I can make that change once I get to my level of success. I just want to change everything. I want to change the poverty in America. I want to change the bullying in adolescent years. I want to change the confidence that we instill in our children from young. I want to change all of that.*

I feel like a lot of us are...I don't want to say damaged, but I feel like [there's] something within our generation. All of us are always so...hurt. And a lot of that needs to change because it stems from when we're young...it's something that I observed throughout my years at school. Me personally, I know that on the outside, [when] I'm being social, people probably think that I'm the happiest person in the world and that I'm fine. But I'm honestly not. In this generation, we're good at covering up how we feel and not showing everything, and sometimes that can be detrimental, but I just feel like we're really good at hiding things.

Actually, I think social media has done everything to make things worse as far as communication. Like regular, face-to-face communication is so hard these days. I know sometimes I have really bad anxiety, like I get really nervous for no reason. But it's because we're always in front of phones or in front of our computers or something. We're not always talking to people, we're typing on our small keyboards, so it's hard to even talk to a stranger or a new person or stuff like that. I think we've kind of gone backwards as we've gone forward.

Erica: *One thing I've learned is that conversations with other people - transparent conversations - they're so amazing. There are so many people out there who can relate to what you've been through. But in the culture today we're so used to putting up the facade like, "Oh I'm fine. I'm good, nothing's wrong" and just going about our day. But if we truly took the time to open up to others and really get to know them, and the things they've struggled with, it's truly a tremendous help to learn and see their experiences like, 'oh, that's what they did.'*

Safiya: *Granted, I'm happy with where I am right now because I've come a long way, but there's a lot more that I can do. Every time I go on social media, I kind of like feeling that I'm not doing enough because it pushes me to do more. I believe that it's better to be positive about it and raise up people's success and congratulate them, because I feel like we're all winning as a team.*

Maybe that's just me, but I feel like...if she's doing good, then we're all doing good. That's how I feel. I don't really know how to explain that feeling, but that's just how I feel. In her doing that, she's inspiring others to do more based on what they want to achieve. Her every achievement is just another reminder that it's not time to stop, it's not time to be stagnant. It's time to be very aggressive about your dreams because this is the time you have to do it. You don't want to wake up and be like 40 years old and looking at those old Facebook photos and saying to yourself, "Wow I should have done something. Maybe if I had spoken to this person or gone to this event..." Shoulda, coulda, woulda...there's a whole bunch of those. You might as well do it now.

Raven: *I don't know, I think it's something about that halfway to 50 that just gets me. But you're not 30 yet, right?! And I feel like at 25, you probably don't know what your life is going to be. You might not even know what you really want your life to be, but you know who you are.*

And I think that's the big thing with me. After 21 years, I still don't know who I am. I think I know who I am, but I really don't know who I am. So, I can't really expect to be perfect, because I don't know what the perfect me is going to be, or what the perfect me is. It can be perfectly imperfect, but I still don't know what it is. You should never be the final version of yourself, you should always be striving to be something better. But you should still know who you are. Like, what do you stand for? What makes you tick? What makes you essentially you? And what doesn't?

Krystal: *I feel like one of the main things - and it's something that not only myself, but a lot of people around my age struggle with - is commitment. We say that we want to do this, and we want to help people, and blah, blah, blah...but we never pick one thing to be committed to. It took me a long time to figure out that you have to commit to something, or you're doing nothing. 'Cuz when you're doing all these little things, you feel as if you're making an impact and you're doing all this like, "I'm doing community service every weekend."...But honestly, are you really helping? What impact are you leaving by just doing things here and there?*

...Before you commit to anything, you have to know yourself. You have to know your strengths and your weaknesses and what you want. And a lot of people don't know that. So, they make decisions, and they dibble-dabble in different things because they see other people doing it. I feel like it starts to become this one big competition of accolades like, "Oh I did this!" And, "I did this on Saturdays!" And, "Every year at Christmas I do this," and blah, blah, blah...And you want to post it all over Instagram, and post it all over Facebook. It just becomes one big competition like, 'who is doing the most?' Instead of, 'who is making the most impact?'

The Heart of the City

I f you can make it *here*, we can make it anywhere. Many of us are familiar with the proverb, *"the grass is always greener on the other side."* We often feel its underlying message most keenly when we are thinking about where to live, especially when we're stepping out into the world on our own for the first time. It's easy to imagine that a more fabulous version of our lives awaits us in some other location, where the opportunities are many, and the worries are few.

For many young people, that other location is a large city. A city they've seen on TV and in movies. A city featured in picturesque Instagram feeds and glossy magazine covers. A city where their favorite entertainer grew up. A city where people are working and things are happening.

We believe that *there* will be better than *here.* Sometimes it is. Other times, we discover that *there* and *here* are more alike than we thought. We learn that constructing a life anywhere involves negotiating a series of tradeoffs; learning what you need to live, and what you can live without.

The essential question we each have to answer is: *What do I need in order to live?* For those of us who live in cities, the essential question is: *What do we need in order to live together?*

Can we live together if you have nowhere to live? Can we live together if I have nothing to eat? Can we live together if you are in danger on your block? Can we live together if I am only safe in my neighborhood?

Is it possible for us to live together if I spend money with you, and you spend no money with me? Is it possible for us to live together if you have offered charity, when I have demanded justice? Is it possible for us to live together if my presence is questioned anywhere, and your presence is welcomed everywhere?

Nationally publicized events in cities around the country in recent years should have disabused us of the notion that not only is the grass not greener, but for some Americans, there is no 'other side.' The living conditions which restrict people's experience of life, liberty, and the pursuit of happiness are present in every city in our country. As we have witnessed time and time again, many cities are only one tragic incident away from civil unrest.

The hope for this country lies in our life-supporting responses to the life-suppressing realities of people who live only a few zip codes away.

CHICAGO

Bernadette: *I think [the city] is misrepresented. I think the information that people hear about in the media, and that they're reading about; there's truth to [it], but that's only one perspective. As someone who grew up for a portion of my life in the city and a portion of my life in the suburbs, a lot of things that people are experiencing in the city from what you're seeing in the media were not my experiences in my life growing up here.*

Recently my husband and I traveled to Ft. Lauderdale, and when people asked, "Where are you from?" We'd say, "Oh, we're from the Chicagoland area." And you could see their expressions like, "Are you okay?!" And I'm looking at them like, "I'm good. My neighborhood is not what you'd expect. It's a quiet neighborhood. I live a nor-

mal life. There aren't gunshots ranging through my existence. I didn't grow up with that."

...So, when I hear people say different things - and yes there's truth to it - [but] how much more do you know about it? You maybe know about something that you've heard about a couple of different small areas of a large city. Have you ventured out to see what the other neighborhoods are like? Chicago is composed of various neighborhoods. There are so many surrounding suburbs. There are so many different parts of town. Someone's lifestyle in the Austin area of Chicago is not going to be the same as someone who lives in Hyde Park, and they're only about a 30-minute drive from one another.

So, it's all about, one - how that person is perceiving things in their day, and if they're having that half-empty or half-full perspective about their life. And it's also about what they're surroundings are. So, I just think people need to educate themselves more. People from Chicago get a little bit defensive when it comes to their city. We don't necessarily approve of the things that happen here, but...I know what happens in my city because I see a lot of local news that tells me, but I can't really say what's happening in your city, because I'm only going to see the major events. I'm not going to see the things that you may see on your local news. If someone from another city is informed about something that happens in my city, they're seeing the publicized event. They're not seeing the other numerous good things that are happening. All of the numerous organizations that are doing outreach to try to combat some of the problems. They're just seeing the big crisis at that moment.

Neiko: What do I see in Chicago? All I see is death around here. Death and negativity. And that's all it is out here. It's death, shooting, gang violence, and none of it is being taken care of. Living in Chicago, you try to be around positive things, because all I see out here is death and negativity. So, for that to change, we gotta have all these big time people...all the people who are from here...they've got to stand up for what's right at home before they can go out and try to correct something.

I was always taught, make sure your home is corrected before you try to do something else. With me being from Chicago, and we've got all these civil rights leaders and whatnot...home is not corrected right now. It's going down the drain. And it's sad to say, our government, they are watching this. And they're just letting it happening...What I would like to see in Chicago is people standing up for what's right here. Let's try to calm down some of this killing, some of this violence. Let's try to 'kill' that first, and then reach out to the other places. I mean, don't get me wrong, I'm all for them trying to help people, but let's start with home. Take care of home first. Once you take care of home, then you can do whatever you please.

Courtney: *I'm like a mixed basket on this one. I've heard - and have been using - the term 'Chiraq' long before Spike Lee got his hands on it, you know? It's really close to home. Obviously, it's not a positive comment, and certain groups of people in Chicago embraced it kind of as an expression of, "This is where I come from." You have to be built of steel to last in Chicago right now. You have to be fearless or 'savage' - that's a term everybody's using. It's kind of a source of pride for some, but I don't take it as such.*

I think that the climate in Chicago has been crazy the past few years, and it's getting consistently worse. My husband always reminds me that in the late '80s and early '90s, when the projects were fully occupied and all that, it was way worse. Gangs were completely overriding everything. So, in that perspective it's not as bad, but because we have social media amplifying everything, and you can log on to your Instagram and you can see people who you actually know who knew 'Pookie and them' who just got killed...it touches very close to home. But I think it's sad. It's sobering. It's scary right now.

Kevin: *Honestly, I'm seeing - especially with Chicago - it's nothing but negativity. It goes beyond that. We have people out here who are not doing what you're seeing on the media, what the media makes us think everyone is doing. The whole south side of Chicago are not hooligans. Numbers don't lie, you've heard that before, but they can be manipulated. So, with Chicago and how I'm looking at it, it's better than what it [seems], but it could be a lot better than what it is. It's not all about violence here. We have people that are trying to start up businesses. There are a lot of different good stories out here, but they're not [portrayed].*

If [I had to use] one word, I would say I see unfairness. The reason I'm saying this is because back in the '90s, the crime rates were much, much higher than they are now. But you would think that this was the most murders ever in the world, within the last couple of years in Chicago. But nah, in the '90s the percentages were much higher. One year it reached almost 600 killings in Chicago.

Right now, let's say a 14-year old turned on the TV and they saw the news that "in Chicago over the weekend there were four killings in 12 hours." Can you do a different story? I know that sells probably, and it has something to do with social media I guess. [Social media] does expand it, makes it a little more, and amplifies it a little. I just don't think it's fair how all the negativity is brought out about Chicago. I don't think the city is that bad.

James: *I'm finna hit two points on this one. First point: I see a lot of death. I see too much of it...not to be directed towards any race or [anything], but Black people want to march for everything. They want to march for everything that has nothing to do with [us]. But right here in Chicago, I think we've already had over 300 shootings in Chicago, and maybe 50 people have died [from] these shootings. They won't march for all the shootings that go on [mostly] on the south side of Chicago, but you'll march for something that happens all the way in*

Ferguson, [Missouri]. That has nothing to do with us. Why are you fighting a battle that's not even near you, but you won't fight the battle that's right here at home? There's a civil war going on in Chicago and you won't fight it. You won't protest against it, you won't do anything.

There are cops...cops are killing people. I'm a person who - if I was a cop - and I had a partner who was about to do something dirty or wrong, I would pull my gun out on them and tell them: "Stop. Stop, think about what you're about to do, because what you're about to do is wrong. If you break the law, I will turn you in personally myself." Because if you can't trust the person that's supposed to protect you, what kind of system do you have?

This place is a circle of death, somebody is always getting killed. Whether it's the person who is supposed to protect you from it, or you doing it yourself because there's too much hatred in the world. Everybody hates each other. There's no love anymore, nobody cares about each other because they're only worried about 'me, me, me...What I want. What I feel. What I need. So, I'm going to kill somebody to take what I want. Oh, this person did this to me, so I want revenge, I want to kill 'em. It's all about me.' We have a selfish generation…Nobody owes you anything. You owe everything to yourself. Everything. If you think [that if] you wait long enough, that somebody is just going to come and give you something, you're going to be waiting a long time because the only thing that's free is the air you breathe.

Maya: *There are so many terrible things going on in Chicago. So many terrible things that have gone on in Chicago. Police relations going back years, and now the relationship that police have with communities - mostly of color - not necessarily on the north side or the Gold Coast...but the relationship that police have with people of color is very discouraging in Chicago, and [in] the country.*

We see what's happening, and it's very easy to get so discouraged and be afraid. Which, I mean...I am. I mean to be very honest, I'm discouraged. It's very sad and unfortunate that we're at this point, that we have not evolved to a greater point. As citizens of this world, it's really unfortunate that money has become this thing that moves everyone and makes people really terrible. To be honest, it's very discouraging, but I'm so encouraged by the work that people are doing here in the city. That people are standing up, demanding that things change. That things aren't done on the backs of poor, working people...on the backs of people of color. People are demanding change. That corporations pay their fair share. That we have elected school boards. You know, those sorts of things.

Christina: *When I look out into the city...I was just posting about this the other day. I was listening to the radio and they were talking about how so far in Chicago, we've had over 1,000 shootings and it's only June [of 2015]. It kind of makes me nervous. Chicago is such a great city, but it's just like we have this violence that's going on and it's not even summer yet.*

That's why I feel like it's important to get involved in the community, and with the youth...so I guess that's what really stands out to me about the city right now. You know people are in controversy about the whole term 'Chiraq'...people have kind of compared the violence that's going on in Chicago to the war violence that's happening in Iraq. Especially in the hip-hop world, they have turned the name Chicago into Chiraq, to show all the violence and the shootings and the death that has been happening in the city...along with other things that are going on.

We've had closings of schools where [Chicago Public Schools] has combined a lot of different schools, so a lot of schools have closed. [And] a lot of closings of mental health facilities. Recently, there's been talk of closing a lot of homeless shelters, which kind of brings a lot of volume to the medical field. A lot of these people have nowhere to go, so they are coming to the hospital. I work at a small community hospital here on the west side, and we see a lot of psych patients, we see a lot of [people who are] homeless, we see a lot of drug patients. They know exactly what to say: "I have chest pains and shortness of breath," and they get a few days in the hospital. Then maybe like a month later, you'll see them again. And you can't really blame them because they don't have anywhere to go, and all those resources are being minimized.

So, I guess when I look at the city, that's kind of what I'm seeing now, just a lot of work that needs to be done. And I just hope that, in the medical field, I can make my mark because these people deserve quality care, and to be treated fairly also. So, I try to make that my motto when I'm dealing with my patients. I know it can be a struggle to deal with that patient population, but it's important that they get quality care and someone who looks out for them and advocates for them also.

Neiko: *I moved over into the Garfield Park area, that's an area in the city of Chicago. It's not the safest place, but it's not the worst place either.*

This is just how I am, because I don't want my kids to be involved or see the stuff go down in front of my house. There's a group of guys out here selling drugs right by my house - like right by my alley - and it dawned on me, 'I'm about to be bringing my kids in here.' I have a three-year old, a two-year old, and a one-year old. My three-year old is my son. He's the oldest and that age, whatever he sees, he soaks it in. I care about my life, but when it comes to my family, that over-runs everything.

So, I went to the group. I came at them respectfully and I just had a word with them. And I told them, I said, "Look I don't knock y'all for being out making your money doin' what you gotta do, but I got three kids I'm bringing in here. They're babies. Three, two, and one. I can't have what y'all doin' right here, I can't have them seeing this." *Because my son will try to mimic it, and he will soak it all in. And he will talk about this every day, you know what I'm sayin'?"* So, I said, *"Look y'all can keep doing what you're doing, but can y'all just move that down the block? Go across the street to the vacant lot?"* And you know, some of them were heated, but I guess the leader was like, *"Hey man, no problem. We got you. We're going to take care of that."* And I haven't had any trouble since.

Shantel: *I'm a suburban kid, so for me Chicago is this idea of fun. This idea of really good energy. Even now, a lot of good streetwear brands are from our city, and a lot of indie artists are coming up from our city. So, it's like you go to the city to get that. To consume that, to see that, to enjoy that. So, I see a lot of positive things from our city. I know that there are a lot of negative things that are put on the news, and shown across the nation about our city. And it's unfortunate. You can't hide it, you can't lie about it, you can't fake it. Especially the violence, and our politics. So, there's a mix of it, but I see a lot more positive than negative for sure.*

Katie: *I go out in the world and I say, "Oh, I'm from Chicago" and people are like, "Oh my gosh, like, are you okay?! Are you coming to live here?" I'm like, "No, I'm going back...I love the Chicagoland area. Hello America, it's okay. We are okay!" So, it's not the best, and that's because that is what's advertised.*

NEW YORK CITY

Toshawna: *I see everybody hustling to stay alive. I think that's syn- onymous with New York. When you say New York, you hear hustle. I'm saying that both literally and figuratively. The poverty rate and all these other negative, systemic issues are way too high. You can't go an entire day in New York without seeing at least five homeless people, in my opinion. Maybe a lot of them still hustle, or a lot of them have given up the hustle, but they still have to fight to stay alive.*

You have the people who work every day, which is also a fight; because I'm sure a lot of people don't really love their jobs. Maybe a few of them do, but I'm sure a lot of people don't love their jobs because they have to pay all these bills, and they owe so much because America is a country built upon debt. They owe someone something, and they have to hustle so they can keep their homes. Or make sure their families are fed. Or keep a roof over their head. Which is like everywhere, but in New York it's especially hard, you know? Especially being a commuter city, you have to travel everywhere, and everywhere you go you're processing so much. You're processing the poverty. You're processing sickness. You're processing all these things being sold to you via advertisements.

I don't know...when I look out at New York, I see people trying to be happy and have that American Dream, and I feel like it's really hard because you're fighting every day. And I don't think you should have to fight to be happy, it should just come naturally.

Devin: *In actuality, for the producers of tech - for your programmers and your hardware guys - New York City actually has a vibrant programming community. There are Meetups almost every other week. So, a Meetup - the name is taken from [the website] meetup.com - is where a group will meet up at an open space...we all just sit around and talk about what we're working on, share some coding tips, or things like that. Or it could just be a whole bunch of people hanging out at a bar after work for happy hour who just happen to share the same interests...but the cultural space is only one part of the equation. The other part is providing accessibility to practice these things.*

So, let's say a young person wants to learn how to write a [computer] program in C++, one of the staple computer programming languages. They wouldn't be able to do that on their own at their house, there would have to be a program at the school, or at a not-so-fairly funded New York City library. A library could definitely play a potential role. It's a central meeting space; there are tons of books available there. Also, you have the internet connectivity there, you have computers that can be used [in case] you don't have a computer at home, and it's not like a PC cafe where you have to pay by the hour to use them.

Erica: *I see two different [sides] essentially. On one side, I see a plethora of young people who are kind of lost in a sense, and are just aiming and looking for the answers, exploring so many different things, dibbling and dabbling in this and that. You know, just looking for answers in life. So, I see that side. Then I also see a more affluent side because of what I do for work, and the communities that I'm exposed to.*

Primarily the two communities I'm in on a day-to-day basis are Park Slope and Crown Heights/borderline Brownsville. Where I currently live is Crown Heights/borderline Bed-Stuy/borderline Brownsville. It's not far from the 'hood…where I live is actually two minutes away driving from the [youth] detention center that I go to every week. I moved here a couple of weeks ago, and that was kinda funny to me because I know the neighborhood now in Brownsville, where it's like projects, people hanging out on the streets, just all kinds of things going on. And then Park Slope, it's a completely different area. It's full of affluent people. Everyone is like…friendly.

…For example, I can walk down the street in Park Slope and give a smile to everyone, and they'll give one back. But if I'm walking in my neighborhood, I have to be careful who I'm smiling at, because you never know who is who. You have to have your guard up, so to speak.

Those are the two elements that I experience on a daily basis. It's very interesting to have two different worlds collide like that for me every single day. It kinda hurts me, in a sense, to see it. Again, I feel like it all boils down to that love factor. If we all just had that, so many things could be so different on so many different levels.

Joshua: *When I see New York City, I see a diverse, modern city. A city with potential, but I feel like it's far from perfect. I love the convenience of New York City, but there are a lot of issues that people don't really pay attention to because they're so enamored with it being modern and the fast pace of it all.*

In terms of Brooklyn, I see a small neighborhood that's misunderstood. When I tell people I'm from Brooklyn they're like, "Oh my gosh, you live in a ghetto" or, "oh my gosh, there must be shootings all the time." Especially when I tell them I'm from Bed-Stuy they're like, "Oh no, I feel so sorry for you. Like how are you still alive?!" And my personality is very reserved in a way and I'm like a kind person or whatever, and they have this mentality that everyone from Bed-Stuy is like...they know a gang member or something like that. It's like, "No, it's not like that at all. I was never in fear of my life." And I tell them, "Oh come visit me; everything is fine." The look in their eyes...it's like, "No, I can't do that!" It's funny and it's annoying, but I deal with it.

Ebonee: *The Bed-Stuy I grew up in was live! It was so nice. Nice sunny days, good people, good community. Not too much happening. You could always walk outside to a smiling face, [people] playing music, Biggie bumpin', reggae bumpin'...that's what my 'hood used to be. Man listen, I love my corner stores, the bodegas. Now they're switching it to all these cafes. All these [new] people, gentrification, I'm not feelin' it. I don't know about the borough, but as far as living in Marcy now; when people from out of state come to visit, they usu-*

ally tend to have this vision in their head that I know Jay-Z! That Jay-Z defines Marcy, and that is not the case at all! Living in Brooklyn, a lot of people assume that you have this persona, like you're 'hood'. I'm not really hood. I'm just like everybody else.

Faith: *I look out on my city and I see a lot of people doing positive things...we have that power, but there are not enough of us. For us to get to that ultimate goal for everything to be positive and for things to change, we all have to come together. We all have to start our own projects and our own forums and our own things in our little communities.*

Even if it's just in your apartment building, it starts at home. In your home, in your apartment building, families sitting down and just saying, "Hey, we're going to have a night where everyone sits down and talks about their days." Where everyone sits down and talks about something they would like to change in their lives. Even if it's something that's nationwide and they can't change it at the drop of a dime, but the fact that everyone sits down and discusses their situation and talks about it, I think that would be great. My city is not bad. We have a lot of crazy stuff going on, but my city has potential. It's just, how are we going to get there?

Kasim: *I was born in Kings County Hospital, so I could say that I'm from Flatbush, Brooklyn. I stayed in Flatbush for the first three years of my life. After that I moved to Crown Heights, where I currently live. I've been living there for the past 17 years or so. [Describing] Crown Heights...it would have to be a bittersweet kind of description, because we're going through a process that's called gentrification.*

For those who don't know what gentrification is, it's pretty much this process where people of higher income move into areas of lower income. Because of this, because of their higher [incomes] moving into this low-income community, this causes a boost in that particular economy. Which can actually [have] a negative effect on the people who originally resided in that area. So, it will cause positive things, like more businesses being opened, more food spots, there's going to be a safer environment...things like that. But the bad part is that, as a result of all the improvements, there's an increase in rent. And that causes the people who originally resided there...they can't keep up with all the constant rises in rent.

Say they were used to paying $1,000 in rent before gentrification. After gentrification, it might just go up to $2,500. And when they can't keep [up with] that, they're forced to move out, and in the worst-case scenario, they become homeless. That's why I say it's bittersweet. I see this every day. I'm currently living in it. Just about a month ago, we got renovations in our apartment and our rent had to go up. Just because of renovations, and we've been here for 17 years. But you're starting to see changes. Although there are better food spots and it's not as bad as it used to be, the fact that it feels like I'm adapting to this environment...I've lived in this environment for the past 17 years of my life, but essentially it still feels like I'm trying to adapt to this environment because there's such a change in the culture. That's the part that kind of busts my brain.

Khalid: *I'll tell you what I see in New York, since that's the place I most identify with. I see us [being] pushed further, and people who wouldn't have been there 10 years ago when I was growing up, are there now. I go home and visit, but I haven't lived there in four years. Then I come back, and I see everything changing, but I still see struggle. I still see me walking down the block from downtown Brooklyn to my house at two o'clock in the morning, and I'm still looking over my shoulder every time I cross the street, to make sure I don't get robbed. So, I still see a hunger, and I still see the struggle, but I also see hope. Right now, there's a Planet Fitness on my block that wasn't there two* or three years ago. So, I see progressive change, but I still believe that we can do a lot better.

I don't like the fact Brooklyn has become the new Manhattan...I'll give you an example: My grandma has a two-bedroom apartment. The size of the apartment...there are studios in Jacksonville, North Carolina that are bigger and you pay way less money [in rent]. You pay [around] $900 a month. For that little two-bedroom apartment that she lives in, she pays $2,000 a month. I tell you, the apartment is not worth $2,000 a month. There are houses out here that you pay $900 towards your mortgage each month, and you've got her paying $2,000 a month and she doesn't even own the building. It's just rent that she's paying, plus utilities and all the other expenses.

So, gentrification is affecting Brooklyn hard, like there are all these brownstone buildings there now, it [costs] so much money just to live in Brooklyn. And it's like, if I'm paying all this money, I'd might as well live in Manhattan because it's a different aspect [of the city]. That's what I mean when I say Brooklyn in the new Manhattan. Everything now....all the prices are going up; the rent is going up. All that stuff is telling people that we might not have opportunities as [people from] other races have, and now we're being forced to either leave New York, go to the Bronx or Queens, or just struggle every day to make rent.

I see the same struggle I saw when I left, and it's getting worse. But I also see hope in the sense that, even though everything is changing, there are plenty of Black people who still live in New York and are making ends meet. No matter what they've gotta do to make ends meet, there's still hope. I think that hopefully 10 or 15 years down the line, there won't be as great a struggle as there is now.

Janelle: I just really want to talk about Brooklyn in general. Right now, I'm kind of disappointed as to where Brooklyn is going...there's a lot of gentrification going on right now, and it's just really disap-

pointing to me. Growing up in Brooklyn all of my life, you just see it a certain way, and I see where this is going already. Now there are a whole bunch of people moving out. It doesn't look the same anymore. It just looks like this isn't even Brooklyn anymore, it's like some suburban sort of area that I'm just not used to. Even though gentrification does have its benefits, where it makes the neighborhood look much better, it's just going to keep happening where it's just going to keep kicking people out of the area.

...On U Street [in Washington, D.C.] I could definitely see that some of [the new residents] had just graduated from college not that long ago, probably grad school, and they had become the gentrifiers. And that's where you see...not even just White people, but you just see other races walking down the street too. And you're just like, 'you look very well-educated. You look like you have a high-paying job. Yeah, you probably graduated from college not too long ago or just left grad school, and you moved out here and you're moving out all of the people who were living here already. You are a gentrifier.' I could very well be a gentrifier to somebody else. I hope that I won't be, because I would hate that existence. To think that I could really push somebody out and displace them, that's a reality I would not want to deal with! Like, "Damn, I just put somebody out of their home."

Chelsea: *Now, living in Bedford-Stuyvesant, it's crazy because...I was away at [college] for three years. Of course, I came back home for spring break or winter break, but only briefly. So, I remember coming back home, I think it was winter break, I was sitting on my porch and I saw this little White boy on his skateboard with a dog, and it was about three in the morning. I'm like, 'okay, wow, this is different.' Now the corner store delivers. They have organic food. The buses are running on time. It's like a completely different environment. They're opening a bunch of different cafes with Wi-Fi. You know Kennedy Fried Chicken? That was probably on every corner in Bed-Stuy! Most of those are gone. I guess it's beneficial, because I can go to the corner store and get decent food. But that says a lot. Why weren't these places available for us before?*

Felice: *I think the thing I'm seeing that's breaking my heart is how much New York is changing. Being from somewhere, I guess maybe it's a human thing to kinda always want it to stay the same. You kinda gotta accept that stuff evolves and things will change. But every time I go back home, it feels like I'm not there anymore. It feels like I'm on a TV show or something. It's just so different. I'm starting to realize [that there is] a huge influx of New Yorkers coming down south, trying to get our own and make our own here, which I think is pretty cool.*

Erin: *I live in Bed-Stuy, gentrification is crazy out here. But at the end of the day, I still see originality. It's trying to come out of this concrete. It's trying to stay alive, and I'm here for it. But we need a couple of people to water this originality for it to stay fresh here in Brooklyn. That's my concern. Brooklyn is my heart forever. I'ma live here forever, I'ma die here. Hopefully I get buried in my backyard, I don't care. But I see originality trying to come back into place.*

What's Going On, America?

"What do you see?"

Our boys' varsity basketball coach paces along the court's sideline, walking parallel to our school's freshman point guard, who is slowly dribbling the ball towards half court. Both are calm and focused as our coach begins talking to the rising star. Everything around them, however, is far from calm. The outcome of this closely contested game has implications for the upcoming citywide playoff tournament. So, in the early evening of a late winter day in Brooklyn, this cramped New York City elementary school gym is hot and loud. Most of the fans - students, parents, teachers, friends, school principals - are standing along the painted brick walls and cheering. The visiting team's coach shouts instructions to his team as they set up on defense. Our point guard crosses the half court line and pauses.

Some of my favorite memories from my years of teaching came during the school's basketball games. They were hierarchy-flattening, egalitarian settings where the focus on victory, and the prerequisite of enthusiasm, was distributed equally among all in attendance. Basketball games allowed the various members of our school community to see each other - and be seen by each other - in a new light. The head coaches of our girls' and boys' varsity basketball teams were each standout high school and collegiate athletes, and could have rested on the laurels of their personal achievements in their approach to coaching.

But they were teachers.

At most high schools in our country, coaches are teachers of the game. Coaches work to help their players develop fluency in their understanding of the game. They assist players in translating lessons from the game into lessons for life. At the high school level, effective coaching is often evaluated in the same manner as effective classroom teaching. In high schools, and in K-12 education more broadly, effectiveness is not determined by the pedigree of the teacher or coach. It is not measured by what schools the coach attended, or by how many degrees the educator has accumulated. Effectiveness is not measured by a teacher's physical appearance or economic status.

We measure effectiveness by what our young people are able to produce. When a player can analyze game situations, in real-time, under pressure, and make the right decisions; then we say that the player has been well-coached. When a student can apply the critical thinking and communication skills they practiced in the classroom to develop responses to real-life situations; then we say that the student has been well-taught. The goal of parents, teachers, and coaches is to move young people from simply answering the questions we ask them, to asking the questions they will seek answers to.

The questions our young people choose to ask will determine the society they choose to create. The questions from our young people that we choose to ignore will reveal the limitations of a society that chooses to not be exceptional.

What do you see?

STAY WOKE

Jasmine: *Definitely, the way I see the world has changed. That's in light of everything that's going on. When I was younger, I used to think America was like the greatest country in the world, that it was the best place to live in, and that I loved being an American. But now that's kind of changed a lot. Like America really isn't as great as I thought it was. I think that just comes with growth, and being more aware and socially conscious. It's not this big, picture-perfect world that they paint it out to be.*

And that's another thing, I think in history class - or any other class - they paint America to [be a place where] we have all these rights, and all this freedom...when really, that's not the case at all. I don't know how to describe it, but I'm definitely seeing the need for change. In the sense of the justice system, the laws...everything. There needs to be a serious change in the country. I don't know exactly what it's going to take, but it's something that needs to be, and needs to be done soon. But it doesn't happen overnight.

I wouldn't say that I'm optimistic, but I do see the potential. I see a lot of people in my age group who are stepping up and taking a stand against injustice - organizing and protesting and stuff like that. So, I see the potential. I just think we need more people to kind of band together and get on that bandwagon. I think it will happen, eventually. We're going to get it together.

Ethan: *I see for the first time in a long time, people are starting to be honest...What I feel is happening since it became the Internet Age, is [that] everything the country's been hiding or trying to cover up, it's coming out now.*

...A lot of people were under the misconception that "Oh, you know, everything's all sweet and we're past that." And this was a wake-up call like, "My brother, no it is not! We're not doing as well

as we think, beloved." We've got to get it together. Things are not always what they seem, and this proves it more than anything.

It is an eye-opener, 'cuz a lot of people don't travel to other parts of the country. If you just go to Texas or Louisiana, and you go to the right neighborhood, you'll see these kinds of people. You'll see these things. A lot of people just don't know. It's a good thing, and a bad thing.

...I feel like the change isn't necessarily in the election. Like, yeah, we get a new president and whatever but they're only there for four years. I don't know, I just feel like the change is deeper than a presidency. It's the people, at the end of the day. I feel like we gotta make change in the people. Anyone who's striving to really make a difference, like yeah go out and vote, but do something too. To me, voting just ain't enough. That's not changing someone's reality. Like it may change [for] the few, or certain things may affect certain individuals, but I'm talking like going to this town and directly affecting the lives of people. I want to be on that level, that status. I would just hope that more people of my generation will see the youth as the gold mine for change for the future. They are the future essentially. That's where it all starts.

Felice: *As of right now, I feel like we're in such a weird place with the whole political thing that's moving about. Not even so much with where these politicians stand, but the fact that where they're standing is bringing out the real kind of mindset of the nation, and kind of exposing how they really feel and what they've been trying to keep under wraps, [but] can't keep under wraps anymore. I think it's kind of bringing the nation into - how can I put this? - into a different type of view.*

Amanda: *For me, I see a world that is going to change very, very, very quickly. A lot of things are about to happen. We're about to get a new president. It just seems like every single day there's a new thing with terrorism. So, I feel like things are about to pop off, and some people are not going to be ready for it, and others are...if they're fortunate enough.*

We already see bits and pieces of it, like how technology is just booming. We're not in Kansas anymore. This is not the [1930s]. We are just on a whole different playing field with the amount of technology that we have and how advanced things are. And I think that all those advancements are going to lead to really radical changes. We live in a world where you can't even get a job without a master's degree anymore. Like, you can't work at McDonald's without a college degree. So many things are changing. It's pretty radical.

Phillip: *I need to be on top of what's going on in the world, what's going on in the community, what's going on in different cities. In this climate right now, with the value of life, whether it's civil rights, human rights, Black Lives Matter...it's a new narrative now from our side, from the side that I am more conscious [of], that I can relate to. And there's another side that's saying, "No, all lives matter," and [they talk about] black-on-black crime, and Black lives vs. Black Lives Matter.*

I listen to a lot of talk radio. I do. I listen to...what the callers are saying...I still want that conversation. At least I want to be aware of it. Because if you are not aware of the conversation, that can hinder you. Information is power. Obviously, so much information is hidden in books that are put in libraries, or information is hidden on the internet. If we're not aware of it, how can we create change? How can we teach children? How can we be active in our community?...There's so much and we need to have the facts. We need to be believable.

Massamba: *Right now, I think there's a big misunderstanding and disconnection at the same time. I think the world is clustered into different groups. You can say [the groups are] the developed countries, the developing countries, and the Middle Eastern countries. That's how I see the world being clustered. I feel like each one of these three groups has misunderstandings about the other groups. I don't think we fully understand who they are and what they mean.*

I also believe sometimes we try - on purpose - to not understand them. Each one of us, we try not to really understand the other groups. And the globalization that we claim, I don't think it's something that we are really trying to do. Each one of these cultures thinks that they have the right lifestyle, the right culture, the right religion, and the right views. I think that's the main, if not only, reason why we have this disconnection.

For example, when I recently traveled to Senegal, they fear that if they keep coming to the U.S. or to other developed nations that they will be changed...that they'll be Westernized and will forget their values, cultures, and religion. If you go to the Middle East, many of the people think that coming to the Western world, or to developed nations, means losing yourself and losing your values. If you look at it from the standpoint of living in the U.S., I think that we kind of look down to other [cultures]. Even if we don't say it directly, I think that we have the sense that they are under-developed, that they are beneath us and should leave their culture and values. So, each one of these [three] clusters...if you go there, they don't want to associate with the rest. I think that's the main difference, each one of us thinks that they are better than the rest.

Bernadette: *I know other people look at this country as a land of opportunity, and that there are so many different opportunities to do things. But people didn't show up in this country to deal with the same things they could have dealt with back home. We didn't get sent* to this country, and helped build this country, for us to not even be looked at as important in this country. So, it's sad.

We just had a Fourth of July, everybody's watching red, white, and blue...but...there's not a sense of belonging. There's not a sense of pride anymore, as I may have felt 10 years ago. I understand that people say, "Well crime was happening then too, but you didn't hear about it because of social media and other things." But there has been some sense, to me, that things are getting worse. And it's just sad because, as you get older, you just don't think about it in terms of yourself, you think about it like, "Do I want to raise a child in this city?" What if I have a son and I have to explain to my son at six years old, "[This is] what you need to do if this happens"? That's something that you shouldn't have to tell kids. There shouldn't be a difference between a kid that grows up in one suburb, and a kid who grows up in a different suburb. It shouldn't be that way.

It's an issue of fear for some of us, but it's also an issue of not hitting home yet for others. But the key word there is 'yet'. So, it doesn't matter to you right now, because you're not burying your family member. Then when it's your time to have to do so, now you want everyone to feel bad for you, but you didn't care when it happened to someone else...It's disappointing.

It doesn't mean that it's all bad, because there's a lot of good in the world. There are a lot of people committed to making change and doing better. We don't hear as much about all those people because they're getting overshadowed by the cuckoos out here who want to consistently do damage to our world. Maybe if we focus more on the positivity, people could see that more and people can copy that behavior.

Joshua: *Racism has been an issue since forever, and it's still an issue. People like to say, "Oh we have a Black president so racism is over.*

Let's stop talking about it." But that's just not the case. The way I think about it, racism didn't go anywhere. It evolved.

When we have an event, something like a shooting by a White person...you see the media, they describe them as "confused youth who lost their way and who needed help" or whatever. But when someone like Mike Brown or Eric Garner or Darrien Hunt, when they're shot and killed, the media describes them as 'thugs'. It's those sorts of ways where we feel like racism has evolved, and it's right there in the open, but people will find ways to justify the death of a Black person, and they will humanize a person who shot up an elementary school. That's ridiculous...What happens to them, could happen to anyone.

When Trayvon Martin was shot, Mike Brown was probably watching the news thinking, 'that could be me.' And it was him. Just because something happens miles and miles away doesn't mean it doesn't affect you. You can't just not care. I remember I was in school and there was a Black Lives Matter protest, and some girl was just like, "Oh these protests are so annoying, you know? Traffic is stopping, I just wish the protesters would stop, they're so annoying." And I so badly wanted to respond to her, because the whole point of a protest is not to be convenient, it's to gain awareness. And you're not going to gain awareness if you're stuck behind barricades. I just feel like you can't just not care. This is your country. People are suffering. You have to speak up about it.

Kiana: I'm seeing a lot of destruction, and I mean that in all aspects. Whether it's [a certain presidential candidate] and the whole campaign and nonsense that goes along with that. Or whether it's the fact that I feel our Black lives are not being as valued as they should be. Especially for all the contributions that Black lives have made to this country, for them to treat us the way that they do, I feel like it's really disgusting. I feel like there's a lot of destruction in the world right now that needs to be fixed. Like it needs to. It's ridiculous.

Haniyyah: *And it's interesting because now that I'm an adult, and in school of course you learn about all the things that happened in history, and now it's like I'm a part of history. And you're finally understanding what it's coming from. And it's like the same things are happening all over again. I think seeing it in real life, everyday...the injustices...that's what I see. That's what I'm living. That's I'm breathing. But then I'm also seeing a lot of positivity, and the people who are doing great things. You see it, and they shine, and you see through the conversations that they decide to have, and all the movements that are happening and, you know, a lot of people are very impressed with us millennials now that we're talking about these things on social media! We're starting all these hashtags and now the old folk wanna be down with the millennials, and talking about the hashtags!*

Maya: *That's very encouraging to me, to know that we have people organizing in Ferguson. I mean I really hope that we're able to sustain that momentum that's going on, because I think we're on the precipice. I think people are really starting to realize and understand that, no, everything is not okay. If this is supposed to be it, then we're not there because there's still so much work to do. I think people are finally starting to realize that it's not just okay because we've got [President] Barack Obama...What does that mean? That means that can't be the end-all, be-all. That means that we're not at the promised land.*

I think we think of our country as being so post...everything. And we're not. I mean, we're not 'post' it, we've just put it in a closet...we've kind of shoved it away. We wanna gloss over it, but the thing is, there are those differences. And we have to acknowledge them, and we have to do meaningful work around that.

Kasim: *I guess you're starting to see society become more aware of what's going on. I'm starting to see more moves for the better. It started from seeing a Black president get elected. That's something that people never, ever thought would happen. It's a privilege seeing a Black president be elected. Kinda bitter that it's his last run, but now we could see a woman in the White House. So, we're starting to see changes.*

We're starting to see more versatility, and this could speak volumes because people could look at that and be like, "If a Black person and a woman could be president and could run America, the country that is so used to Caucasian presidents, then I could do that." It's definitely possible, but it would be harder to believe that if you only see Caucasians being presidents over and over again, especially as an African-American or any other race or whatever.

[Even with] the negative things too, it's starting to become obvious...with the killings like Eric Garner and Trayvon Martin - you know, brothers like that - you're seeing the police brutality. You're seeing that it's pretty much like racial profiling. That could speak volumes because we're starting to be aware. We are on the backburner of society - us as African-Americans - we're at the bottom of the food chain. They're out here to get us. I feel like that's powerful because we could really convert that, and come together. Hopefully if we see that everybody's against us, we'll know that we have to be there for each other, so we can take each other to the next level.

I guess seeing all these changes, and seeing all these events happening right in front of our faces...You see it every day now. It's almost like the curtain has been opened, we just see everything now. We're more aware, so now it's up to us to make that move. And I think that since we're more aware of what's going on, we have the ability to make the move, or at least we have the motivation and the reason to make that move. You would think that leaders like Dr. Martin Luther King and Malcolm X - people who sacrificed themselves to get us to where we're at now - from then we should have been aware. I guess it took longer than it was supposed to, but at the end of the day, now we're clearly seeing it. Hopefully now we make the move that we're supposed to.

Krystal: *What do I see now? I'm not even sure. I see a lot of people who...I could say that they want change, that they would like to be a part of change. I would say that they want to uplift. I feel like, as a country, we have so many wants. We want everything to happen right now.*

We're getting impatient and we just want to see results, but I still see that we're focused on ourselves. What I'm trying to say is that I don't see a holistic view. Like even though everyone likes to say that they have a holistic perspective, I feel as if each and every day we don't act in that way. We act individually. If it doesn't pertain to us, if it doesn't affect us, if it doesn't have an impact on us, then we turn a blind eye to it. But when it does affect our community, or has some- thing to do with someone that you personally know, then that's when we're gung-ho and ready to go. For a period of time, of course, be- cause it just seems to fall off.

I feel like that's where we are now. I feel like people are noticing that, but it's like, how do you change that? Because everyone is doing it. No matter what, you're going to care about yourself and your family and things like that. We're not thinking of a holistic view of how to help America and how to help everyone. We're not acting in that way. Because no matter what, we're still more concerned about the things that affect us.

Silver: *I see people who struggle with communication. Communica- tion is very important. It's just like [what occurs in] interpersonal relationships, people are struggling to communicate with the world around them. Whether language barriers or cultural barriers, there's a lack of communication.*

I would know, because I struggled with that. Communicating was very hard for me, and I realize now how important being able to talk to someone is. Not saying this 'at' them, but being able to get a message 'to' them. Hearing what they have to say, being able to transfer those ideas and understand them for what they are, and being able to work past whatever conflicts or issues [may arise]. Right now, there are a lot of people who are just saying things at each other, who have these messages that they've told themselves are true and correct. And they won't necessarily accept anything else. They say those things over and over again, and they're not necessarily communicating with it, you know?

I'm not really sure how we can get the world to start communicating more...What I would love to see, is people communicating. People being able to say what's on their minds, say what their real problems are, and just be able to listen to others. It's very important. I can't stress that enough. I know what it's like to not be able to communicate with the people who are very close, and I regret not being able to talk and listen.

The older I get, the more I realize that other people are just other versions of you. They have their own problems. They have their own desires and goals and inspirations. I regret not being able to hear them out for who they are, because when you've created a story for someone, you've kind of destroyed them in a sense. Or at least destroyed who they are...their truth. You've kind of limited yourself from understanding who that person is. And there are a lot of situations in the world...I'm not the most political person, but I think that anyone who has a conscience, or a state of mind, or a state of being, can know that something's not right.

Malika: *I see something that's broken. Something that needs a sense of unity to fix. Something that there's no universal language for, that people are trying to fight against. I feel there are a lot of things that were previously deemed out of our control, that citizens are realizing that, 'no, we are the people who can change this.' I'm seeing a shift of consciousness...I think that consciousness was always there.*

I mean you go to a young Black boy, he can probably say, "Oh yeah, this kid said he doesn't want to be my friend because I'm Black." There's his first experience of racism. So, they have an understanding, but they don't have the language yet. And I feel like that's the case for a lot of situations in a lot of underprivileged areas – where they see what's going on with them but they don't have a language for it. Or when they try to express that language, it turns into this horizontal oppression where they're not harming those above them, they're harming other people within their same group. Because that's the way that they're able to kind of overcome themselves and their own pain. There's so much potential for something more. I can see that.

Chelsea: *One of the biggest things that I see is that people aren't really aware of what is going on around them. The lack of focus on mental health issues, especially in the African-American community...I really wonder, why aren't mental health issues treated? For instance, if someone had cancer or diabetes, there is so much more importance placed on that. I think that your mental health should be just as important.*

The people you see on the train just talking to themselves or running up to people, and it's normal. It's like, 'oh okay, this person is just crazy, it's alright.' But it's not okay, you know? Just looking out [at the society], that's one of the biggest things, the fact that we ignore it. I think your mind, your brain, your mental health, is like one of the most important things. Yet, it's one of the biggest things that we just neglect as a community.

Dante: *I'm less concerned about 'sticking it to the man'. I don't really have that same sense of 'stick it to the man and show them what's up.' It's important to get in the practice of having your voice heard, but I also think change is a more collaborative process than 'you just gotta show them what's up and they'll back off and then they'll change things' Nah, I don't think there's a 'they' out there, I think there's a lot of 'we'.*

That said, there are certain practices I still think are important. I think the [2014] Millions March was important. I think it was important for all the youth in New York - for the city - to have their voice heard...In a democracy people have to have their voices heard. And you have to do what's necessary to do that. No one wants to shake things up too, too hard, but you gotta rock the boat a little bit and you can't be afraid of doing that in order to win people over. I think it's important to do it in a respectful manner...people have to have their voices heard, but there isn't a man out there to stick it to. And sticking it to people is not really the process that forms true change. It can be the spark that gets the conversation going. That's why things like the Millions March are important, why Occupy [Wall Street] was important. Even though I didn't take part in Occupy for the most part, I thought it was at least important to initiate the conversation and let people know - let young people know especially - that they can have their voices heard. That they are listened to. That they can do things. That they are, in fact, powerful.

HOW IT IS

Leodus: *I think everything is wide open man. Because there is a very small percentage of people who are actually doing things. You see a* lot of people who are showing things and trying to make things appear to be a certain way, and they're nothing like that. [Trying] to make other people feel bad, or [trying to] be up there with the Joneses. Most people out here are trying to make you believe they are doing something that they are not.

And the people - to me - who are out here making the biggest moves are not out there trying to show you anything…The people I know who have the most money, [looking at their] social media, you wouldn't know that they had money. You wouldn't think they were broke, but they're not out here trying to show you shoes and little trinkets or whatever. They're not bragging, they don't even talk that much. Or if they do talk, it's about getting some money.

Most people out here - to me - are living a lie, in my opinion. And so, they're not willing to put the work in that it takes to get real money, to become very rich. They put so much effort into just making it seem as though they are rich. And they only seem rich to other poor people, because only people who don't have anything are impressed by shoes. I don't care if you have $1,000 shoes on.

…If you're impressed by a car, and you're impressed by some shoes, or you want to hang with me because of that superficial [stuff]…it's cool. The car looks good, it's cool to wear shoes and nice clothes and stuff like that. I'm not telling you not to do that, but look at what somebody owns. The guy who owns these urban clothing stores never has on the urban clothing, if you ever notice that. Or if they do wear it, they wear it so that you'll be more inclined to buy it. And so, I'm more impressed with the guy who owns the store, than the guy who buys the shoes every time they come out. Because the guy who has the store has access to everything. He doesn't have to stand in line for Jordans. It's his store. And he can make you wait as long as he wants to. That's the power right there.

Steven: *I think I see a house of cards. I think I see a lot of illusions, a lot of false realities, a lot of misconceptions, a lot of broken down communication. Nowadays, I truly believe it's sad that there's no foundation to a lot of the things that people are doing. For the times now, Black people, African-Americans, people of color...I think the thing we lack the most is foundation. History. A starting point.*

I believe every person of color, at a certain point, feels like they are the one that is starting new. My generation starts with me and my wife and my kids. We are going to be the new ones. And their kids say, "We are going to be the new ones." No one is building upon anything solid, everybody's just [breaking] new ground. Everybody's trying to recreate the wheel, when the wheel's already created.

One of the things I learned in college was that it wasn't [so much that] the people who weren't of color were better off than I was, it was that at a certain point their families started to build on top of the preceding generations growth. 'If I went to high school, my kids went to college. If I went to college, my kids graduated from college. If I got a regular job, my kids got a great job. If I got a great job, my kids got an excellent job. If I didn't travel, I made sure my kids traveled.' Each one taught down into their generation, so kids knew their grandparents, they knew where their family history came from. They knew their family tree. That was something that I never knew.

And even now, having a wife, I say those same things, "It starts with us. We have to make the decision that the things we do now...generations to come will have, because we made the decision." And it takes a people to make a decision to say, "This is who we are." And I don't think that's happening, and because of that, it's overflowing into everything we do. We're going into the same pitfalls. We're hitting the same traps. We're saying the same things as the generation before us.

Krystal: *I feel like a lot of people like to blame this new generation, [like] "We're so self-absorbed, we're so this, we're so that." But it's like, "Who raised us?!" You have to point the blame somewhere else! Like I'm sorry, we can't take that whole 100%, we need you to take like 50%!*

Because if you go back to the generation before theirs, they had to work so hard for everything. That's the way it had to be. They had to join together in order to get anything done, you know what I mean? One person just couldn't make an impact. You needed to be a movement. You needed your neighbor. To raise a family, you needed your whole neighborhood. You needed everyone. Then, after that, I don't know what happened.

People were telling their kids, "No, you're beautiful by yourself. You're independent. You can do it." And then they told us that, and we ran with it. It's like, "Okay, I can be smart. I can be pretty. But if I don't have any of that stuff, I can just buy it. I can make money, why do I need to help anyone else?" And then when you feel that entitlement, it's like, "Well, I worked hard, so why aren't you working hard?"

We don't even know what real hard work is! Our work hard is, "Ooh, we went to college." Meanwhile they were like, "Ooh, running from 'Massa." You know what I mean? When you put it in that perspective, it's like we didn't really do anything!

That's the thing, it's like what is the bar? There is no set bar. We just set a bar for ourselves and once we get there, it's like, "Boom! We made it. That's it. You can't tell me nothin'!" And it's like, how can you in the next breath say, "Power to the people! We're a movement! We're going to this!"

...It's way too contradicting. I'm not saying I'm not like that either. I'm admitting that I am. And it's like, how do you change that? Because it just comes out, you don't even realize it. It takes a lot of reflecting. How do you get the entire world to reflect on what we need

to do? Because that's going to be the only way that we figure this out. But that's going to take time.

Ashley: *There are two sides to this coin. I see a lot of potential, a lot of talent, a lot of creativity, a lot of grassroots activism going on, and that makes me really excited about the future. I think we are in a space and time where equality for all people, no matter [their] race, gender, [or] sexual orientation is so important to so many people, and they're letting it be known. And that's great. On the other side of the coin, there is just a lot of sheer ignorance. And unfortunately, I think it's because so many people have this platform called the internet where they can get followers by doing ridiculous things, and the more ridiculous and ignorant you are in some spaces, the more popular you are. And I think that's terrible, and it's causing really intelligent, bright, creative people to be viewed as - or to portray a role of being - dumb and ignorant just for the sake of popularity. And that makes me really sad.*

Safiya: *What I see out here is change. There's a lot of change, and without change there is no growth. That's what I believe. I'm seeing a lot of change within people around my age. Not necessarily the entire generation, but specifically around my age I see a lot of people becoming more conscious and aware of what's going on around them.*

To be honest, when I was in high school - or possibly even two years ago - I wasn't that aware of what was going on around me. I was kind of in my zone. I was kind of not really interested in what was going on around me; but the truth is, it doesn't matter how far [away] you think it is, it will eventually affect you in one way or another. I see that happening in society in my age group. I see a lot of people becoming more aware of things that are happening around them, near and far.

I want to say that I'm optimistic for our generation, but truly - at this point - I'm not, really. I'm not too optimistic about how far we are going and how intensely we are becoming more aware...because you have this large, large percentage...this large, large group...where all they care about is how to whip and how to nae nae, right?! And then you have this smaller, smaller group of people who are all about Black Lives Matter, and Bernie Sanders 2K16, and about all these things that would actually matter to us, and will affect us in the coming years. I feel like the smaller percentage is doing what they can to inform the larger percentage, but I feel like the larger percentage - whoever they may be - are just becoming too hard-headed and too into themselves and into pop culture, and not enough into news and important events that are happening around them. And that can actually end up hurting us as a whole.

I believe that if we don't do something about it now...even if my friends and I did everything in our power to inform everyone we know on the street, I still don't feel like it's going to make a large difference. I feel like the only way that we can make a huge difference in that is to hit the mainstream media, and hit the [media that] the larger percentage give themselves access to - what they watch, what they listen to. If we can alter that, then we have a chance. But other than that, I don't think we do.

Salihah: *I don't know...I see a lot. I see young people who are ready to make a change and who are really involved. I see older people who are willing to embrace that younger generation and want to be involved. I still see people who are kind of stuck behind the times and don't quite embrace diversity. I still have people who give me dirty looks and make comments under their breath. But in that same day I can have someone come up to me like, "I love you. You're my sister. The Quran has nothing negative in it."*

So, I think we're always going to be dealing with such a mix of people who understand what's going on and are ready to make a change, and people who remain ignorant despite the wealth of information and resources around them. It is really interesting to see what's going on, especially in New York where we've experienced so many different things over the years. I would like to be optimistic. I think sometimes I am optimistic, but I'm only human, and I definitely have those moments where I look around me and I'm like, 'this can't be real. This can't be the world I'm living in.' It becomes very easy to lose faith in people, in the world. To become apathetic. It's been a bit of a tug-of-war for me lately, if I'm being honest...between that and being optimistic and trying to find ways where I can be useful and of service. But yeah, it's hard. It's really hard.

Maryka: *I see we [are] all hustlin'. I see all of us trying to grind to reach this one common goal, which is internal peace and happiness. I feel like America is a hustle. The government is a hustle. Our parents going to work every day, us going to school - and going into debt for it - I feel like what I see in America is that we're all just trying to make it out and hustle and not be a statistic.*

I can't say that's for everyone, but I feel like even the drug dealers that I know...I feel like they're hustling. That student who's at Columbia University, he's hustling too. They're two different hustles, but we're all trying to achieve the same thing. Sometimes I feel like that can get messed up with human ego and greed, and things can just turn. Power in itself can just change people's motives. Yeah, we're all trying to seek success and be happy, but sometimes it turns into something negative. Mainly though, all in all, I see that we're all hustling.

Faith: *I'm seeing a lot of people and a lot of souls who need mentorship, who need guidance. There are a lot of awful things happening in the world and a lot of things happening where you could say, "Oh, we're living in the last days." I feel like we lack mentorship. We lack togetherness. If we were to take a pause and assess the fact that we have the power to change things, we would definitely be able to grow as a people, grow as a community, grow as a nation.*

I see a lot of people who want to have that mentor, who want to have that guidance, who want to have that connection with each other...and everyone is just afraid to step outside of that box to grab that connection. To say, "Oh, I'm an older male, let me see if I can find someone to mentor." I feel like everyone is not necessarily looking internally and saying, "You know, I have the power to change something or change someone." When I look out on my city, I see a lot of people who want to have that mentor and [be] that positive influence on someone else, but they just don't know how to go about it.

Amadu: *People are not being vulnerable [about] what they're experiencing in their lives. You'd be surprised how much help you could receive once you put yourself out there. Honesty is also really important. If you're walking around doing dishonest deeds, then obviously you don't want to be vulnerable because then all the skeletons are going to come out of the closet. However, the sooner all the skeletons come out of the closet, the less you have to carry it around on your shoulders and your chest...and be able to breathe for a second.*

Patrick: *Social media is one of my biggest problems right now. The influence that the younger generation is getting from social media...it's sad to say, but I don't think we're going in the right direction right now because of the influence and the hold it has on them. A lot of kids now, they don't want to go to school. They go to school, and you have kids fighting teachers nowadays. When I was growing up, you didn't think to fight a teacher. Now, children think they have that power to get up and say and do whatever they want to do, because nothing's going to happen to them. And social media is kinda what built up that mentality.*

You gotta know to respect an adult. Kids nowadays, they don't respect adults. They will walk in a room and start cussing out adults, spitting on them - I've seen some things like that - it's just sad to see that. It's sad to know that there's not a clear hope for the younger generation. You're not 100% sure that they're going to be successful because of how they're behaving now. When I was growing up, if you did something, you couldn't fight your parents. You couldn't cuss them out because you know they would drag you in the back room and wear your butt out.

Parents nowadays allow their kids to do whatever they want to do, and they reward them. They don't take things away from them. They just give them whatever they want. You can't do that to them. I will make sure my son is rewarded for whatever he needs to be rewarded for, but when he acts out and does something that he's not supposed to be doing, things will be taken from him. He will be disciplined in the most appropriate way possible. I can't have my son running around thinking he can do whatever he wants to do. It's not healthy.

Now, with what's going on with the police, and especially being a minority, they're afraid of us...because of how we portray ourselves on social media. And they shouldn't be...Honestly, everything starts in the home. How do you raise your kids in the home? How do you treat them in the home? That's what they're going to go outside and do.

Parents are the biggest influence on their children. They teach us the first rule about life, and most rules about life come from them. It comes from being able to discipline your child when they need to be disciplined. It comes from allowing children to understand that an adult and a child are not equals. Children need to know that they're expected to go to school, get an education, and come out and get a good-paying job. Parents have the responsibility of going out to work, providing a healthy household for their child, teaching them the right ways in life, and teaching them how to follow the right path.

Ebonee: *I see darkness. My goal is to move out of the state of New York, and if I can, to move out of America. I have a son. I have an African-American son. I have a daughter. I have an African-American daughter. I cannot raise them in these streets. I cannot raise them here. I can't do it. At the rate that the world is going right now, I can't do it. I can't. It's scary. It's definitely scary. You see all these young boys dying on TV, that's scary. And to live in the projects and to see somebody die, it's scary.*

You know, you never want anything bad to happen to your kids, and you can't protect them all the time. There are going to be times when my daughter is going to want to go out by herself and I'm going to be scared. This is why I need a house. I can't let her go outside and just run the streets, run the projects, and be here and be there. You know, it takes a village to raise a child, but it also takes a parent to raise a child. What am I doing that I can't go outside with my kid? Why would I send her outside by herself? Why? No, I can go outside too. We can go outside together.

A lot of people lack togetherness with their kids. Everything is like, get your kids dressed and send them outside. That's what I see a lot of living in the projects. I see a lot of motherless children. And my kids will not be motherless children. When I say motherless, I don't mean like your mother passed and you don't have her. I mean, your mother is too wrapped up in being young. And that's what we tend to forget as young mothers. Like okay, yeah, we're the type to have kids young, and that doesn't mean that our childhood is over, but that doesn't mean it's always turn up time.

A lot of young mothers have this thing where you leave the kids with the grandmother, and you leave them with this one and that one. All these bad things are happening to these kids, 'cuz you're just leav-

ing them with whomever. And it's like, "Son, sit down. Sit down and be a parent." Sometimes you gotta know when to sit down and be a parent. When I first had my daughter, I was one of those young mothers going out like, "Mommy, watch the baby." And then one day, my daughter was playing with her doll baby. And she said [to the doll], "Here, you go to grandma. I'm going outside." That's when I realized, I can't do this anymore. I'm staying in the house with my baby. 'Cuz if she sees that, and that's her idea of what being a mother is, then what am I doing as a parent that this is what my child sees? That made me change. That definitely made me change.

Quaneesha: *I see confusion, I don't really know where we're at right now in this world because there is so much going on, of course with the presidential election and we're seeing the divide again between Blacks and Whites. I'm kinda scared to see what the next couple of years are going to be like. It might go back to how it was in the '60s and '70s. I don't want to say it will be that bad as far as racism and the divide between Black and White. We do see people coming together, but then you see a lot of people in the divide. I just don't know what to expect. It's one of those things where it's kinda scary, but then again you can't wait to see what it will be like.*

Bernadette: *It saddens me that we are where we are in our country. I always listen to my grandmother tell me stories about when she was a kid and how she grew up in the '50s, and how she came here to get a better experience. She didn't want her children to grow up in the environment that she grew up in. So, she put them in activities...to have a better life, and not to have to deal with the racism and injustice issues that she dealt with. Now, to be her grandchild, and we're having to deal with some of the same things that she dealt with in the '40s...it's sad.*

I feel like a lot of people think that we've made it. And I just don't mean 'we' as Black people, I mean 'we' in general. [The mindset] of, 'I have this job, and I live in this neighborhood, and I have this.' But then you go into a club and it gets shot up. Or you're walking or driving down the street, and because your radio and your bass is bumpin' a little bit, because something just came on the radio and you're like, "Yes, this is my song!" And now you're pulled over and you may not be able to come home to your family. It's disappointing, because a lot of times we have the perspective that, because I live in this suburb, or I live in this area of the city and I can pay this much for rent, that I'm protected from that. And you're not. And until we start looking at things like 'our' problem and not 'their' problem, we're still going to have a problem.

It's like everyone wants to have private conversations about their solutions to things and what we should do, but there are so many individual conversations. There are so many individual organizations like churches having these discussions, but no one is having a group discussion. So, it's like too many hands in the cookie jar trying to figure out what to do, instead of everyone sitting back and saying, "Okay, let me hear what you have to say. This is what I have to say. Let's try to find common ground."

Mikal: *It's tough. You see a lot of bad situations. As far as the racial climate, things get really ugly and you'd like to see more peace, but it's kinda weird. It doesn't really seem like there's an answer. Nothing seems to work. You kinda just wish you could see a utopia when you look at the world, and find something better. Something where people can get along, [where] nobody's getting hurt…*

Katie: *Unfortunately, it's really not the best. It's very hard to see, you know? It's like, "No indictments again." And it's kind of like, ugh…an every single day sort of thing. It's really hard to see, and it wears you down. I feel like a lot of people close to me know how I feel about everything that's going on, but I don't really share it all out on social media like that.*

...I've been hearing - well actually, this is from <u>The Hunger Games</u> - but, [the rulers of Panem] were talking about setting up the Hunger Games and the people were getting unsettled, and they wanted to revolt. So [the rulers] were just like, "Fear...pump more and more fear into them! It will be great, they'll do what we want." And they were like, "Snuff out all the hope." I feel like that's very similar to what is going on today. There's a lot of fear, and people are just so fearful and they just don't see any hope. I definitely see the fear, but I also see the hope. Being surrounded by great people, I am hopeful about them and what they can accomplish.

...I will say something about our generation, we expect things to happen right away. I think social media, and media in general, has damaged that aspect of seeing an injustice, [and] being like, "This is not right! It's been brought to people's attention, now fix it immediately!" Unfortunately, that is not how it works. We're going to be fighting battles until the day we die, and sometimes what we want to happen is not going to happen like that.

There are plenty of people from the Civil Rights Movement who did not make it to today. We have benefitted from their fight, and what they've done, but they didn't get to live to see any of those rewards. To some people that's discouraging, like why fight at all? But for me, I like to think about others. I like to know that I'm fighting today, I'm fighting for justice for my niece and nephew. Like okay, I might not get to see this just and perfect society - which it will never be because we're humans and we're flawed - but knowing that it might be a little better for my nieces and nephews is worth it. And other kids, and other people...I have to think about them. Even though I don't know you, I want the world to be a better place for you. Be-

cause I have been so lucky and so blessed, and I just want other people to have that and to experience that.

Courtney: *Lots of unrest. I think people are just crying out right now. I think...I don't know...it's very somber to me. The world doesn't seem like such an exciting place, like it used to. To me it seems very somber. I think people are fed up with a lot of different aspects.*

The racial struggles and tensions that have climaxed in the past year or so are definitely not lost on me, it's definitely very real. I think African-Americans are resisting the whole, "You guys have come so far, and you're equals" and all of that. It's like a joke now, and that's come front and center with the various police brutality issues and the media's exposure of them.

I think that even with the different transgender issues that are going on right now, and the visibility to transgender equality and gay rights...I just think that there's something brewing, you know? I think there have been a lot of important decisions that have been made on Capitol Hill, and a lot of important regulations that have come forth for equality and freedom for certain groups of people. I think that's good, but I think that people are really starting to demand more, and everybody is so aware of issues of justice, issues of equality, issues of...freedom.

Even the conversations now about allowing Syrian refugees into America are sparking these conversations about, "Well, what is America? What was America created to be? Who is America for?" I just think it's so...heavy...but I think that something's brewing. People are not going to be settled [by] the junk that the news has been feeding them. People are not settling for anything anymore. And I think that's a good thing, but I think that there are some interesting, and possibly dangerous, times ahead of us. I feel deeply burdened by a lot of it.

But I'm also encouraged by the vibrancy of so many young minds about activism. So many young people are just getting involved, and being passionate, and finding a cause, and rallying with it at such a young age. And that's powerful to me. I think we're in an age where corrupt politicians are going to get away with less and less. The government, if they're not doing something for us, they're going to get away with less and less and less. Because we have so many young people who are cued in and paying attention to it. And I think that's a great thing.

Casey: *I am optimistic for my generation, but I think there are a lot of problems that still exist that definitely need to be solved before we can truly move forward. Not only as African-American people, but just the American population in general.*

If you look on certain social media outlets, or [traditional] media outlets, you still see a lot of hatred towards certain groups. A lot of people say a lot of things, and in a world of technology, I guess this is one of the cons of the internet. A lot of people feel that they can - or should - voice certain opinions that aren't necessarily appropriate to certain situations.

...There was a GoFundMe page set up for the cop who shot [Michael Brown Jr.]. The comments [posted] with these donations were kind of ridiculous; and it was like, wow, there are really people out here who feel this way towards the African-American race, or toward other races in general. That was eye-opening for me, because I'm aware that we have moved forward, but not as far forward as some people may think. That just showed that, wow, there are still people like that out there, and it was pretty sad to see that, honestly. I'm not sure if all those people who were donating are from my generation necessarily, but there were definitely people of my generation who would go, "Yeah! They're right! They're doing the right thing. This cop is a hero!" And it's just like, 'c'mon man. Not at all.'

Devin: *What do I see? I see a system...well, correction...a failing system that is on the verge of terminal collapse. And that system is, of course, society's rules and regulations on the handling of Black people.*

I mean with all the recent incidents...no, it's not really recent, it's pretty much been a murder every couple of months of young Black men and women all across America. It's just sad that there's just a constant flow of misinformation from the media...because as a young African-American growing up in America, the media always likes to highlight the bad parts of a Black person whenever they are on the news for whatever reason. Specifically, when the case is a murder, or an arrest, or a death...they always highlight the bad...which I find very sad. We all live here, and one group should not be held over another group just because of the color of our skin. We're all humans, we've all got red blood flowing through us. We bleed when we get cut. There are honestly no differences.

Alberto: *I'm seeing a lot. One of things I'm seeing that bothers me the most...is a lack of resources for those who need it. Not just in this country, but in the whole world. When you think about the number of people who are not going on to be their best selves...*

For example, me, the community college student. There are a very low percentage of us - minority students of color - that go to community college, graduate, and transfer to a four-year [university], and graduate. Go out there and just look at the numbers. When I say lack of resources, I mean for things like that. When I say lack of resources, I think of [people] around the world, and seeing how we have all of these very innovative people who have all these good ideas, but they're stuck. They're stuck because they don't have enough support, or the resources needed just to move forward.

It's not just [about] making them successful. A lot of these people have innovative things to share that would make society a better place for all of us, you know? The lack of access to education for a lot of people out there is just sad. There's a huge lack of empathy. There's a huge lack of awareness about [the problems] with access to education. That's what I see, and it deeply saddens me.

HOW IT COULD BE

Jason: *My argument is, if it's taught in schools...if the national government decided that every person in America - like they did with the Common Core standards - would [take] cultural education classes and would learn about Native American history, Asian American history, Mexican American history, African American history, African history, cultural education in general...people would be much better off in my estimation. Because there would be more of an appreciation for everyone's culture.*

So, the whole conversation of inferior and superior man, of racism, those things would diminish over a period of time. I think if more people were 'conscientized' and no longer relied on the information they get from the television...if we are knowledgeable, if we read the books, if we understand the history - the true history - the truth essentially...If we understand the truth, then the concept of racism would eventually start to dissipate, in my estimation. But we have to get people conscientized first. We have to put the knowledge in the schools.

People have to know from birth that they are human beings, that they are valued. That they have value. That they matter. Black lives matter. People have to be taught that...and that's the only way you're going to deal with racism. We all have to be valued, 'cuz we all are valuable. We all have made contributions to the advancement of humanity, because we're all human beings. People lose sight of that.

Atisha: *When I look at the United States in general - I have to be honest - right now it's hard for me to see a lot of progress, because we're being set back so many years based on the current events that have taken place.*

It's been breaking my heart to see certain news stories that have been popping up on my news feeds, like the [death of] Sandra Bland. It just makes me so sad to the point that I get a little bit hopeless. I'm sure that a lot of people have felt this way, but I know that it's really not helping to feel hopeless and to just give up. Lately that's the way I've been feeling a lot, but I do know that there are some things that I can do to help in small ways. If we help in small ways, it can make a big difference.

I can't say I'm going to go out and change the world by myself, or try to change government policies by myself, because I'm not in the position to do so. I'm not making the laws; I'm not part of the people who do stuff like that. But I am interested in teaching art. I feel like if art becomes a part of every single school's curriculum; that would be amazing for the people who haven't had art classes at all in their school. That was me growing up in elementary school, there weren't any art classes until I got to middle school. Then I went to high school and there were absolutely no art classes. There was like an arts and crafts class, which saddened me a little bit. I think art should be like math, science, and social studies in school.

If everyone is able to have a conversation around art, then every-one would be able to be more open about their feelings, and talking about issues, and less scared...I feel like art is going to be a part of making that conversation more open and informing more people. It's not just going to be Black people talking about Black issues, it's just going to be a conversation amongst everyone. Because we can't expect change if we're just talking amongst ourselves.

Phillip: *What I see is a need for the Black community to have its own representation in stores. We need Black businesses. I saw similar things when I was a kid in Chicago. I saw fast food restaurants where you can't sit down and eat, and you have to order food from a window. I see that up here [in St. Paul]. But in my area, I don't see drugs, Thank God. I don't see gangs, or little children walking up the street doing vandalism or anything like that. Thank God. And we're going to fight to keep that out.*

In Minneapolis I see crime, drugs and other things, and gangs. I hear about it in the nation. But I do see the rich getting richer and the poor getting poorer. It is uncomfortable, because I'm at the age now where I'm 30. I'm not 21, and I'm not 22, where I had the aspirations that I could get a good job graduating fresh out of college. That was my plan, my goal: 'Oh, I'm going to have a degree now. It's going to be like how it was when my parents were young adults. I'm going to get a good job here.' That's not there anymore. Especially when you don't have a focused degree, and you're not focusing on an industry - engineering, finance, whatever. So, it's very frightening.

I want to make sure that I'm doing my part and taking care of my family, because I know how easy it is for people to move in and change the landscape of a community. I don't really like what I'm seeing, because this narrative with people blaming police officers...there have been instances...my brothers had an experience and they could have easily been an Eric Garner. It can easily happen. You know, my son walking to the store with his friends, it's scary. So, I just communicate with them about how to speak to an officer, how to speak to adults, what language to use, stuff like that. So, it's kind of uncomfortable, but I think with more conversations like this, I think we all can be prepared and just change the landscape and have a better tomorrow.

Joshua: *I see a really diverse country, with different states that have different issues. I don't know, I see a country that can do better in terms of LGBT rights. I mean, like how many states have already legalized gay marriage? It's like over 30 at this point. It's going to be legal nationally, sooner or later. I think we're doing well progressively. It's slow, but we're going to get there eventually.*

But I also feel like the U.S. is a country where we're just not politically involved...it's worse for young adults. For young adults from 18 to 24 - that's my age range - only 38% voted [in the 2012 presidential election]. Less than 40% of young adults voted. And these are the same people that are complaining about all of the U.S.'s problems, yet only 38% voted. If you could get 75% of people voting, you're going to see great changes. But people just seem to have lost hope...I think we at least need to find a way to incentivize voting. We're not going to see the country progress in the way that it should if we don't get the people at the polls putting the proper officials in their right spots.

Steven: *I would just like to see people more passionate. I think a lot of things we do nowadays, people do what they think they need to do. They do what they have to do or what they should do, not things that they want to do or wish to do.*

Success is out there for anyone who really and truly wants it, but we are so conditioned to having to make a living. Or we get into circumstances where we say, "This is not for me, let me just hope that my kid makes a different decision." Not understanding that decision is setting our children up for failure, to make the same mistakes we did. I would love to see people just going out there, and being passionate about doing something they love...Because that type of positive energy changes a nation, and changes the people around you.

WE GON' BE ALRIGHT

Erin: *I see hope, kind of. I feel like we're a little lost right now, I'll be honest. But as far as the younger generation, and even my generation, I think it's important for us to come together right now. You know we're going through a lot. The world is going through a lot with all these shootings and everything like that. I feel like it's very important for us to come together. I'm only trying to look at the positive, even though there are a lot of bad things going on in the world. Every time you turn on the news, something's happening. Which is heartbreaking, but I see hope.*

I see us becoming a family again one day. I see that. Hopefully I'm not the only one. It's important for us to get back and actually be a family, and actually appreciate [each other]. Put the guns down, and give out some hugs, you know? Just look at somebody and just appreciate them. It could be a stranger. I do it all the time. I see a beautiful girl, I tell her that. I think it's important for us to give compliments to each other. Even though I say that your opinion of me doesn't affect me, it will be something nice to hear. There's somebody out there that needs to hear that they're beautiful. That they're smart. That they're worth everything that they need and deserve. That they matter, you know? They matter.

Daphne: *I'm seeing a lot of young people doing their thing! Oh, my goodness, it's like overbearing...there are so many people in this world in my generation who are doing their damn thing! I have [girlfriends] who are graduating from college, girls who are in dental school, girls who are doing so many good things. It's just amazing to see, like 'wow, I used to go to school with these girls! I used to play double dutch with these girls, we used to play with Barbie dolls'...and now these girls are living their dreams. And I have some guy friends* too...*everybody is in hustle mode right now. Everybody is doing something, and it's amazing to see.*

Aquillia: *I see game changers. I see people who have been given a system and told, "This is how it is," and they're like, "Nope, I'm just going to go this way and do my own thing." And they're doing it. I see a lot of entrepreneurs [coming] from us. I see a lot of people who are maybe not being entrepreneurs, but [who] are trying to train up the next generation of them. I really see us being innovators. We're doing what we want to do.*

Some of us - even if we are doing it negatively or positively - we're taking our own steps to see what it is that we want to do. For those of us who've decided, "Hey, you know what? I don't really like working, but I still want to make money. Now how can I create an idea that generates money?...and I'm going to go do that." Or, "I really want to see a program that mentors our kids. How can I start this? What do I need to do to do that?" And they just go do it. Or people who just don't agree with what they see or what's given to them or what's shown to them and they say, "You know we're just going to change this. We'll start our own thing. Then you can come join us 'cuz we've already got it moving over here." That's just what I see, we're game changers. We were given something, and now we're making it our own.

Joshua Jackson: *What I'm definitely seeing nowadays, more on the West Coast since I've moved out here, is that a lot of people are more focused on achieving their dreams. They're not really concerned about maybe going to college and getting a post-secondary education. They're more like, "Let me just follow my dreams of being an actor, or a model, or a producer." Most times it's in the entertainment industry, because this is Los Angeles. I run into a lot of people like that.*

Now on the East Coast - and especially in the South - people are taught at a young age that you've got to go to college, you've got to get this degree, etc. So, there's a lot of pressure on that front to go to college. There's nothing wrong with that. I feel like people should go to college and get their degree, but they need to focus on what their dreams are. Their degree needs to be exactly what they could imagine themselves doing in the next few years, or close to that. I know that when people are 18 or 19 - as I was at that age – they just don't know what they want at that moment. So, it's kind of like they're just trying to figure it all out in their teens to mid-twenties. Then by their mid-to-late twenties, they learn "Aha! This is what I want to do."

Quaneesha: *For the most part, I have a lot of confidence in my generation. You see the teenagers, when stuff is going on, they're the first ones to come together. "We're meeting here at this time. We're going to hold a protest. We're going to come together to talk about things that we can do to change people's outlook on us. How can we get everyone to join together? How can we take a stand?"*

Being that social media is the most popular form and way that people interact, it's easier for people to meet certain activists and other teams across the world that are doing so many great things. It's like everyone has come together, and they're talking about the movement for change and trying to get people to see that our lives are important. I feel like our generation...I have so much hope for it. I feel like everyone is doing more for themselves.

So, it's like, this is not happening for us, but they're creating what's not happening. Instead of saying, "You know what? I'm not seeing this", they're the ones saying "[Since] I'm not seeing this, I'm going to make this happen. I have so many connections, how can I build [something]? How can I come up with this app? How can I create something for my generation that they can relate to?"

And it isn't someone who's in their forties and fifties who are creating things. It's [people] who are 18 and 21, creating all this new technology and all these new things for us to be safe. It's like, wow, I wish I could think the way they're thinking. And you see all the activist things that are going now, people are really like, "You know what? We're going to take a stand." And you see a room for opportunity, and people are taking it like, "I'm taking this opportunity. I'm not going to let it wither away." There are so many things that our generation is doing, and I'm just like, Thank You! That we're not just sitting down and moping and complaining. I've seen people who [get challenged] like, "You're writing [about] this, but are you actually doing this?" And they're like, "Yes I am. I'm writing this, and I'm actually doing this. I'm meeting with so-and-so right now, and we're going to have a discussion about how we can change things." So, I love it!

Rima: *I think I'm seeing a lot of good, at least with my generation. Despite us constantly getting the, "Your generation is lazy; you guys don't work for anything. You don't want anything in life; you want it to just be quick and easy" [rhetoric]. I don't think that's really the case. I think we have more opportunities to making it slightly more quick and easy, but even those things that seem quick and easy prove to be a lot of hard work.*

People, for instance, who are becoming super-famous off of YouTube; it's like, "Oh, anybody can sit down in front of a camera and talk." But when you see into these people's lives, when you look at what they do for the projects they work on, it's not that simple. There are a lot of those things that you have to learn how to do. I mean these people gain incredible computer skills as far as filming and editing go, because they do this. So, I kinda feel like a lot of good is happening. And as much as [the media] say that we don't care about our generation and focus on the bad...kinda the, "Oh look at these little hoodlums and degenerates going around doing all these things, cursing at teachers, and fighting and all this stuff." But it's like, these are a small number. There are so many who are out here protesting and speaking for what's right, and we're getting undermined by [statements like], "Ah this generation, they don't know anything."

Maya: *Thankfully right now I have awesome people in my life who have really allowed me to not be completely discouraged by what is going on in the world because I know that they are doing very important work. They are encouraging me to do important work to combat what's going on. My partner has really been a huge source of inspiration because he's really actively working towards changing what our current viewpoint is.*

We're seeing politicians that aren't doing anything. People are coming in, and they don't care. And I think that has really translated...it's kind of trickled down to people. People have kind of grown very fatigued and tired of what's going on. So, to know there are so many people who I interact with often who are changing that...who are doing important work and really challenging me to do important work, to take action steps when I'm discouraged and exasperated by what's going on...And so, for me, that's good and that's a lot of what I see.

Shanai: *I'm seeing a lot. It's one of those things where there's so much going on in one area, and you can't really process it all. I'm seeing everything from the beautiful and the good, people doing well and succeeding and progressing in life. I'm [also] watching a lot of people unfortunately pass away or die young, or have people in their family who are close to them lose children.*

There's so much going on around us, it's hard to emotionally attach to everything 'cuz it's a roller coaster sometimes...Whatever it may be, I have to let the bad come in, and make sure that I put good out. That's how I handle those situations, because some things are heart-breaking. Some things are frustrating. You're human, so you're going to feel some type of emotion, but I at least try to make sure that if there is some way that I can put some good into something, or help someone, or in any way give to someone with the best means I have, then I'm going to do it. And that's how I interact with those situations. But at least I see hope for things to get better. I at least know, for those who are in a bad space right now, that they absolutely have the power, and [that they] are strong enough to get through whatever they're experiencing right now. And to the people who are doing well, I know that they are going to continue to do well and succeed and make a name for themselves.

Raven: *I'm tragically optimistic...I'm an empath by nature, so I feel pain very easily. I feel other people's pain very easily. I still have hope because, shout-outs to us, we're the most woke generation that has ever walked this Earth! That's why I'm optimistic. I just feel that it's beautiful how woke everyone is. And people have the means [through] social media to explode and bust open these issues of police brutality...[and] institutionalized racism.*

I'm proud of so many of my peers. So many of the people in my generation who have decided to use platforms, and even go out and physically protest these issues. And even if they're not, at least being willing to speak on it. Especially because I know so many people who go to predominantly White colleges. I go to a predominantly White college, and I do not hesitate to speak...and so do many of my peers. Even so many of my peers, who might not necessarily be Black - my Asian friends, my White friends - they're just so woke. They understand their privilege and it's beautiful to me.

I always think that for every racist who exists, there's a White person who is also screaming "Black Lives Matter." And that's kind of what makes me have hope in this generation, is that there are a lot more people who care than people who don't...There are a lot more people who are challenging the status quo, challenging [the practice] of not speaking about injustice just because it doesn't directly affect them...because at the end of the day, we are the minority in this country. We need those people on our side, so I applaud those people who aren't even directly impacted by this who are willing to stand up and make a change and make a difference by supporting this cause. I do have hope in this generation. In my peers.

And in this country, eventually.

Acknowledgments

The young people below are the reason this book exists. They believed in me, in themselves, and in the vision for this project. I am inspired and humbled by each person who shared their time and their story with me, and I will be forever grateful for their presence in my life.

Krystal is from Brooklyn, New York. At the time of her interview, she had recently graduated from college, and was living in the Bronx. She spent her days *"adjusting to being a grown up."*

Phillip is from Chicago, Illinois. At the time of his interview, he was living in St. Paul, Minnesota with his wife and four children.

Neiko is from Chicago, Illinois, where he was living at the time of his interview. He spent his days *"working, taking care of his three children, and coaching students."*

Haniyyah is from New York City, *"born in Queens, but raised in Brooklyn."* At the time of her interview, she was a graduate school student living in upstate New York. Her days were spent *"at work, then school, then the library...then rinse and repeat."*

Malika is from Brooklyn, New York. She was living in upstate New York, completing her final semester of college at the time of her interview. She spent most of her days *"running organizations, working as a resident assistant, participating in poetry communities and [other] campus involvements like crazy."*

Maya is from Pittsburgh, Pennsylvania and has lived in Chicago, Illinois *"for the majority of my life."* At the time of her interview, Maya was still living in Chicago and was spending her days *"trying to figure out precisely what it is I want to be when I grow up."*

Maryka is from Brooklyn, New York. She was a third-year college student living in western Pennsylvania at the time of her interview. Her days were spent *"usually working, dancing with my dance team, and spending time with my family."*

Joshua is from Brooklyn, New York. At the time of his interview, he was completing his final semester of college in New York City, and spending most of his days *"studying for the CPA (Certified Public Accountant) exam."*

Jason is from Brooklyn, New York, *"by way of Grenada, West Indies."* He was a third-year college student living in Washington D.C. at the time of his interview, and spent his days *"studying and doing lots of reading."*

Aquillia is from Palmdale, California and grew up in Chicago, Illinois, where she was living at the time of her interview. Her *"days, nights, and some weekends"* were spent teaching ninth grade reading at a high school in Chicago.

Faith is from Brooklyn, New York, where she was still living at the time of her interview. She spent her days *"working, preparing to back to college, and being a full-time mom."*

Steven is from Brooklyn, New York. He was still living in Brooklyn, New York at the time of his interview, and was spending his days *"either at work or with my family."*

Toshawna is from *"a small but really prominent village"* in Guyana, South America. At the time of her interview, she was completing her final semester of college in New York City, living in Brooklyn, and spending her days *"planning, organizing, [and] trying to get a lot of work done for multiple projects."*

Leodus is from Chicago, Illinois. He was living in Chicago at the time of his interview. He spent his days *"renting [out apartments], doing construction, talking to tenants, talking to investors, and building a tech startup."*

Ashley is from the Chicagoland area, and was living in the suburbs of Chicago at the time of her interview. She was spending her days *"working my 9-to-5 and doing work for a master's program."*

Dante is from Brooklyn, New York. At the time of his interview, he was living in New York City and spending his days *"working on an app with a team, running around the city, and traveling."*

Massamba was born in the U.S and spent his childhood in Senegal and New York City. He was living in New York City at the time of his interview. His typical daily schedule was *"work, work out, pray...and movies."*

Shantel is from Oak Park, Illinois and was living in the western suburbs of Chicago at the time of her interview. Her days were spent *"going to work, coming home, trying my best not to bring any of my work home...and on the weekends, making sure I find somewhere really good to eat."*

Daphne is from Brooklyn, New York, where she was living at the time of her interview. Her days were spent *"planning, writing [ideas] down, scheming on the next big idea, the next big goal, the next big dream."*

Mikal is from Toronto, Canada. At the time of his interview, he was living in New York City and spending his days *"hoping Kanye [West] will call and sign me."*

Christina is from the Chicagoland area. At the time of her interview, she had recently moved into her first home in the western suburbs of Chicago.

Amadu is from Brooklyn, New York, and had recently moved to the Silicon Valley region of California at the time of his interview. He was spending his days *"acclimating to the California environment, watching movies, hanging out with friends, and building my network with people out here."*

Atisha was born in Guyana, South America and spent her early childhood years there before moving to Brooklyn, New York, where she spent her teenage years. At the time of her interview, she was living in New Jersey and spending most of her days *"drawing a lot."*

Joshua Jackson is from Jacksonville, Florida. He was living in Los Angeles, California, and had recently authored his first book at the time of his interview. His days were spent *"writing, traveling to different cities, and enjoying eating different foods and cuisines from all over the world."*

Rima is from Brooklyn, New York and was living in Norfolk, Virginia at the time of her interview. She spent her days *"on YouTube...but outside of that, I read."*

Casey is from Brooklyn, New York. At the time of his interview, he was a third-year college student in New York City and was spending his days *"either studying for my economics exams, at the movies with my girlfriend, or just hanging out with my friends."*

Noor is from Saudi Arabia, where she was living as a journalist, educator, traveler, CrossFitter, and aspiring screenwriter at the time of her interview. Her days were spent *"meditating, reading, and trying new things whenever I can."*

Devin is from Brooklyn, New York, and was still living there at the time of his interview. His days were spent *"being a superhero, fixing people's computer problems."*

Erica is from Harlem, New York City. At the time of her interview, she was living in Brooklyn and spending her days *"working, being heavily involved with the young people's ministry at my church, spending time with my sister, and reading a lot more."*

Courtney is from Chicago, Illinois. She was living in the western suburbs of Chicago at the time of her interview, and her days were spent working and raising her two kids with her husband.

Jared is from Oak Park, Illinois, and was living in the western suburbs of Chicago at the time of his interview. He was spending his days *"either working, or taking care of my five children."*

Katie is from Oak Park, Illinois. At the time of her interview, she was living in the Chicagoland area and spending her days *"just trying to make the world a better place through volunteerism."*

Kiana is from Brooklyn, New York, and was a third-year college student living in upstate New York at the time of her interview. Her days were spent *"doing nothing, I don't really have a life. If I'm not in school, I'm not really doing anything...but hanging with friends."*

Safiya is from Brooklyn, New York. At the time of her interview, she was living in Brooklyn as a third-year college student, and spending her days *"working out at the gym, going to school, and staying at home typing up scripts and stuff."*

Kasim is from Brooklyn, New York, and was in his third year of college in New York City at the time of his interview. He spent his days *"usually working...working takes up most of my time. When school comes back, that takes even more time, but I still try to have my downtime and hang out with my friends."*

Khalid is from Brooklyn, New York. He was serving as a United States Marine, based in North Carolina, at the time of his interview. His days were spent *"either working out, reading books, or going to work."*

James is from Chicago, Illinois, and was living there at the time of his interview. He was spending his days *"working, working out, and trying to better myself."*

Stephanie is from Chicago, Illinois. She was living in the Chicago suburbs and spending her days *"working...and when I'm not working, I'm with my son and with my family."*

Chelsea was born in Haiti, grew up in Brooklyn, New York, and was living in Brooklyn at the time of her interview. Her days were spent *"working as a college advisor at a nonprofit, reading a lot, meditating, practicing yoga, and trying to find ways to be better and keep myself grounded."*

Jonel is from Brooklyn, New York. She was living in northern Japan at the time of her interview, and was spending her days *"at work...and if I'm not at work, I'm either relaxing at home, studying more Japanese, cooking, or hanging out with my friends."*

Ethan is from Brooklyn, New York. He was living in Brooklyn as a third-year college student/filmmaker at the time of his interview. He spent his days *"doing what I believe to be the most crucial thing to do at this point in my life, and that's learning and laughing."*

Amanda is from Haiti, and was living in Queens, New York at the time of her interview. Her days were spent *"working in an OB-GYN office...and applying to graduate schools."*

Janelle is from Brooklyn, New York. She was preparing to graduate from college in Washington, D.C. at the time of her interview, and she was spending her days *"mostly...I'm going to be completed honest, I'm tired all the time. That's become a part of my personality."*

Felice is from Brooklyn, New York and was living in Atlanta, Georgia at the time of her interview. She was spending a lot of her days *"trying to make this money."*

Kevin is from Chicago, Illinois. At the time of his interview, he was living in Chicago and spending his days *"working...and when I'm not working, just with the kids, being a family man, trying to do as much as I can possibly do on my weekends."*

Erin is from Brooklyn, New York, and was still living there at the time of her interview. She was spending her days *"right now...cooking, cleaning, getting ready to go back to work, living life, loving life, and spending time with family."*

Jasmine is from Brooklyn, New York, and was living as a first-year graduate school student near Baltimore, Maryland at the time of her interview. Her days were spent *"on a very strict routine, during the school year. I go to work, come home, do my work, and go to class. I try and squeeze a gym day in here and there, but it's mostly studying and going to work."*

Ebonee is from Brooklyn, New York. She was living there at the time of her interview and spending her days *"being a mother...being a friend. I recently got my license to be a childcare provider, so that's kinda cool. I watch kids all day. I love the kids."*

Alberto was born in New York City, raised in Providence, Rhode Island, and spent most of his teenage years in the Dominican Republic. He was beginning his first year as a transfer student at a university in Rhode Island at the time of his interview.

Raven is from Brooklyn, New York. She had recently completed her third year of college in Massachusetts at the time of her interview, and was spending her days *"currently...getting adjusted to this 9-to-5 life. I'm interning in [New York City], so I pretty much just go to work, take naps, and try to eat."*

Bernadette is from Chicago, Illinois, and was living in the western suburbs of the city at the time of her interview. Her days were spent *"advising college students, to build motivation in them, and to try to push them towards something greater in their lives."*

Silver is from Brooklyn, New York. He had recently graduated from college at the time of his interview, and was living in Brooklyn as an animator and illustrator. His days were spent, *"at this point...I spend most of the time just trying to find work, like I think most recent grads are."*

Quaneesha is from Brooklyn, New York, where she was living as an actor at the time of her interview. She was spending her days *"just working...I work every day. And if I'm not working, I'm either in acting class or I'm at home hanging out."*

Salihah is from New York City, and was a graduate school student living in the Bronx at the time of her interview. Her days were spent *"[at] school and work...that's pretty much how I've been spending my time as of late."*

Shanai is from Brooklyn, New York, where she was living at the time of her interview. Her days were spent *"working as a manager at a medical practice."*

Patrick was born in Jamaica and grew up in Brooklyn, New York. He was living in Alaska and serving as a member of the United States Air Force at the time of his interview. He spent his days *"waking up at five o'clock in the morning, going to work at two jobs, coming home...this winter, I want to get into doing some ice-fishing and trying snowboarding."*

Tobi is from Lagos, Nigeria. At the time of her interview, she was living outside of London, England, and had recently launched a social enterprise focused on promoting literacy. Her days were spent *"working part-time, and running an organization."*

Camille is from Brooklyn, New York. She was a college student living in Brooklyn at the time of her interview, and was spending her days *"either working, going to school, or sleeping."*

INDEX

Made in United States
Troutdale, OR
11/29/2023

15021091R00202